Globalization and Regional Integration

How was the European airline industry transformed from national fragmentation in 1957 to a point in 2006 where the European Commission could negotiate with the United States for an Open Aviation Area on behalf of all twenty-five members of the European Union? What can explain the change in mindset that saw conservatism and the tight regulation of the airline industry being replaced with increased competitiveness and the subsequent rise of the low-cost no-frills airline? In his new book, Alan P. Dobson draws from a mass of European documentation, including interviews with officials and airline executives and a unique collection of personal papers, to answer these questions.

Dobson traces the liberalization of the airline industry from the 1970s right through to the present day, illustrating how integration came about and which forces were driving it. The approach is comprehensive, focusing on the work of the Commission, market forces, the voices of airline industry interests and on key individuals in the policy-making process. The story concludes with an overview of the attempts by the EU and the United States to create an Open Aviation Area, which would embrace their respective airline industries allowing free operation of services throughout their territories and mutual ownership and control of each other's airlines.

This book will be of great interest to students and researchers interested in aviation and international policy, as well as academics engaged with European integration, globalism and economic history.

Alan P. Dobson is Professor of Politics and the Director of the Institute for Transatlantic European and American Studies at the University of Dundee, Scotland.

Routledge studies in the modern world economy

1 **Interest Rates and Budget Deficits**
A study of the advanced economies
Kanhaya L. Gupta and Bakhtiar Moazzami

2 **World Trade after the Uruguay Round**
Prospects and policy options for the twenty-first century
Edited by Harald Sander and András Inotai

3 **The Flow Analysis of Labour Markets**
Edited by Ronald Schettkat

4 **Inflation and Unemployment**
Contributions to a new macroeconomic approach
Edited by Alvaro Cencini and Mauro Baranzini

5 **Macroeconomic Dimensions of Public Finance**
Essays in honour of Vito Tanzi
Edited by Mario I. Blejer and Teresa M. Ter-Minassian

6 **Fiscal Policy and Economic Reforms**
Essays in honour of Vito Tanzi
Edited by Mario I. Blejer and Teresa M. Ter-Minassian

7 **Competition Policy in the Global Economy**
Modalities for co-operation
Edited by Leonard Waverman, William S. Comanor and Akira Goto

8 **Working in the Macro Economy**
A study of the US labor market
Martin F.J. Prachowny

9 **How Does Privatization Work?**
Edited by Anthony Bennett

10 **The Economics and Politics of International Trade**
Freedom and trade: volume II
Edited by Gary Cook

11 **The Legal and Moral Aspects of International Trade**
Freedom and trade: volume III
Edited by Asif Qureshi, Hillel Steiner and Geraint Parry

12 **Capital Markets and Corporate Governance in Japan, Germany and the United States**
Organizational response to market inefficiencies
Helmut M. Dietl

13 **Competition and Trade Policies**
Coherence or conflict
Edited by Einar Hope

14 **Rice**
The primary commodity
A.J.H. Latham

15 **Trade, Theory and Econometrics**
Essays in honour of John S. Chipman
Edited by James C. Moore, Raymond Riezman and James R. Melvin

16 **Who Benefits from Privatisation?**
Edited by Moazzem Hossain and Justin Malbon

17 **Towards a Fair Global Labour Market**
Avoiding the new slave trade
Ozay Mehmet, Errol Mendes and Robert Sinding

18 **Models of Futures Markets**
Edited by Barry Goss

19 **Venture Capital Investment**
An agency analysis of UK practice
Gavin C. Reid

20 **Macroeconomic Forecasting**
A sociological appraisal
Robert Evans

21 **Multimedia and Regional Economic Restructuring**
Edited by Hans-Joachim Braczyk, Gerhard Fuchs and Hans-Georg Wolf

22 **The New Industrial Geography**
Regions, regulation and institutions
Edited by Trevor J. Barnes and Meric S. Gertler

23 **The Employment Impact of Innovation**
Evidence and policy
Edited by Marco Vivarelli and Mario Pianta

24 **International Health Care Reform**
A legal, economic and political analysis
Colleen Flood

25 **Competition Policy Analysis**
Edited by Einar Hope

26 **Culture and Enterprise**
The development, representation and morality of business
Don Lavoie and Emily Chamlee-Wright

27 **Global Financial Crises and Reforms**
Cases and caveats
B.N. Ghosh

28 **Geography of Production and Economic Integration**
Miroslav N. Jovanović

29 **Technology, Trade and Growth in OECD Countries**
Does specialisation matter?
Valentina Meliciani

30 **Post-Industrial Labour Markets**
Profiles of North America and Scandinavia
Edited by Thomas P. Boje and Bengt Furaker

31 **Capital Flows without Crisis**
Reconciling capital mobility and economic stability
Edited by Dipak Dasgupta, Marc Uzan and Dominic Wilson

32 **International Trade and National Welfare**
Murray C. Kemp

33 **Global Trading Systems at Crossroads**
A post-Seattle perspective
Dilip K. Das

34 **The Economics and Management of Technological Diversification**
Edited by John Cantwell, Alfonso Gambardella and Ove Granstrand

35 **Before and Beyond EMU**
Historical lessons and future prospects
Edited by Patrick Crowley

36 **Fiscal Decentralization**
Ehtisham Ahmad and Vito Tanzi

37 **Regionalisation of Globalised Innovation**
Locations for advanced industrial development and disparities in participation
Edited by Ulrich Hilpert

38 **Gold and the Modern World Economy**
Edited by MoonJoong Tcha

39 **Global Economic Institutions**
Willem Molle

40 **Global Governance and Financial Crises**
Edited by Meghnad Desai and Yahia Said

41 **Linking Local and Global Economies**
The ties that bind
Edited by Carlo Pietrobelli and Arni Sverrisson

42 **Tax Systems and Tax Reforms in Europe**
Edited by Luigi Bernardi and Paola Profeta

43 **Trade Liberalization and APEC**
Edited by Jiro Okamoto

44 **Fiscal Deficits in the Pacific Region**
Edited by Akira Kohsaka

45 **Financial Globalization and the Emerging Market Economies**
Dilip K. Das

46 **International Labor Mobility**
Unemployment and increasing returns to scale
Bharati Basu

47 **Good Governance in the Era of Global Neoliberalism**
Conflict and depolitization in Latin America, Eastern Europe, Asia and Africa
Edited by Jolle Demmers, Alex E. Fernández Jilberto and Barbara Hogenboom

48 **The International Trade System**
Alice Landau

49 **International Perspectives on Temporary Work and Workers**
Edited by John Burgess and Julia Connell

50 **Working Time and Workers' Preferences in Industrialized Countries**
Finding the balance
Edited by Jon C. Messenger

51 **Tax Systems and Tax Reforms in New EU Members**
Edited by Luigi Bernardi, Mark Chandler and Luca Gandullia

52 **Globalization and the Nation State**
The impact of the IMF and the World Bank
Edited by Gustav Ranis, James Vreeland and Stephen Kosak

53 **Macroeconomic Policies and Poverty Reduction**
Edited by Ashoka Mody and Catherine Pattillo

54 **Regional Monetary Policy**
Carlos J. Rodríguez-Fuentez

55 **Trade and Migration in the Modern World**
Carl Mosk

56 **Globalisation and the Labour Market**
Trade, technology and less-skilled workers in Europe and the United States
Edited by Robert Anderton, Paul Brenton and John Whalley

57 **Financial Crises**
Socio-economic causes and institutional context
Brenda Spotton Visano

58 **Globalization and Self-Determination**
Is the nation-state under siege?
Edited by David R. Cameron, Gustav Ranis and Annalisa Zinn

59 **Developing Countries and the Doha Development Round of the WTO**
Edited by Pitou van Dijck and Gerrit Faber

60 **Immigrant Enterprise in Europe and the USA**
Prodromos Panayiotopoulos

61 **Solving the Riddle of Globalization and Development**
Edited by Manuel Agosín, David Bloom, George Chapelier and Jagdish Saigal

62 **Foreign Direct Investment and the World Economy**
Ashoka Mody

63 **The World Economy**
A global analysis
Horst Siebert

64 **Production Organizations in Japanese Economic Development**
Edited by Tetsuji Okazaki

65 **The Economics of Language**
International analyses
Edited by Barry R. Chiswick and Paul W. Miller

66 **Street Entrepreneurs**
People, place and politics in local and global perspective
Edited by John Cross and Alfonso Morales

67 **Global Challenges and Local Responses**
The East Asian experience
Edited by Jang-Sup Shin

68 **Globalization and Regional Integration**
The origins, development and impact of the single European aviation market
Alan P. Dobson

Globalization and Regional Integration

The origins, development and impact of the single European aviation market

Alan P. Dobson

LONDON AND NEW YORK

First published 2007
by Routledge
2 Park Square, Milton Park, Abingdon, Oxfordshire OX14 4RN

Simultaneously published in the USA and Canada
by Routledge
711 Third Avenue, New York, NY 10017

First issued in paperback 2014

Routledge is an imprint of the Taylor and Francis Group, an informa business

© 2007 Alan P. Dobson

Typeset in Times by Wearset Ltd, Boldon, Tyne and Wear

All rights reserved. No part of this book may be reprinted or reproduced or utilized in any form or by any electronic, mechanical, or other means, now known or hereafter invented, including photocopying and recording, or in any information storage or retrieval system, without permission in writing from the publishers.

British Library Cataloguing in Publication Data
A catalogue record for this book is available from the British Library

Library of Congress Cataloging in Publication Data
A catalog record for this book has been requested

ISBN 978-0-415-37338-8 (hbk)
ISBN 978-1-138-80685-6 (pbk)
ISBN 978-0-203-94657-2 (ebk)

This is for Bev
May we long continue to fly together

Contents

Acknowledgements	xii
Freedoms of the air	xiv
Abbreviations	xv
1 Airlines and the European Community	1
2 After the French Seamen's case 1974–84: the market, member states, and the voices of aviation interests	21
3 Tentative moves towards a common transport policy in aviation 1974–84: the European institutions	45
4 The single market and the reaction to Memorandum 2	61
5 Achieving the first package of reform	82
6 Receiving Package 1: delivering Package 2	106
7 Package 3: delivery in 1992	134
8 Impact and developments after Package 3	149
9 External relations and the SEAM	166
10 Concluding thoughts: the dervish shall whirl again	185
Postscript	190
Notes	194
Bibliography	216
Index	222

Acknowledgements

Funding for the research for this book was generously provided by the British Academy in 2000, which enabled me to conduct a wide range of interviews with EC, British and US government officials and airline executives. I am also grateful to the Carnegie Trust, which also provided funds for interviews in Brussels, conducted in September 2006. The book actually draws on over twenty-five years of research and interviews on aspects of the international airline system, and although the immediate research for the project was accomplished during 2000–01, it all took a little longer than I expected to complete the book. This was largely because of my taking the Chair of Politics at Dundee University and becoming involved in various initiatives that that prompted.

Towards the close of my writing in 2006, I was grateful for some last minute research assistance from one of my research students Gavin Bailey and I greatly benefited also from comments on the draft of the first five chapters from Steve Marsh of Cardiff University. But most of all, I would like to acknowledge two other debts of thanks. First one is owed to all those I have interviewed over the years, who have been unfailingly helpful. For this work, the most important of these is undoubtedly Frederik Sorensen, who allowed me to interview him on no less than three occasions. The second is to John Loder without whose papers much of this would have appeared rather impoverished research. The John Loder Collection was offered to me by John and eventually purchased for my use by the University of Wales Swansea Library. It provided unique insights into many of the crucial issues that contributed to the creation of the SEAM.

This is my third book on the airlines. My first was *Peaceful Air Warfare* with Oxford and the second was *Flying in the Face of Competition* with Avebury. They dealt successively with the Anglo-American moulding of the international civil aviation system and the story of deregulation, which largely drew on the US experience during 1968–94. This present work in a sense completes the stories related in my first two books by explaining the liberalisation of the European airline system, the creation of the SEAM, and EU–US attempts to create an Open Aviation Area in which their airlines can have freedom to compete as they will. Research for and the writing of these three works span twenty years of my career, and it is with some sense of nostalgia that I acknowledge that this will almost certainly be my last full-length study of the politics and diplomacy of international airline policy making. It has given me as much, if not more, satisfaction and fulfilment as any other aspect of my research career. At times it, of course, has not been easy, but throughout I have always been refreshed and renewed by the loving support of my wife Bev. And it is to her that I dedicate this book, the last of my major works on the airline industry. Among other reasons why it is appropriate to do so is that after nearly twenty years of her fretful fear of flying such fears have fallen away.

Freedoms of the air

   i the right of innocent passage or overflight
  ii the right of technical stop for repairs or refuelling
 iii the right to pick up passengers from an airline's country of origin and disembark them in another country
 iv the right to pick up passengers in another country and disembark them in the airline's country of origin
  v the right to pick up passengers from another country and carry them forward to a third-party destination
 vi the right to pick up 'gateway' passengers in a foreign state and bring them to the airline's country of origin for transfer to another flight with a foreign destination
 vii the right to commercial carriage between two states, neither of which is the airline's country of origin
viii the right to carry passengers between two points within a state other than the airline's country of origin, commonly known as cabotage

Abbreviations

AA	American Airlines
ABC	Advance Booking Charters
ACE	Association of Independent Air Carriers in the European Community
AEA	Association of European Airlines
ARB	Air Research Bureau
ASAs	Air Service Agreements
ATC	Air Traffic Control
ATK	Available Tonne Kilometres
APEX	Advance Purchase Excursion (fare)
ATFM	Air Traffic Flow Management
BA	British Airways
BABS	British Airways Business System
BATA	British Air Transport Association
B.Cal.	British Caledonian
BEA	British European Airways
BEUC	*Bureau Européen des Unions des Consommateurs*
BM	British Midland
BOAC	British Overseas Airways Corporation
CAA	Civil Aviation Authority
CAB	Civil Aeronautics Board
COREPER	Committee of Permanent Representatives
CRAF	Civil Reserve Air Fleet
CRSs	Computer Reservation Systems
CTP	Common Transport Policy
DG 4	Directorate General for Competition
DG 7	Directorate General for Transport
DG TREN	Directorate General for Transport and Energy
EATCHIP	European Air Traffic Control Harmonisation and Integration Programme
EC	European Community
ECAC	European Civil Aviation Conference
EEC	European Economic Community

EFTA	European Free Trade Area
ERTI	European Round Table of Industrialists
EU	European Union
FATUREC	Federation of Air Transport User Representatives of the European Community
FEDEX	Federal Express
FFP	Frequent Flier Programme
GNP	Gross National Production
HLG	High Level Group
HMG	Her Majesty's Government
IATA	International Air Transport Association
ICAO	International Civil Aviation Organisation
IGC	Inter-Governmental Conference
KLM	Royal Dutch Airlines
MEP	Member of the European Parliament
NGOs	Non-Governmental Organisations
NPRM	Notice of Proposed Rule Making
OAA	Open Aviation Area
Pan Am.	Pan American World Airways
SAS	Scandinavian Airline System
SCO	Show Cause Order
SEA	Single European Act
SEAM	Single European Aviation Market
SWISS	Swiss International Airlines
TAP	Air Portugal
TCAA	Transatlantic Common Aviation Area
TDRs	Traffic Distribution Rules
TWA	Trans World Airlines
UA	United Airlines
UK	United Kingdom
UPS	United Parcel Service
US	United States
UTA	*Union de Transport Aérien*
VAT	Value Added Tax

1 Airlines and the European Community

> Just as it's not supposed to be physically possible for a bumblebee to fly, it shouldn't have been *politically* possible to deregulate the airline industry.[1]

How did we get from there to here? How was the European airline industry transformed from national fragmentation in 1957 to a point in 2006 where the European Commission could negotiate with the US for an Open Aviation Area (OAA) on behalf of all twenty-five members of the European Union (EU)?[2] How was the European airline system changed from a limited number of connections, predominantly between capital cities, to a rich cross-cutting mosaic of regional and metropolitan routes? How were national airlines transformed into Community airlines with equal rights of establishment and commercial operation throughout the Community? How was price fixing changed to price competition and more flexible capacity introduced – more seats on more airlines? How were important commercial practices harmonized and how did the Commission tackle the problem of aviation relations with countries outside the Community? In short, how was the rigid conservative mindset that had insisted for so long on tight regulation of the airline industry replaced by a more competitive and efficient integrated Single European Aviation Market (SEAM), characterized by a liberal regulatory touch exercised by the European Commission rather than by nation states?

A simple answer to those questions would be that the European Commission's three packages of reform, beginning in 1987 and culminating in the creation of the SEAM in 1997, largely accomplished most of those things. However, even though the years between the mid-1980s and the mid-1990s are rightly seen as the heyday of the Commission's power and influence for further European integration, it would be misleading simply to identify it as the primary dynamic in the creation of the SEAM. The packages of reform provided the crucial architecture, but acknowledging that still begs the questions as to how these architectural packages came about, what changed the majority of the Member States from opposition to grudging support for reform and what contributions to the momentum for change came from other sources. In short, one still has to ask: What forces brought about the creation of the SEAM and how did they change over time? Did the Member States provide the political dynamic for change? How important were individual officials and politicians? Were the institutions of the European Community (EC) primarily responsible? What role did non-governmental organizations (NGOs) and interest representation play both at the level of what we might call civic or public interest and at industry level, either through individual airline corporations or through industry institutions such as the Association of European Airlines (AEA), the International Air Transport Association (IATA), the International Civil Aviation Organization (ICAO) and its sister, the European Civil Aviation Conference (ECAC)?[3] And, finally, given that many see market liberalization as the driving force of European integration, what was the impact of global market forces?

Scholars in this and in other fields of focus have struggled with questions like these in trying to explain how European integration has come about. There is a vast and varied literature of theories, which seeks to provide either a key to explaining how matters unfolded and moved integration forward or, less ambitiously, insights into such processes. This study takes a rather different approach. It has no pretensions to theory. Instead it offers a detailed historical explanation of how and when policy developments occurred in the European civil aviation system. In doing so, it may provide evidence to help demonstrate when functional, intergovernmental and other factors were significantly in play in the integration process and provide sufficient detail to evaluate efforts at more limited illumination of sector integration and the effectiveness of EC institutions in policy making.[4] However, the main aim is to provide answers to questions about how the SEAM came about through historical explanation.

While this work does not operate at the level of generalization of integration theories, some general claims can be drawn out from the detailed evidence. In particular, along with individual human agency, four important dynamics for integration emerged in the course of the research, and these can be conveniently summarized as state, EC institutions, the voices of aviation interests and market forces. There is a broad claim that runs through this study that these four dynamics generated, in an ever-changing matrix of interplays, the forces that created the SEAM and, furthermore, that whether and when these dynamics counted often depended on powerful and influential individuals. The problem is trying to establish which dynamic was powerful, to what degree, when and why. The rest of this book is devoted to explaining this complex and changing amalgam of forces, which created the SEAM.

The early years and little progress on the common transport policy

On 25 March 1957, the Treaty of Rome established the foundation upon which the EC would be built. Its aim was to establish 'a common market and an economic and monetary union' by implementing common policies that would nurture sustainable prosperity in an ever-closer union of states characterized by economic and social cohesion and solidarity.[5] An integral part of that vision was a common transport policy (CTP), something that was essential for opening up the inward-looking state-centric transport systems of the Member States and for promoting cohesion, economic mobility and the reality of a single European market.[6]

Transport is important. In the mid-1980s, it accounted for about 6.5 per cent of the EC's gross national product (GNP), and as the SEAM finally began to take shape in the early 1990s, it was estimated that ten million jobs were related to the availability of an efficient air transport system.[7] Transport has broad economic, social and political benefits, but they can only be realized in a system whose components have a coherent make-up, work efficiently and relate to each other. From the outset in 1957 it was realized in principle that a CTP would be cost effective and would foster integration by facilitating the mobility of labour and by helping to develop a greater sense of unity. It would help to equalize opportunities between the industrial and commercial heartland and the outlying regions. It would create a level playing field for transport competition throughout the Community and provide a larger operating base for firms, including airlines. Yet, despite all these benefits, the political will to develop a CTP has been exceedingly difficult to muster, even though the Treaty of Rome established a framework that provided for a fully integrated market free of distortions to competition (Article 3).

The Treaty insisted on the free movement of workers and on a right of establishment of companies anywhere in the Community (Articles 52 to 58), which, among other things, logically entailed the idea of Member State airlines operating from anywhere and to anywhere within the EC. This was directly at odds with the then-existing system, which restricted airlines to operating from their country of ownership and control. The Rome Treaty also had a section specifically devoted to transport (Title 4, Articles 74 to 84) and provided rules governing competition, which prohibited cartel arrangements and abuses of the market by those holding dominant positions (Articles 85 to 91). These provisions were also directly at odds with the then-prevailing anti-competitive practices in Europe, where airlines pooled or shared revenue, agreed to restrict capacity through limiting the number of seats available and fixed prices through the good offices of the IATA.

Notwithstanding the obvious clash between the practices in the airline market and the prescriptions of the Treaty of Rome, the latter was not used to much effect during the first two decades of the Community's life. Problems ranged from the technical to the nakedly political. It has not been easy to harmonize, let alone integrate, the national transport systems of the Community. For example, national railways were designed primarily for the state, and not for interstate intercourse. In an effort to compensate partly for the inadequacy of the rail network in the context of the EC, liberalization proposals were put forward to encourage road haulage. But several countries immediately became concerned about the negative impact such action would have on their heavily subsidized railways. Problems like these stymied the growth of a CTP in the land, rail and inland waterway sectors for many years; for air and sea transport, matters were even worse.[8]

Prima facie, one obvious way to proceed, in order to enhance the transport of people between the Member States, was via the airline industry. The airlines and the infrastructure already existed. Unlike the railways and the canal system, whose infrastructures were not generally designed to cross borders, there was not the same need to build new and expensive infrastructure links for airlines, at least not initially, and not until traffic grew dramatically and new regional routes flourished. All that was needed was the political will to give new direction to the airline industries of the several states making up the Community and to improve the use of the already existing infrastructure such as equipment, routes and airports. However, that was hardly forthcoming. Indeed, in Title 4 of the Treaty of Rome, which dealt with transport, it was specifically acknowledged that there would be a two-track, two-speed approach: for rail, road and inland waterways the provisions of Title 4 would apply immediately; but it would be left to the discretion of the Community's Council of Ministers to decide how to proceed in the case of sea and air transport. 'The Council may, acting by a qualified majority, decide whether, to what extent and by what procedure appropriate provisions may be laid down for sea and air transport.'[9] For over twenty years the Council barely acted at all. As late as 1973, when it received proposals from the Commission on a CTP, it refused to take any action for air transport.[10] It was recognized from the outset that air transport posed complex and difficult political problems, and if we are to understand how the SEAM eventually came into being, it is necessary first to explain the general conditions that existed between 1957 and the mid-1970s in the four dynamics that have been identified and why conditions prevailing then did so much to inhibit the development of an integrated EC airline system.

The market 1957–74

One might have thought that the international civil aviation market would have epitomized the idea of globalization with its ability to cross frontiers and bridge cultural divides with ease. Nothing could be further from the truth. Civil aviation functions at the interface of commerce and politics and has always had military, strategic, national status, safety and public service factors associated with it. The result was ubiquitous state interests, for the protection whereof states imposed regulations that compromised competition and fragmented the marketplace. As a report to the European Commission put it in 1994:

> In its early days as an infant industry, air transport depended on state support. It developed as a highly protected area of national economies, an integral part of government policy. All over the world, states exercised their right of sovereignty over airspace and their privilege to set up national carriers. Almost regularly, these carriers were used by governments as an instrument to promote their 'own' aeronautical industry, or foreign political links or domestic employment – all without regard to the economic implications or commercial significance.[11]

A senior United Airlines (UA) executive put it more pithily when he said that the first thing that newly independent states do as a sign of national virility is to set up a major steel plant; the second is to launch a national airline.[12] The exclusion, or near exclusion, of competitive market forces from the airline industry stretches back to its origins, and vestiges remained in 2006. The starting point in many ways is the Convention Relating to the Regulation of Air Navigation, signed in Paris in 1919, which specified that airspace over a state came under its sovereign control.[13] The assertion of sovereignty over national air space dictated that international civil aviation would be dependent upon a multilateral agreement of regional or global reach that would promulgate the rules of commercial intercourse or else governments would have to negotiate bilateral mini-treaties, or air service agreements (ASAs), to the same end. Until the regional reach of the SEAM, states opted for the bilateral route in their commercial relations. Bilateral negotiations had to take place between governments to determine under what conditions they were willing to exchange rights for commercial entry into their respective sovereign national airspace. Before the Second World War, this resulted in a highly predatory series of bilateral negotiations where the politically strong exploited the weak. At the International Civil Aviation Conference in Chicago in 1944, members of the United Nations (UN) under US leadership tried to institute reform and create a more orderly multilateral framework.[14] They failed in the commercial field because of disagreement between the two leading players – the US and Britain – but created ICAO for the technical side of aviation; and later IATA, whose membership comprises the majority of the world's scheduled airlines, came into being in 1945. It began to provide for price fixing subject to government approval. These two institutions helped regulate post-war airline operations, but they only touched on the commercial side with regard to fares. The main commercial operating standards were not set until Britain and the US signed the Bermuda 'model' bilateral ASA in 1945.

The Bermuda Agreement was more or less dictated by the Americans. They played on the British post-war need for dollars for reconstruction, to extract from them an agreement on a system that was highly favourable to the US and which allowed its airlines to exploit the world market. Bermuda provided for airlines, 'substantially' owned and controlled by either state party to the bilateral agreement, to operate on a basis of 'fair and equal opportunity' through the exchange of five freedoms. These five freedoms provided for (i) innocent passage or overflight, (ii) technical stop for repairs or refuelling, (iii) the right to pick up passengers from an airline's country of origin and disembark them in another country, (iv) the right to pick up passengers in another country and disembark them in the airline's country of origin and (v) the right to pick up passengers from another country and carry them forward to a third-party destination. Other rights, which later became significant under a more liberal dispensation, are (vi) the right to pick up 'gateway' passengers in a foreign state and bring them to the airline's country of origin for transfer to another flight with a foreign destination; (vii) the right to commercial carriage between two states, neither of which is the airline's country of origin; and (viii) cabotage, namely the right to carry passengers between two points within a state other than the airline's country of origin.

Under the Bermuda Model, fares were recommended by IATA tariff conferences after agreement among the airlines, subject to ratification by both government parties to the ASA: a system of double approval. Control over passenger capacity, the number of seats an airline could fly into the bilateral partner's country, was intended to be permissive as only *ex post facto* adjustments were supposedly allowed, i.e. after it could be shown that there was over-capacity or that one side was unduly damaging the other's operations. However, this notionally liberal model, which the US urged the rest of the world to adopt, was open to interpretation, and some analysts believe that any bilateral system has a tendency to conservatism and protectionism.[15]

What happened to Bermuda-type agreements, according to one highly experienced airline official, was that airlines and governments sat down and said, 'whatever this agreement meant to say we aren't going to let you do more than we want to do.'[16] The result in Europe was a pattern of collaboration and collusion between governments and their airlines and among the airlines themselves. This continued after the creation of the European Economic Community (EEC), even though it was committed to an integrated market and a CTP that should eventually be subject to the competition rules of the Treaty of Rome. Those rules largely prohibited commercial collusion and the abuse of dominant market positions, but airlines in Europe still operated under the aegis of their respective governments (i.e. national flag carrier airlines – favoured instruments) in dominant positions and free from competition thanks to regulations that carved up the market and stifled development.[17] Foreign routes were largely limited to capital cities. Capacity was controlled and divided between national carriers operating under a near-universal single designation regime in which only one airline from each country was allowed to operate on routes between the two parties to the agreement. In 1982 only six routes could be identified in Europe where there was dual designation, and that was only possible by treating London's four airports as one destination.[18] Revenue pooling and other arrangements that flew in the face of normal commercial practice were commonplace. Under pooling arrangements the two airlines that operated a route agreed to divide revenue, often in accordance with the specified number of seats or capacity offered by each, and to coordinate marketing and schedules. Once a route operated under a pooling arrangement there was no incentive to allow new airlines entry as part of the pool would have to be reallocated away from one of the original pool members to the newcomer. Regarding other un-commercial practices, a good example is British European Airways (BEA) in the late 1960s, which was obliged by government to maintain non-profitable services and to buy British made aircraft for the sake of the health of the British aerospace industry even though BEA did not want them and thought they would not be commercially successful. In return BEA was subsidized, cosseted and protected on its routes and allowed, indeed encouraged, to collude with its European counterparts. All its European routes were operated on a 50–50 pooling arrangement. Rates were kept high by both airline collusion through IATA and restrictive national licensing policies, which prevented entry of newcomers into the marketplace. Competition was virtually non-existent except from charter airlines and high speed rail links. European operators were state owned or controlled and frequently subsidized. Even during a decade of prosperity, 1955–65, and even though IATA operated on a cartel basis, its member airlines were so inefficient that they only managed to average an operating return of 3 per cent compared with an average of about 7 per cent in other industries during the same period.[19] In short, there was an inefficient cartel-type operation that was not responsive to public needs, that was organized round the individual states and not the EC, and that was non-competitive.[20]

In addition to the problems with the operating system, the European airlines also had structural problems with a diversity of air traffic control systems, congestion at national airports, and expensive user charges. In 1991, even after some reform in Europe, the operating costs of its airlines were still high compared with their American counterparts: total operating costs in US cents per available tonne kilometres (ATK)[21] ranged from 59.6 to 110.3 for British Airways (BA) and the Scandinavian airline SAS respectively in Europe and 32.6 and 51.8 for Southwest and UA respectively in the US. Among major airlines the lowest airline operating costs in Europe were just short of 8 cents *more expensive* than *the highest US airline operating costs*.[22] Even ten years after Britain had joined the EC, anyone wishing to fly abroad on a scheduled airline service from Britain had to go through one of London's four airports – Heathrow, Gatwick, Stansted, Luton – or from Birmingham, Manchester or Glasgow.[23] Those were the options. Treating London as one, there were only four possible geographical connecting points between Britain and its European partners. There was virtually no choice of airline in Europe. People had to fly the national flag carriers with only few exceptions such as British Midland (BM) in the UK. Routes and route entry by airlines were tightly regulated. Fares and costs were high. In short, there was little or no competition through new entrants on routes, or through the establishment of regional route alternatives by independent private airlines, or through competitive fares, or through one airline offering increased capacity at the expense of another.

Market dynamics seemed impotent, stifled by cartel-type arrangements and government regulations and requirements, and they appeared unable to provide impetus for change. However, a struggle had been enjoined by reformers at the end of the 1960s in the Netherlands and Britain, and, more importantly in some ways, in the world market leader in civil aviation – the US. The main impact of developments there was not fully felt in Europe until after 1978; but it is important briefly to assess the changing mind-set that gradually developed in America because it encouraged both existing and infected new reformers in Europe as well. It was also characteristic of the bourgeoning power of globalization as significant economic ideas in one part of the world had accumulating impact elsewhere and eventually universally.

In 1969, the incoming administration of President Richard Nixon was admonished by its own transitional task force '... to take a fresh and objective look at the role of private enterprise in transportation'.[24] Notwithstanding the US' oft-repeated declaration of commitment to liberal and competitive international airline services, US airlines were never run on anything approaching market lines. The Civil Aeronautics Board (CAB), an independent government agency, ruled the domestic and overseas operations of US airlines with a rigid regulatory hand and had done so since its creation by the Roosevelt administration in 1940.[25] Now, however, the Nixon administration was prompted by its own Task Force to review the situation. Concerns underlying its recommendation included terrorist hijackings, the impact of competition from charter airlines on scheduled airlines, increasing disquiet over IATA fare setting, and growing unrest among US bilateral partners with the Bermuda Model because of the scope of operations it gave to US airlines. In addition, the industry was also still suffering from the fuel price rise and economic down-turn caused by the 1967 Arab-Israeli Six-Day War. The effects were particularly damaging as costs rose and passenger numbers went down just as airlines were trying to absorb the costs of re-equipment with Boeing jumbo 747s and to adjust to the quantum leap in increased capacity that they introduced. When the Yom Kippur War of 1973 further exacerbated problems, the result was that thirteen carriers operating with Boeing 747s across the Atlantic flew the equivalent of twenty-five of every fifty-one of them empty.

Transportation Secretary John Volpe was charged with carrying out a review of US international aviation policy. One of Nixon's assistants, Peter Flanigan, played a key role in that review as he both chaired the Steering Committee that was set up and liaised between the Department of Transportation and the White House. At first, things appeared to be going well for those who favoured reform, namely, Flanigan, the Justice Department's Anti-trust Division, and the President's Council of Economic Advisers. Flanigan was robust in his desire to see more market impact within the airline industry. He also thought that US airlines were missing an opportunity. In September 1969 Ernst van der Beugel, who had been President of the Dutch airline KLM in the early 1960s, advised him that US airlines were being increasingly disadvantaged by the bilateral system. 'Because of the greater strength of US civil aviation which cannot be matched other countries are forced to take defensive measures.' He recommended 'substantial liberalization' through the negotiation of a new international multilateral agreement.[26] While Flanigan did not think that a new multilateral agreement was a practical option, he did want liberalization, which would open up more opportunities for US airlines to exploit their superiority over foreign carriers. However, there were strong conservative forces and vested interests, which staunchly resisted changing the status quo. Most of the airlines and particularly the industry's unions opposed liberalization, the Department of Transportation was lukewarm about reform, and the CAB was stubbornly set against change. Nixon appointed Secor Browne as Chairman of the CAB in the hope that he would change its attitude towards competition, but Browne proved to be something of a disappointment and only moved slowly. In August 1970 Flanigan wrote to Nixon:

Browne should *continue* to clean out the staff to provide the most competent people who agree with the free enterprise philosophy, …. Then the Board's policy is to provide the greatest freedom possible to make its business decisions. The lines, not the Board should run their business.[27]

This was radical. The idea that the airlines should run their own business was what deregulation was to become all about in the US in the late 1970s. In 1972, however, it was too early for such radical measures and the airlines were in too parlous a state to endanger further by introducing unsettling change. As a result, for example, the US Statement of International Air Transportation Policy of the United States proved to be anodyne and inconsequential.[28]

For regulatory reform and more competition to be pushed forward ruthlessly in the US, two different and incompatible political types were more appropriate than those generally found in the Nixon administration. The first of these was the neo-conservative: 'Capitalism is based on self-interest and self-esteem; it holds integrity and trustworthiness as cardinal virtues and makes them pay off in the marketplace, thus demanding that men survive by means of virtues, not of vices.'[29] As Flanigan had put it more mundanely: 'The lines … should run their business.' The second political type was more socially concerned and looked to the free market, not so much as a moral good in itself but as a good when it produced good results; and it was felt that a freer market in the airline industry would achieve that by delivering benefits to the consumer. As this political alliance gradually formed and gathered strength in the US, so the cause of airline regulatory reform progressed as well. The Nixon administration did not immediately empower market forces in the airline industry, but there was a shift in thinking. More people on both the Right and the Left began to view the airlines in a more critical light. The coalition of forces in favour of the status quo was capable of preventing immediate reform, but it proved unable to keep the cork on the thought bottle: the genie of deregulatory reform was now out and about in the marketplace of ideas. This genie would eventually contribute significantly to the growing momentum towards globalization of the airline marketplace.

Member States 1957–74

The longstanding general default position on airlines, in the US no less than in Europe, was that they were not like other commercial businesses and did not operate in a way that could gain from economies of scale. They should be positively shielded from the forces of competition, which, if left unchecked could have adverse safety implications and, in Europe, threaten the viability of national emblems – the state owned flag carriers. Apart from the Netherlands and Britain, all the Member States were regulatory conservative in civil aviation and stubbornly remained so. This majority position was buttressed by a combination of vested interests among dominant national flag carriers, and political ideologies unsympathetic to market reforms such as socialist *dirigisme* in France and the influence of social democracy and trade unionism in Germany. Even after deregulation in the US indicated that it could deliver economies of scale and benefits for consumers and airlines, the regulatory conservatives were still reluctant to fix something that did not appear broken in Europe, and were further deterred from change as it would be politically controversial with both airline management and workers. Unlike Britain and the Netherlands, they would not embrace the radicalism needed to change the system. They did not have the particular perspective on the need for a more open market to benefit their national flag carriers, which both Britain and the Netherlands had, and unlike Britain they did not have any tradition of trying to cultivate a national multi-airline system, nor again unlike Britain did they generally have effective airlines other than their national flag carriers. In Europe the major airlines had always been state owned, and the airline industry was well embedded in a culture that rejected the idea that they should be operated like any other business.[30] Treating them in such a way was beyond the pale for most Member States and their airlines. It was desperately radical for the US airline industry, never mind Europe's. The USA, with over 40 per cent of the world's entire airline market, was clearly the market leader and as such had more influence than any other state on the condition and character of the international airline industry. Once it embraced deregulation, it inevitably had impact elsewhere; but if there had not been sympathy for liberalization in the Netherlands, Britain and elsewhere in Europe, then developing the SEAM would have been a much longer drawn-out process than it actually was.

Prior to Britain's entry into the EC in 1973 there was only a lone voice from the Netherlands that showed any inclination to reform the Community's airline system. However, its voice was not powerful enough to move things along and the other Member States saw Dutch policy as narrowly self-interested. Given the tiny size of their domestic airline system, the Dutch attempted to make Schiphol Airport the equivalent in the international airline market to the one that the port of Rotterdam played in the international maritime trade. The vision was the same. Schiphol would become one of Europe's great international transit centres thus expanding the market available to KLM. 'The Dutch were in favour of liberalization because they saw it as the only way in which they could develop Schiphol and KLM. [But] ... they from time to time tempered their enthusiasm [for reform] by more realistic elements so as not to make it too difficult for KLM.'[31] There thus arose specific liberalization ambitions for KLM, modelled on the long-standing maritime policy of the Netherlands.

With Britain in the EC, the voice of reform became more powerful and more persuasive in the sense of a realization that benefits could accrue to a wider constituency than just a national airport and a national flag carrier. In fact, notwithstanding its reputation as a 'poor European', particularly under Prime Minister Margaret Thatcher, Britain from 1979 onwards was the most powerful and consistent promoter of the SEAM among the Member States through its national policy and through its officials in the Community. In the latter case, the UK was fortunate in having a succession of able people in positions of influence on transport in the EC, for example Raymond Le Goy, who was Director-General in the European Commission Directorate General for Transport (DG VII) in the early days of attempts at reform. He was an expert in air transport and was keen to see change.[32] The voice of reform was strengthened by the Thatcherite commitment generally to a freer market and in particular to privatizing BA and liberalizing regulation of the airline industry. In urging integration in the airline sector, Britain was the good European, countries like France, Germany and Italy were not. This irony did not pass unnoticed among British Ministers. In July 1980, Transport Secretary John Nott, speaking of Britain's desire to integrate and liberalize the European aviation system, observed, 'when we seek to open up competition in areas where we are in the ascendant position, we find a total incapacity, or unwillingness, to follow our lead'.[33]

Britain was in a better position to exploit a single competitive airline market than any other country in the Community because, in addition to its national flag carrier,[34] it also had successful independent and charter airlines to such an extent that other Member States did not have; it had a vast international network thanks to its imperial history and in virtue of being one of the international pioneers of air travel and because Heathrow was the largest international hub in the world and also the gateway to Europe for much of the North American market. Once these factors combined with both the good fortune of strategically important transport and competition appointments in the European Commission and the Thatcherite ideology committed to liberalization of the marketplace, there then emerged a potent concoction of forces that would eventually have enormous impact on the liberalization of the whole European airline system. Britain did more than any other Member State to bring about the airline sector's integration.

Rather oddly, the first significant move for competitive airline reform in the UK came towards the end of the term of office of Prime Minister Harold Wilson, whose Labour government was not favourably disposed towards freer competition and which had taken restrictive decisions in the earlier part of the 1960s. The Edwards Report, which Wilson commissioned to look into Britain's civil aviation industry, issued its findings in 1969. It acknowledged the need to meet demand at the lowest cost compatible with safety, adequate return on investment, stability in the industry, and appropriate contributions to the economy and in particular the balance of payments. But, it also added that there should be:

> the minimum of restriction ... imposed on it [the airline industry] or on the users of its services, and that arrangements which restrain competition or innovation should be tolerated only to the extent that they are necessary to achieve the main objectives of policy.[35]

Recommendations were one thing, what the Wilson administration might implement was something else. As things turned out, it had no opportunity to do anything substantial because the Conservatives under Edward Heath won the General Election in 1970, much to the surprise of many, and their mission to modernize Britain took a robust line on the airline industry and its reform. Four significant changes now transpired. First, BEA and the British Overseas Airways Corporation (BOAC) were merged to form BA in 1974. Second, a Civil Aviation Authority (CAA) with considerable independence was established with licensing powers, subject to the issuing of guidance by government. The CAA developed its powers over the years in a way highly supportive of more competition. Third, the government adopted a policy of double designation and established a 'second force airline' in the form of British Caledonian (B.Cal.) to encourage competition with BOAC and later BA. Caledonian Airlines took over British United Airlines to form B.Cal., routes were taken away from BOAC and given to B.Cal. and B.Cal. was licensed to operate on the London to New York route in direct competition with BOAC. And fourth, the CAA licensed Freddie Laker, who had previously been restricted to charter operations on the Atlantic, to run a scheduled service from Stansted to New York. Laker was a pioneering champion of low-cost flying and his transatlantic Skytrain service posed a major challenge over subsequent years to the cosy regulated environment enjoyed by the well-embedded scheduled airlines. When compared with what came later, the policy of the Heath government looks like rather thin gruel, but at that time it was seen as quite a rich diet of reform. The Heath government had established a framework that could challenge the rigidity of controls that had stifled competition and efficiency for so long.

Unfortunately for the forces of liberalization, the changes achieved little of substance in the short term. The US CAB refused to grant Laker traffic rights, some of B.Cal.'s routes also failed to gain traffic rights and some of the routes that it did launch on the North Atlantic were soon abandoned as economically unviable. A serious problem for the British was the appearance of enormously expanded capacity on the North Atlantic because of the introduction by US airlines of Boeing jumbo 747s and the entry of new US airlines such as National on Atlantic routes. This led the Heath government, notwithstanding its more pro-competition policy, to adopt a highly restrictive interpretation of the Bermuda Agreement in 1972. It departed from the principle of restricting capacity only *ex post facto* and attempted to foist a unilaterally predetermined level of capacity on the US, in part by reducing National's Boeing 747 flights from seven to four a week.[36] Several months had elapsed before a compromise emerged whereby the US agreed to restrict jumbo 747 flights, but even then they flew with load capacities of barely 40 per cent.[37] The recession that deepened in the airline industry as a result of the Yom Kippur War made everything even more difficult and change to a more competitive dispensation particularly so. The Conservative Government and its policies were not unaffected by these economic difficulties and the government began to back-track on its reform programme. Enthusiasm for the free market waned and in 1974 the Conservatives introduced a statutory prices and incomes policy. The industrial unrest, which followed in its wake, unseated Heath and returned Wilson and Labour to power. Successive Secretaries of State at the Department of Trade, Peter Shore and Edmund Dell, according to one senior member of the CAA, wanted 'to undo as far as they could the work of the Heath government' in the airline industry.[38] That judgment might have been a little harsh so far as Dell was concerned, but the flurry of activity for regulatory reform seemed to have petered out without substantial achievements. It was unlikely that the British Government would now be a powerful voice for reform within the EC. The Labour Government was not only regulation-minded, but it was also ambivalent in its attitude towards the EC, so much so that Wilson held a referendum on 5 June 1974 over whether or not Britain should even remain a member.

The voices of aviation interests 1957–74

For the purposes of this study, the influence of NGOs such as IATA and international institutions such as ECAC are corralled together with conventional interest groups. The power of interest groups within the EC can be expressed through two main conduits: indirectly through the organizations of the nation states or directly through the organs of the EC in Brussels. Greenwood, who has done the definitive study to date of interest groups in the EC/EU, describes them as the natural constituencies of the Commission and the Parliament and adds significantly for this study that 'a liberal market discourse' is at the core of the EU agenda. Two important considerations arise from these judgments. First, the airline sector between 1957 and the mid-1970s was clearly an exception to the rule about liberal market discourses and was so for a variety of reasons. As the review of the general condition of the airline market disclosed, there was no liberal market discourse there and while the Council of Ministers refused to take action in the field of aviation policy under Article 84(2), those who wanted to start such a debate felt that it was not possible to do so. They were unable to locate discourse about the highly regulated air transport industry within a context conducive to reform: the power of vested interests and the conventional wisdom that the airline industry could not be run on market lines because of the lack of economies of scale to be reaped, safety, national interests and public service reasons were simply too strong. The default position in the airline industry in other words was not, like most other economic aspects of the EC, a liberal market discourse, but a tight regulatory dispensation and it was difficult to see how that default position could be changed. Second, while the Parliament and the Commission are well placed to engage with organized interests as allies in their ambitions and the EC/EU system is clearly not insulated from organized interests, it is neither driven nor captured by them.[39] There may be occasions when interests determine policy, but they do not routinely do so, largely because of the 'multiple level architecture of the EU' and the fact that 'the grand bargains of European integration are influenced more by open political debate, and resolved in *fora* in which private interests are no more than background influences'.[40] Even during the heyday of interest group influence, when Jacques Delors was President of the Commission 1985–95 and momentum developed for the Single Market, the much vaunted role of one of Europe's most powerful industrial interest groups, the European Round Table of Industrialists (ERTI), was over-exaggerated by commentators and only one of several factors, some of which were more important than pressure from ERTI, that progressed integration towards the realization of the Single Market.[41] Thus while the EC/EU may be open to interest groups, it is difficult to generalize about their actual impact over time and in different issue areas.

As far as civil aviation-related organized interests, institutions and NGOs were concerned, between 1957 and the late 1970s there seemed to be a heavy preponderance in favour of the status quo. Contrary to the impression sometimes given, ECAC was generally highly conservative: 'ECAC being liberal ... is absolute utter nonsense.'[42] In 1982 ECAC did contribute to the change of mindset that was so important for regulatory reform, but this was because an important review that it set up was hijacked by British pro-reform officials, something that will be examined in more detail in the next chapter. IATA and the AEA, which were well-established and influential by the 1970s, were both firmly set against regulatory reform: IATA in particular was fearful of fragmenting the market and was content with the 1967 Paris ECAC Multilateral Agreement on Procedures for Establishment of Tariffs for Scheduled Air Services, which provided for various procedures for interline consultation and government double approval of pricing and reaffirmed IATA as the preferred means of setting fares.[43] Regarding the latter institution, one British official was later to comment: 'it's [i.e. IATA is] totally reactionary'.[44] There was no groundswell of public consumer interests, partly because most members of the general public only used air travel for holidays and there they were well served by the charter airlines, which operated under the permissive rules of Article 5 of the Chicago Convention on International Civil Aviation and IATA resolution 45 of April 1949, amended in 1953, and which then ran through until 1972. These provisions allowed charters to develop operations that looked increasingly like scheduled operations and to offer much cheaper fares than the scheduled airlines. By the mid-1970s the conditions under which consumers could purchase charter airline tickets were so flexible that to some observers it was impossible effectively to distinguish them from scheduled air services. In fact charter innovations had to be copied by scheduled operators in order to keep up and compete with them, hence the introduction of advance purchase excursion fares (APEX) in order to respond to advanced booking charters (ABCs).[45] Consumer groups such as the British Air Transport Association (BATA), the Freedom of the Skies Campaign, the Federation of Air Transport User Representatives of the European Community (FATUREC), the European charter lobby group the Association of Independent Air Carriers in the European Community (ACE), and the *Bureau Européen des Unions des Consommateurs* (BEUC), either had not been formed by 1970 or else were ineffective. In 1974 only Britain among the Community's Member States had an air transport user group.[46] In fact the main form of lobbying felt by the Commission was from the Member States 'to prevent us from doing anything'.[47]

EC institutions 1957–74

Before assessing the positions of the European institutions in the period between 1957 and the mid-1970s, a brief outline of their powers and areas of competence needs to be given. The main institutions of the EC/EU are the Council of Ministers and the Committee of Permanent Representatives (COREPER), the European Council (1975), the Commission, the Parliament, and the European Court of Justice, but there are also several other specialized institutions such as the Economic and Social Committee (1958), the Committee of the Regions (1994), the European Investment Bank (1958), and Europol (1999).

Decision-making power lies generally in the hands of the Council of Ministers, which is not one but many councils made up of the appropriate ministers of the Member States for the topic under discussion. From the outset decisions were made through a mixture of unanimity and qualified majority voting, but crisis with France in 1965–66 resulted in the Luxembourg Compromise, which stipulated that when very important issues were at stake the Council would need unanimity to make a decision. It was not until the Single European Act (SEA) came into force in 1987 that the scope for qualified majority voting was substantially expanded. The Council of Ministers is serviced by national delegations of professional diplomats who form links between Brussels and the governments of the Member States, keep business moving, set agendas, have decision-making powers on low level issues, but more importantly can often have important influence on highly important decisions taken by the Council of Ministers. They meet weekly in the COREPER. The President of the Council of Ministers, who can be a major influence on policy developments, holds office for six months. The presidency changes every six months by rotation among the Member States. The other major input from the Member States into the decision-making process comes from the European Council. It is in effect a twice-a-year summit of the political leaders and foreign secretaries of Member States and the president and vice presidents of the Commission. Formed in 1974–75 to give stronger leadership to the Community, it has grown in power and influence over time at the expense of the other European institutions.

The Commission is the guardian of the treaties. It has the obligation to ensure that their provisions and Community laws are implemented and properly applied and it holds the power to initiate new laws. Community laws take the various forms of Regulations and Decisions, both of which are binding on the Member States with the former being broader in scope than the latter; Directives are also binding, but it is left to the Member States to decide how to implement them; and Recommendations which are non-binding are usually a means of testing opinion towards possible new policy departures. The Commission has no direct power of enforcement. In these roles the Commission has to work closely with the Member States, the Council of Ministers, and the European Court of Justice and as such is central to the everyday workings of the Community, which also places the President of the Commission, potentially at least, in an important power position.

The Parliament at the outset with no elections and no powers over revenue-raising or the introduction of laws was by far the least effective institution in the Community. The fact that its administrative headquarters is in Luxembourg, its chamber in Strasbourg and committee meetings are held in Brussels does not particularly help matters either. The Parliament has the power to dismiss the Commission with a two-thirds majority vote, but this is an extreme measure that has never been used, though in January 1999 political pressures in the wake of corruption charges were so great that the Santer Commission resigned *en masse*. In the beginning, the Parliament had to be consulted by the Council in a small number of legislative areas, but these areas and its powers in decision making have grown over the years. In particular it gained budgetary oversight powers after the Hague Summit in 1969 and the phasing in of provisions for 1 per cent of value-added tax (VAT) from the Member States to go directly to the Community budget. Its powers also increased generally after the introduction of direct elections in 1979 and with the provisions of the SEA in 1987, which conferred more power and influence on the Parliament over legislation. The Parliament has thus grown in stature, influence, and the role it performs; however, in its early stages it was little more than a talking shop. It had little effect unless it could work in tandem with the Commission on a shared agenda.

The European Court of Justice has the power of judicial review in those areas where the Member States have ceded sovereignty to the EC/EU. It thus has the final say on interpreting the treaties and Community law. Community law will be held to prevail in any sphere of Community competence where there is a conflict with a Member State's national law. Its role may seem quite straightforward, but in fact it has been complex, technical and difficult, – so complex and difficult at times that the full implications of its decisions were not fully appreciated. A good example of this is the AETR case in 1970. The facts of the case involved crews operating cross-border road haulage in the EC, but a general principle that was promulgated would have important consequences for the SEAM. Essentially the Court ruled that Member States could not make agreements with third parties outside of the Community in any way that would run contrary to common policies established within the Community. This became an important sleeper in the development of aviation integration, which awoke in the 1990s and troubled even those keenly in favour of liberalization because of its implications for sovereign control over external aviation relations.[48]

Within the Community, underlying the problem of creating a CTP in aviation was the fact that the Council did not act under Article 84(2) to lay down appropriate provisions for air transport, even though it was directly empowered to do so by the Treaty and had no need of the Commission to make legislative proposals. There was ambiguity in that the Treaty of Rome set out a CTP as one of its objectives in Articles 2 and 3(f), but at the same time Article 84(2) seemed to indicate that in air and sea transport this should only occur as and when the Council thought appropriate. In other words it was generally believed that the competition rules were rendered inapplicable by Article 84(2) until the

Council of Ministers acted under its authority and therefore: 'In the absence of any Council action under Article 84 there was doubt as to the applicability of the Treaty [of Rome] to aviation.'[49]

However, in February 1962, the Council of Ministers adopted Regulation 17 implementing the competition provisions of the Treaty of Rome and for a short time this looked promising for the liberalization of the air transport market. Certainly on one reading it could have had important consequences for air transport because of the possible application of the prohibitions in Articles 85 and 86 of dominant positions and 'all agreements between undertakings, decisions by associations of undertakings and concerted practices' that prevent restrict or distort competition within the common market. On the other hand, the airlines could have been exempted from the application of the competition rules by Article 90(2) if they were deemed to have been 'entrusted with the operation of services of general economic interest'. In fact the Council ensured that there would be no need to consider either of these possibilities because in November 1962 it adopted Regulation 141 which retrospectively withdrew both sea and air transport from the scope of Regulation 17 'it was felt that ... some kind of Community policy should be developed before competition rules could be applied usefully in that area'.[50]

The problem thus remained, but there were Commission officials, in particular in Directorate-General IV (DG IV) for Competition and DG VII, who believed that the competition rules applied to air transport:

> the Commission always thought that the Treaty applied to air transport. Even one of the first transport commissioners ... said it very clearly in speeches even in Communications to the Council, but the Council ... did not take any note of it.[51]

In October 1973, shortly after Le Goy had become Director General for Transport, the Commission sent a Communication to the Council of Ministers in an attempt to get things moving on a CTP. It included specific mention of air and sea transport for the first time. The programme presented was discussed by the Parliament and the Economic and Social Committee over the following two years and was 'substantially approved. The Council of Ministers however, did not wish to commit itself to such a comprehensive and fundamental programme.'[52]

Even if the Commission, as guardian of the Treaty, tried to take Member States to task over non-implementation of Treaty rules in air transport, it had no independent means of doing so. As the Council of Ministers had not conferred implementing powers under Article 87 on the Commission for air transport, if the Commission took it upon itself to try to apply them, it would have to rely on Articles 88 and 89, which required it to work in collaboration with the Member States in attempts to get them to use their own national powers to implement Community law. Given that the Member States, with the exception of Britain and the Netherlands, had firmly set their faces against regulatory reform that would facilitate competition in the airline sector, the auguries did not look good and the Commission did not stand on firm ground.[53] In the meantime, the airline industry was going through some remarkable technological changes and passenger numbers were increasing steadily, but air transport remained untouched in the Community for over a decade and the Transport Directorate General, DG VII, did not even have a civil aviation section.

In the light of the Commission's own limited powers and the reluctance of the Council of Ministers and the Member States to act, there seemed no way forward. Then in 1974 things began to change, albeit glacially. Matters did not become entirely clear, but they at least became slightly less opaque. A case was adjudicated in the European Court of Justice concerning the legality of a domestic French law, which reserved quotas for French nationals in the manning of French merchant ships. This, the so-called French Seamen's Case, was not a test case conjured up by pro-liberalization forces: it 'came out of the blue'.[54] The issue was: Did the quota contravene the provisions of the Treaty of Rome governing the free movement of workers within the Community? Even though the general rules on services were excluded by the Treaty of Rome from application to transport, and air and sea transport were then excluded from the special provisions on transport by Article 84(2), nevertheless the Court declared the French quota law illegal. It did so on the grounds that air and sea transport 'remains, on the same basis as the other modes of transport, subject to the general rules of the Treaty. It thus follows that the application of Articles 48 to 51 to the sphere of sea transport is not optional but obligatory for Member States.'[55] This by no means dispersed entirely the ambiguity surrounding air transport and its relationship to Community rules, but it did edge a little further towards the idea that the competition laws might be applicable to air transport. Unfortunately, for integrating the sector, the Court failed to express clearly what it meant by 'subject to the general rules of the Treaty'. Nevertheless, the judgment provoked considerable discussion about what the actual situation might be and added fuel to the thoughts of those in the Commission who were obligated under the Treaty to ensure its proper application. Those who held their assumptions comfortably, that Community law would not require change to the status quo, were made to feel slightly less comfortable, but they could rest well, at least so far as the Court was concerned, for another twelve years before it issued a clearer and far more discomforting judgment. Complacency, however, did not govern in the Commission or the Parliament, both of which then began to develop more momentum for change.

Up until 1974 there were no strong dynamics for change in evidence in the European air transport sector.

The market was badly troubled in the late 1960s and early 1970s with recession, rising costs and diminishing load factors, and many thought that the unique nature of the airline industry made liberalization unwise on safety and national interest grounds, that airlines would not flourish in a freer market and that unlike other economic activities economies of scale did not apply to them. At this point no one had ever experienced the operation of a large deregulated airline market and there was thus little evidence either to demonstrate its possible advantages or to dispel the claims made in favour of sustaining the status quo. Those with the temerity to advocate regulatory reform and the nurturing of more competition in the US and in Britain had been rebuffed by the conservative power of vested interests and the uncertainties and problems that had wracked the industry. Little progress had been made, but widespread disillusionment with Keynesian economic policies and their apparent inability to deal with stagflation – rising inflation and declining out-put and demand – turned many economists to a more market-oriented approach that embraced privatization, deregulation and free enterprise. These ideas were soon to impact in a more successful and radical way on the international airline market than anything that had occurred under Nixon and Heath. In 1978 the US unleashed forces in its domestic market that soon thrust out into the international marketplace as well. These forces impacted on the operations of European airlines, on the airline system generally in the EC, and more globally.

The new economic ideas that began to emerge in the mid-1970s were particularly influential among organized interests. Those that existed during the period 1957–74, were overwhelmingly in favour of the status quo and consumers were generally content, largely because of cheap fares from the charter airline industry. However, as the new thinking began to gain purchase on a wider public, consumer groups began to press for regulatory reform in order to deliver the benefits to the consumer that the new economic dispensation so loudly claimed were there for the taking in a deregulated airline industry. New economic theory also had massive impact on politics in Britain and the US. Eventually it also drew many in the EC to the conclusion that Europe must respond to the challenge of globalization and the robust market forces that had been released through what was popularly referred to as Reaganomics and Thatcherism.

As we have seen, the Netherland's position was somewhat compromised because of its obvious self-interest regarding KLM and Schiphol and, while Britain's position was stronger, it was a newcomer and its commitment to the EC, especially with the return of the Labour Government in 1974, was still in question. The fact that Le Goy was the Transport Director-General was significant, but that alone was not enough to move things along within the EC. However, Britain was soon to take significant steps within its national sphere to modernize its airline industry. Forces were thus brought into play both within the European airline system as well as from outside from the US and soon they began to tell. So, while most of the Member States of the EC favoured conservative regulation for the air transport industry and were reluctant to develop a CTP and apply the Community's competition rules to it, they were about to be challenged in a way that they had never been before by Britain, the Netherlands and a combination of forces from the market, and organized interests. This took some time to materialize, but by the early 1980s forces were beginning to coalesce to form a point of attack on regulation and changes within the institutions of the EC were to provide a strategic way forward for them.

As changes in the market, among organized interests and in one of the key airline players within Europe developed, the European Court of Justice diminished the ambiguity of the Community's institutional position on the CTP, and in particular on air and sea transport. The French Seamen's case gave heart to those in the Commission and the Parliament who favoured change and the application of the competition rules to air transport, but change was still both slow in coming and dependent on a complex interplay of dynamics and it was far from clear just how far it might go.

2 After the French Seamen's case 1974–84

The market, member states, and the voices of aviation interests

> In the history of aviation, until 1978, there was never a significant market that was not developed through regulation.[1]

It is only in retrospect that 1974 can be seen as any kind of starting point for the SEAM. The French Seamen's case was known only to a handful of experts in the Commission, but those experts and the Director-General for Transport, Le Goy, were keen that things should be moved along. Generally within the Commission there was a feeling that 'now is the time, we have got a court ruling and we need to do something and we need to see if we cannot get the ball rolling'.[2] Whether they could do so or not, however, remained doubtful. Outside of the European institutions the ruling provided little scope for regulation reformers and was too technical to lend itself to easy exploitation by those lobbying for change. It had little impact among the Member States and in the same year in which the judgment was delivered Labour returned to power in Britain and there was a reversion to more traditional civil aviation policies. In the Bermuda 2 negotiations with the USA, 1976–77, the British argued strongly for single designation and a general reduction of opportunities for competition. The Chair of the Civil Aviation Authority (CAA), Lord Boyd-Carpenter, did all he could to try to rescue as much as possible of the Heath Government's legacy of a more liberal dispensation, but he was on the defensive, particularly while Peter Shore was Secretary of State for Trade and Industry.[3] So, with the reform impulse weakened within what had been the most reform-minded Member State, the prospects for significant movement within the Council of Ministers looked remote. The prospects for reform generally within the Community still looked poor and the Commission's position was not strong.

In 1974, if there had been a clear indication that the competition rules could be applied to air transport, the Commission might have been able to seize a real initiative and develop a strategically important negotiating position vis-à-vis the Member States. However, the Council of Ministers refused to act under Article 84(2), and the French Seamen's Case did not provide a clear enough mandate for the Commission to achieve anything by itself. As a result, there was hardly a viable negotiating situation discernible, particularly after the return of Labour to power in the UK and the onset of economic recession, both of which tended to gag discussion of regulatory reform and to confirm the near-unanimous preference among the Member States for the status quo. Even though airline regulatory reform was of low salience and a complex issue, both of which were often seen to benefit the Commission's hand; in fact, low salience in this case made it difficult to mobilize consumer and political interest behind reform and, with little or no expertise within the Commission in the early days, it is difficult to see how it could have taken advantage of the technical complexity in civil aviation. A modestly successful low profile leadership strategy on air transport did begin to emerge within the Commission during the decade between 1974 and 1984, but that did not really begin to take shape until after 1977, when a civil aviation section was established in DG VII. Even then, developments took place both in the marketplace and among the more liberal Member States and a clearer voice heard from reformist interest groups before any real momentum was created.[4] It was only after the impact from these several sources that the Commission was able to make moves on air transport, which stood a remote chance of success, and it was the marketplace impact, more than anything else, which ruffled the feathers of regulatory complacency between 1974 and 1984 and began to beckon to a way forward.

The marketplace

By the mid-1970s new economic theory was emerging particularly from the Chicago School in the US, which challenged the conventional wisdom of Keynesianism and the idea that regulating industries, like civil aviation, was necessary for public and consumer interests.[5] The newly discovered Laffer Curve, which predicted macro-economic benefits through lower taxes, along with privatization, deregulation, and the supply side revolution, framed the dominant position of economic theory and supposedly also spoke to the requirements for political liberty as well. The consequence for the airline industry was that two of the leading traditional arguments in favour of regulation were now challenged. The idea that competition on thin routes would eliminate services altogether, as they were deemed capable of sustaining only one operator, was set aside in favour of freer competition and pricing to decide which operator should run the route. This argument was buttressed by the claim that competitive prices would stimulate demand and transform thin into fatter routes. The general benefits of regulation were also challenged by the argument that regulation nurtured vested interests, which operated contrary to the public interest, for example, by price-fixing and pooling arrangements on single designation routes, which artificially raised the cost of flying for the consumer and eliminated competition. There were also 'mystery factors' involved in all this because there had never been a large deregulated civil aviation market before. No one really knew what the net effects on the airline market would be if it were to be deregulated. It needed a politician to take a leap of faith to consummate reform and let the market take its course, whatever that might actually turn out to be. The US found such a politician in President Jimmy Carter.⁶

Though Carter was a Democrat, and Democrats favour more government intervention than Republicans, he acted more robustly on deregulation than either of his two Republican predecessors. He was an interesting mixture of fiscal conservatism and populism that made him dislike economic power blocks, especially when they were inefficient and did not promote the public interest. By the time he came into office there had been a shift in economic theory and in the public mood: both were now critical of regulation and of the tightly regulated airline industry in particular. Carter and his aides conceived of a win-win situation where they could improve the efficiency of both the airlines and the economy in general and gain popularity from the voting public for delivering benefits to the consumer. In his first message to Congress on 4 March 1977 Carter announced:

> One of my Administration's major goals is to free the American people from the burden of over-regulation. As a first step toward our shared goal of a more efficient less burdensome Federal government, I urge the Congress to reduce Federal regulation of the domestic commercial airline industry.⁷

It took nearly two years before the Airline Regulatory Reform Bill became law. There was considerable opposition to overcome, both inside and outside government, but there was determination on Carter's part and among a group of his close advisers to push reform through the Congress. Carter also made a key appointment to the chairmanship of the Civil Aeronautics Board (CAB) in the person of Alfred (Ghengis) Kahn. Kahn played a massively important role. He was an economist convinced of the benefits of the deregulated market, and while there was little nationwide evidence of such benefits, there was from airline operations within single states which were not governed by CAB rules. For example, Pacific Southwestern Airlines operated a highly competitive low cost service within California between San Francisco and Los Angeles. Kahn used evidence of those types of operation as ammunition to strengthen his more theoretical arguments in favour of deregulation. The conclusion of his argument was simple: 'It is time to return this industry to the free enterprise system.'⁸ In retrospect Kahn opined in 1983: 'What can be attributed to deregulation is a wider variety of service and fare options, lower costs and fares, and an end to barriers to entry.'⁹ Instead of expensive fares for limited services offered by inefficient high cost airlines, the discipline of the market could produce airlines that were flexible and efficient, sensitive to consumer needs, and offering lower fares while achieving levels of profitability that had eluded airlines in the past. These are the beliefs that he acted on and, even before the passage of the 1978 reform act, he began to use his executive powers to liberalize route entry and pricing. All this was accelerated after the passage of the act, which brought a staged phase-in of an almost completely deregulated market. Its consummation and the expiry of the CAB were both set for January 1985. Any danger that executive action might reverse policy in the same way that Kahn had reversed the thrust of regulation prevailing prior to 1978 was no longer imminent. As Kahn had advised, 'Only Congress can say which of these [regulation or deregulation] it prefers, and make sure this whirling dervish ends up facing in the direction you want it to face.'[10] The Congress duly made its decision and on the domestic front the way things were to go was clearly set out, but there was also the question of the international marketplace as well. This grew increasingly important as the market forces released by domestic US deregulation soon demonstrated what economists had long known: market forces do not recognize national boundaries. The Carter administration developed two strategies to deal with the international marketplace, but US policy was also helped by market forces released by the fait accompli of domestic US deregulation and by the way that those forces began to seep into the international terrain.

For the Carter administration, the international airline market was clearly more intractable than the US domestic market. Their scope of action was more constrained and, as the ill-fated – so far as the US was concerned – Bermuda 2 negotiations with Britain demonstrated, international relationships sometimes had an awkward tendency to produce results completely at odds with what the US actually wanted. Nevertheless, it was unavoidable that the US would have to conduct a wide series of bilateral re-negotiations if it were to change, albeit incrementally, the international marketplace and create an operating environment that efficient US airlines could exploit to their advantage. The passage of the International Air Transportation Competition Act in 1979 created the mandate for that policy and it has been pursued with varying degrees of vigour ever since. By 1980 a dozen liberal bilaterals had been negotiated and, while most were with fairly insignificant players, agreements with the Netherlands, Belgium and West Germany, all concluded in 1978, were to have important consequences for awakening members of the European Community (EC) to the rigours and opportunities of more competition. This was the first and most enduring of American strategies to deregulate the international marketplace: the second was a Show Cause Order (SCO) promulgated by Alfred Kahn's CAB.

Ever since IATA began its tariff conferences to fix air fares in 1945, its recommendations regularly received approval from the US CAB. This was vital because as it approved it also granted the airlines immunity from US anti-trust laws, which would otherwise have prohibited this cartel-style operation. With Kahn at the CAB things changed. On 9 June 1978 the CAB suggested that IATA fare setting might not warrant anti-trust immunity as it might not be in the interest of the US public. It now issued a SCO requiring IATA to show cause in proceedings before the CAB why this new interpretation of IATA practices should not be applied in the US. The SCO was correctly seen as an attempt by the CAB to stop inter-airline fare agreements and to destroy IATA or at least IATA in its role as a fare co-ordinator.[11] There were three consequences to this. First, an unholy row erupted with criticisms directed against the SCO and the CAB from the international community, from hard-line opponents and some of the more moderate reform elements from within the US and, of course, from IATA itself.

Second, despite the often rather self-righteous defence of its traditional practices, the IATA bowed to the pressure for some reform. Since the mid 1970s it had been subjected to increasing demands for change, particularly in the light of the challenge to scheduled operators from charters and non-IATA scheduled carriers from South East Asia and the increasing difficulty in achieving agreement on tariffs. The SCO precipitated decisions from policy reviews already under way. 'Provisions for the Regulation and Conduct of the IATA Traffic Conferences' were approved by the IATA's executive in the fall of 1978 and submitted to the US CAB in November. Tariff conferences were now made optional rather than obligatory for members and the system of price fixing was made considerably more flexible. Instead of world-wide agreements it now became possible to deal with regions or even individual routes separately and single vetoes over more competitive pricing was made more difficult. Consultation procedures were broadened and the whole tone of IATA's rigid fare fixing was lowered.[12] Third, recognizing that IATA had acted to reform its operations and, in the light of world-wide opposition, mobilized at least in part by IATA, which had also tried to exploit differences between the US State and Transportation Departments on the one hand and the CAB on the other, the Carter administration and its allies in the Congress began to back away from the more radical alternatives.[13] Provisions prohibiting CAB approval of inter-carrier fare agreements in the International Air Transportation Competition Act were deleted.[14] In fact, the new IATA procedures were granted anti-trust immunity on 14 May 1979[15] and Kahn's successor at the CAB, Marvin Cohen, explained in February 1980:

> The Board was impressed by the support given to the new IATA mechanism not only by many witnesses who are familiar with the industry, but also by our own Department of Transportation and State and other [sic] foreign government leaders who support the pro-competitive policies of the United States.... Diplomatic considerations are primary reasons for our decision to extend immunity to the new IATA.[16]

However, this moderation of the US drive for international deregulation did not apply equally throughout the system: it continued to use the threat of the SCO on the North Atlantic and, as we shall see when we come to examine the role of ECAC during this period, this had significant implications for the beginning of liberalized pricing for the international operations of European airlines. If nothing else, it set an example of what could be achieved though those rigidly set against liberalization had developed such strong ideological perspectives or else believed that they had so much to loose, that they chose only to see damaging chaos and little or no benefits in the new liberalized North Atlantic marketplace.

Acting in tandem with US liberalization strategies ran market forces, some preceding the legal and institutional moves for reform, others released and nurtured by them. In the US there were no state owned airlines, but the operation of many had been heavily subsidized through airmail contracts, and the CAB had tightly regulated entry and exit into the market and controlled prices. So, even in the US, the airlines never operated on commercial lines. There was also a widespread belief that airlines could not reap economies of scale. An airline could get bigger and possibly make more overall profit, but on a *pro rata* basis profit margins would remain constant or more likely would decline as larger operations meant more management difficulties. Getting bigger did not appear to provide opportunities for more efficiency, for example, by increasing an aircraft's load factor, and thus economies of scale did not seem to apply. This conventional wisdom, held widely within the airline industry, was about to be destroyed.

> What was discovered were economies of scale ..., i.e. you organised your system in such a way that you were able to consolidate large amounts of traffic at a point and then redistribute that traffic. For each unit ... that you flew, if you had ... higher load factors on that piece of equipment in effect you had a more productive piece of equipment – a more productive unit of production.[17]

This was the hub and spoke configuration of routes. Ironically, deregulation, in releasing market forces that discovered economies of scale through hub and spoke operations, on the one hand destroyed America's leading traditional overseas operators, Pan American World Airways (Pan Am) and Trans World Airlines (TWA), and on the other empowered its traditional domestic operators, UA, American Airlines (AA) and Delta. They now became major international operators with the efficiency and the networks to challenge the very survival of many foreign airlines, including in Europe, unless their governments were prepared to bail them out continuously with subsidies of ever increasing size or to go down a deregulation path of their own. The way it worked was like this: UA, AA and Delta seized the opportunity offered by deregulation to compete and to expand. With hub and spoke efficiencies, economies of scale made sense and soon all three airlines had major hub and spoke networks that could draw on most of the vast US domestic market. They fed huge numbers of passengers in and out of their hubs along spokes operated by aircraft with higher load factors. Prior to deregulation, load factors over the decade had averaged out at about 52 per cent, while in the six years following the deregulation act it averaged about 59 per cent. Perhaps more importantly, when demand was depressed, post-deregulation load factors were over 10 per cent higher than in similar periods pre-deregulation.[18] And these load factors were with vastly expanded passenger numbers. Inhibitions about expansion were now replaced by enthusiasm to expand in pursuit of more economies of scale, more hubs and spokes, and more profits. As US government policy pursued liberal bilateral ASAs, which opened up more and more US international gateways based on the old domestic carriers' hubs, AA, UA and Delta carried all before them. Well positioned through their domestic inter-connected hubs and their vast number of feeder spokes to assemble large numbers of passengers, there seemed an irresistible logic that the traditional domestic operators should now use their dominance over the US domestic market, i.e. approximately 40 per cent of the entire world civil aviation market, to thrust out their spokes into the international sphere and that is precisely what they did. As Taneja explained in his study in 1988: 'An increase in the number of spokes leads, in turn, to the development of national and eventually international coverage.'[19]

Why restrict operations to the domestic market when they could reap profits from overseas operations? They now entered the international market in a big way to the growing consternation of foreign carriers and to the likes of Pan Am and TWA, which now recognized the strategic vulnerability of their operations and scurried around trying to develop domestic feeder systems of their own through expansion and takeovers. They had to have their own domestic hub and spoke operations, but they had acted too late. Within a decade the mighty Pan Am and TWA were struggling to survive: in the early 1990s they gave up and disappeared for ever. There were those in Europe who had realized, well before those commercial fatalities occurred, that Europe had challenges to which it must respond. As one senior airline executive put it, the new dynamics of competition, released by deregulation in the US, would impact in Europe and either force the airlines there to become more competitive or cause them to require larger subsidies.[20] John Steele, the European Commission Transport Director-General (1981–86), in retrospect said more or less the same thing, namely that the beginning of reform in Europe 'was a reaction to events in the USA and the realisation that the same concerns existed in Europe and that unless the system was made more flexible it would break'.[21]

An important coda needs to be added to this account of the rise of the US domestic carriers into international mega-carriers. None of this would have been possible without a quantum leap forward in the technology of computers. The complexity of running an airline on a hub and spoke system was intimidating. Ensuring that passengers fed in through multiple spokes for a common destination and then speedily fed out on the relevant spoke to that destination could not have been done without computers. By the mid 1980s the major computer reservation systems (CRSs) could 'juggle one hundred million fares at a single time'.[22] CRSs became a key weapon in the newly competitive airline industry and this also was to have impact in Europe.

By the end of the 1970s, EC officials and members of the travelling public were beginning to absorb what was happening in the US and to consider the implications for Europe. As a senior European official put it:

> The new aviation policy of the Carter Administration has its influence on the European scene. European governments and airlines have to react to the challenge coming across the Atlantic. The European public asks whether the advantages, which the new developments on the other side of the Atlantic apparently have for the passenger, could not be had in Europe as well, especially for the intra-European traffic.
>
> The European politician cannot remain indifferent to this growing concern of the European citizen on matters of civil aviation.[23]

Between 1974 and 1979 nothing was more significant for promoting action, or at least thought, within the EC on regulatory reform of the airline market than the changing attitudes towards regulated industries, wrought by new economic theory, the changes that they helped to produce in the US airline industry, and the significance of competitive market forces that those changes unleashed into the marketplace. By 1983 articles were appearing in academic and business journals that specifically discussed the lessons that Europe might learn from the US experience. Some pointed out the different conditions in Europe, namely its collection of only partially integrated nation states, high levels of regulation, less efficiency in its airline industry and government ownership.[24] There were also issues such as the greater strength of the trade unions and stronger commitments to social goals in Europe. All these factors and others were taken into account in the growing debate about reform in Europe and modified what eventually happened there: there was no US style deregulation in Europe. However, for those who favoured any kind of substantial reform, there was no denying that there were lessons to be learnt and benefits to be reaped from the American experience: 'Possibly the most important conclusions from the US airline deregulation are that it has resulted in increased efficiency of the industry as a whole, and that it has broadly confirmed economists' views on how markets work.'[25] In contrast, those staunchly in support of the European status quo argued that US style deregulation was simply not applicable to the different conditions in Europe, pointed only to its actual and potential negative effects, and used it as a kind of bogeyman to scare people away from any kind of liberalization in Europe.

Over the following years US liberal ASAs sought incrementally to adjust the international aviation system to facilitate the impact of competitive dynamics. The US always acted, however, with a careful eye on the overall interests of its airlines. It is important to note that neither the Americans nor the several European states nor those who spoke on behalf of the EC were without hubris. All parties, including the Americans, had some aspects of the marketplace that they wanted to protect, either for the benefit of their own airlines or on national interest grounds. As the EC/EU progressed down the road of reform, negotiations with the US were often fraught with difficulties and, so far as at least some European Member States were concerned, the US position on cabotage, ownership and control, the requirement that US officials fly only on US airlines – the fly the flag rule - and restrictions on wet leasing (the leasing of aircraft with crews) were all seen as problematical and curiously contrary to the principle of allowing market forces and airlines to determine business. Ironically, when the EU and the US finally came to discuss such matters face to face, it was the Europeans who trumped the Americans at their own game of liberalization, but that was not for another twenty years.

Britain: the key Member State

Britain had the potential to be, and later became, the key player among the Member States in the reform of the Community's air transport system. The decade between 1974 and 1984 witnessed radical government shifts in policy away from liberal reform and then back again, but it was not to a position without difficult complications. The liberal reform agenda for airlines in Europe was never straightforward anywhere, even in Britain. Shifts in British policy were propelled by pragmatic considerations of the health of British airlines as well as by ideology. In order to appreciate Britain's key role in promoting liberalization of the airline industry in Europe, it is important to appreciate the impact of such factors, which determined what at times appeared rather contradictory, and which were always complex, policy positions.

When Labour came into power in 1974, the Secretary of State for Trade and Industry, Peter Shore, and his Parliamentary Secretary, Stanley Clinton Davis, set about a review of civil aviation policy. It soon became clear that Shore wanted to revert to a policy of tight regulation.[26] In part this was justified by a serious downturn in the market after the recession that followed in the wake of the Yom Kippur War. There now seemed to be less scope for competition and Shore reversed the Heath government's policy of direct competition between B.Cal. and BA, and in its place reintroduced single designation and spheres of influence for each airline. On 11 February 1976 Shore announced this new policy and most controversially of all he withdrew Laker's licence to operate his low cost service Skytrain between Stansted and New York.[27]

While the CAA recognized that market conditions were difficult for introducing more competition, it nevertheless felt that the government had gone too far in re-regulation. In the wake of the downturn of the market, sensing that Skytrain's low-cost service posed the threat of inviting retaliatory competitive fares from foreign operators and of diversion of passengers from other operators, BA had appealed in 1975 to the CAA to revoke Laker's licence. 'Diversion', or siphoning off, was a commonly used euphemism by regulators. They ignored the idea that it was possible to have a more efficient competitive airline that would not only deliver benefits to the consumer but generate new customers as well, and instead they emphasized the negative effect of the 'diversion' of passengers from existing airlines. The CAA acknowledged the dangers identified by BA and cautioned that new operations should not be introduced in 1975 because of difficult market conditions, but it refused to revoke Laker's licence. In fact, Laker had been unable to mount the service anyway because of procrastination by the US CAB and its failure to grant him traffic rights. Then ironically, just as President Ford appeared set to end those procrastinations and get the CAB to grant traffic rights, Shore's policy guidance seemed to dash any hope of the transatlantic Skytrain becoming a reality.

The CAA was far from content. It tried to safeguard the Heath legacy and Lord Boyd-Carpenter, Chairman of the CAA, expressed dissent from Shore's new policy guidance for the CAA because it 'would have the effect of inhibiting the Authority from granting, even in the most exceptional circumstances, an air transport licence to more than one British airline on the same route'.[28] Boyd-Carpenter feared that any meaningful independence was being denied to the

CAA by the new regulation-minded Labour government. Freddie Laker took heart from the stance of the CAA. He had invested millions of pounds in equipment for Skytrain and was too resilient a character to give up at this stage. Laker took the matter to court claiming that Shore had exceeded his statutory powers in ordering the CAA to withdraw his licence. Both the High Court and the Appeal Court agreed. The 1971 act that had established the CAA provided that the Secretary of State could 'give guidance to the Authority so as to amplify and supplement ... four objectives [set out in the 1971 Civil Aviation Act], in more detail and so as to cover also the Authority's functions in other areas'.[29] The court ruled that the requirement that the CAA should withdraw Laker's Skytrain licence was not guidance but a diktat and as such *ultra vires*. Laker could have another try at launching Skytrain. Largely because of this, Laker became an important factor in the re-negotiation of the Anglo-American ASA over the next twelve months.

The Bermuda 2 negotiations, as they were universally known, were conducted under the auspices of Shore's successor Edmund Dell. Dell had denounced Bermuda 1, thus forcing a wholesale renegotiation of the ASA with the Americans, largely because of national balance of payments reasons and the hope of gaining more of the transatlantic market for British airlines. He was deeply concerned about the airline industry and that led him into advocating various new regulations. For example, he introduced Traffic Distribution Rules (TDRs), which tried to restrict or at least control access to Heathrow and spread airline operations to the other London airports. The TDRs and their consequences became a perennial issue in UK–US negotiations and they also had implications for the SEAM. In addition, Dell felt that US carriers had too large a share of the transatlantic market. His position thus looks like that of a conventional government regulator, somewhat akin to Shore's. However, he was 'rather unhappy about what Peter Shore had done' with Laker, and he also knew that Shore's single designation policy was problematic. In particular 'to achieve single designation on the New York-London route would have been a miracle'. The Americans just would not accept that. In fact, he might be more accurately described as an advocate of regulated competition (especially when British interests were thereby served). The exigency of the negotiating situation with the Americans on airline designations demanded that Britain should have a competitive second carrier on the main transatlantic route. Dell thus decided that Laker should be Britain's second carrier and he argued the case in Cabinet Committee and won.[30] In September 1977, Skytrain began operations under the new Bermuda 2 regime. With his usual flourish Laker announced that he and Skytrain were liberating the imprisoned travelling public, who had been locked into high prices through IATA's cartel price-fixing operations for over thirty years. In fact, Bermuda 2 was generally more regulatory than Bermuda 1, but Laker and Skytrain introduced a highly competitive element that was to have impact on the North Atlantic routes, albeit for a short time, and set another example of what might be done.

A rather strange configuration of factors conspired to maintain some competitive forces in British civil aviation, despite Shore's policy, and to provide potential for developing more. The CAA had dug its heels in and thanks to the ruling in the Appeal Court had achieved a degree of independence from the government, which held out the possibility of more pro-competition policies emanating from the CAA in the future. More specifically and immediately they had helped to launch Skytrain. That in the end was made possible by a switch away from a rigid policy of single designation by Dell because of his need to match two US carriers on the main transatlantic route with two British carriers. However, all this was something of a struggle. There were no strong moves emanating directly from British government policy that would be likely to influence the EC to move on airline regulatory reform. In 1979 that was to change again and the potential that had been preserved for regulatory reform and increased competition was now seized upon robustly by the new Conservative government of Margaret Thatcher.

Thatcher wrought radical change throughout the British economy, and civil aviation was no exception to that generalization. The emphases on market forces, self-reliance, and individual enterprise were ubiquitous. However, the government was not so ideologically blinkered that it could not appreciate that there would have to be a gradual move towards a freer market in civil aviation. That does not mean to suggest that change should not come as quickly as feasible but that it had to be managed carefully, particularly with regard to international and European operations and to the intention of privatizing BA. Overseas markets in Europe and wider a field would need to be carefully adjusted to so as not to be to the disadvantage of British airlines, and it was no good pushing BA into a competitive marketplace only to see it fail. Thatcher's controversial economic reform agenda could not be endangered by the perceived possibility of a spectacular failure if BA were privatized and then failed. Considerations of the health and welfare of BA continued to have regulatory implications for British policy until the early 1990s and placed something of a brake on those fervently seeking liberalization at home and in Europe.

The civil aviation bill introduced by Secretary of State for Trade and Industry John Nott clearly spelt out the way things were to go. BA was to be privatized. The CAA was to be given more independence and authority. Guidance from the government was to be replaced by a periodic statement of licensing policy from the CAA, the interests of consumers were to be given equal weight to those of the operators, and there was to be much more emphasis on competition. Nott made it clear that liberalization at home and abroad were the objectives of the government.

> The United Kingdom cannot force other Governments to loosen the constraints of regulation. All that we can attempt to do is to persuade other Governments to follow our course.... Meanwhile it is the Government's intention to keep up pressure on other Governments, particularly within Europe. Government shareholdings in national airlines should not deny air travellers the benefits of competition which apply in other industries.[31]

As Nott acknowledged, Britain could not unilaterally change the system outside the UK domestic airline market, but it could bring pressure to bear upon the EC through its officials there. John Steele took over from Le Goy in 1981 and continued to argue strongly in favour of liberalization. The British Presidency of the Council of Ministers in the latter half of 1981 was also used to try to push things along. However, of equal, if not greater, importance were the changes that the Thatcher government crafted in the British airline market and in its approach to ASAs. Nott supplemented legislative with executive action and in 1980 took the controversial decision to override the CAA and allow multiple designations on the London–Hong Kong route by authorizing licences to Cathay Pacific and Laker, thus allowing them to join existing operators BA and B.Cal. There was a similar decision in the domestic sphere when Nott's successor Lord Cockfield reversed another CAA decision and allowed BM to mount a service from Heathrow to Glasgow in 1982. Some saw these decisions as the beginning of a highly competitive policy, but they were just isolated decisions, more important in symbolism than in substance. In the international sphere further deregulation had to be mediated through the need to protect BA,[32] and in the domestic market the independent airlines were fearful that a strong and privatized BA, allowed to compete on any and all routes, might act as a predator and gobble up the smaller airlines. This case was very effectively made by Richard Venables on behalf of Air UK.[33] So far as the government was concerned, economic recession and other factors, both in the domestic and the international marketplaces, temporarily placed constraints on further liberalization; and the situation in the EC in particular appeared to offer no clear way forward. Lord Cockfield commented in the House of Lords in January 1983:

> The competition rules of the Treaty of Rome can only be enforced once it has been determined that they do in fact apply. There has been no decision of the European Court of Justice in relation to air transport which says conclusively that they do.[34]

Just over a year later, however, conditions had changed and Nicholas Ridley took a much more robust line with regard to the operation of the Community's competition rules and their application to air transport. In June 1983 there was a General Election, which returned Thatcher to power with renewed determination to carry reform forward, and conditions were now improving as both the British and the world economy began to revive. The aviation brief was shifted from the Department of Trade to the Department of Transport and, after four months of the new government, Nicholas Ridley became Secretary of Transport with a renewed and firm commitment to liberalization. Largely in response to these developments, the government asked the CAA in late 1983 to make a comprehensive study of deregulation and, in the EC Transport Council meeting in May 1984, Ridley gave clear notice of British purpose when he announced that the Community's competition rules would be deemed by the British government to take precedence over the practice of inter-airline price agreements.[35] Unfortunately, as we shall see in Chapter 4, while there was good intent and symbolic importance to Ridley's declaration, there turned out to be little substance. Nevertheless, with the economy improving and with a renewed mandate from the British people, it looked as if Britain was going to move unequivocally on its uphill journey on the road of regulatory reform towards liberalization.

The CAA's report appeared in July 1984. It favoured nurturing competition and reducing BA's dominant position by redistributing about eight per cent of its routes. Ridley tried to defend the report, but BA's Chairman, Lord King, charged with the job of leading BA through privatization and on to commercial success, had the ear of Margaret Thatcher and the support of Chancellor of the Exchequer, Nigel Lawson, Chairman of the Conservative Party, Norman Tebbit and Michael Colvin, Member of Parliament (MP) who had an influential voice in the House of Commons on civil aviation. There was also an added complication for BA, which had already stirred up King's protective feelings. Freddie Laker, when his Skytrain failed in 1982, brought an action against BA (along with Pan Am, TWA, McDonnell Douglas and others) alleging that they had colluded to set predatory prices to drive him out of the marketplace. This was eventually settled out of court in the summer of 1985, but until then the case hung like a malevolent cloud over BA's future, threatening both its financial viability and prospective buyers of its shares. Those who opposed Ridley were just as committed in general to liberalization, but they were concerned about the possible adverse consequences for the broader economic agenda if BA were privatized and then were it to fail. With such powerful opposition ranged against him and, in the face of devastatingly effective lobbying by BA, Ridley had to give way.[36] The resulting White Paper turned into a compromise. It approved further mild deregulation in the domestic market and created little immediate change in the international sphere because of the need to ensure that, when BA was floated on the open market, it would be attractive to investors and commercially strong. BA was not obliged to abandon routes or weaken its position at Gatwick. However, liberalization was to continue. The CAA was expected to promote change through liberal licensing with due regard to the dangers of predatory pricing and monopoly positions.[37] The government continued to voice the language of reform. Policy was 'to encourage a sound and competitive multi-airline industry ... to promote competition in all markets ... to ensure adequate safeguards against anti-competitive behaviour ... [and] to put ownership of British Airways into the hands of private investors'.[38] There was no denying that progress had been slow and difficult and problems had appeared along the way. After moving ahead of the CAA on liberalization for four years, the government confronted by the need to nurture BA and the possibility of problems that deregulation might spawn pulled back slightly. At the same time it continued to encourage the CAA to be innovative and to nudge things forward to a more liberal dispensation and to negotiate liberal ASAs with European partners.[39]

However, there would be little point in creating a more liberal environment if British airlines could not exploit it. And here the position of BM, one of Britain's strongest independent scheduled airlines, was important. BM had been disappointed with the way the government dealt with the CAA's recommendations about redistribution of routes from BA. In an attempt to encourage competition and mollify BM's chairman Michael Bishop, who was no less a close ally of the Thatcher government than Lord King, BM was granted international traffic rights at Heathrow through a process of rather contorted reasoning. Dell's TDRs stipulated that there should be no new international operators at Heathrow; however, it was now decided that as BM had operated a route from Heathrow to Strasbourg for a short time in the 1970s, which had been disbanded well before the TDRs were introduced, it should have a grandfathered right to international routes out of Heathrow. This was important for the near future because in June 1984 Britain and the Netherlands negotiated a liberal ASA with free route access, no capacity restrictions, and a country of origin, and then a year later a double disapproval, fare regime. With its grandfathered right to international operations BM could apply for a Heathrow–Amsterdam route, which it duly did. On Sunday 29 June 1986 the inaugural flight to Amsterdam took off. BM was thus able to contribute its competitive edge and play a significant part in the British strategy to put pressure on Europe by negotiating liberal ASAs and introducing the forces of the marketplace into European air transport.

Movements in the EC were beginning to open up more opportunities for British airlines and the government was eager to exploit those opportunities. As we shall see in the next chapter three of the key developments in the EC in the aftermath of the French Seamen's case were a regional services directive and two memoranda from the Commission trying to lay out air transport policy. All were supported by the British Government and were partly the result of inputs from its officials. By October 1984 the British government's opinion was that:

> The Regional Air Services Directive of 1983 was a very limited step in the right direction, allowing smaller airlines more freedom to mount services between regional airports in the Community. The Government has welcomed the European Commission's Second Memorandum on a Community Air Transport Policy which should provide the basis for a worthwhile liberalization, though it does not go far enough.[40]

Clearly, by the end of 1984, liberalization had made progress in Britain, but it was not a straightforward affair. It was not simply a matter of abolishing regulations and letting the market have a free hand. Even in the free market heart of the Thatcher government that was never seen as a viable option. In that sense Britain, which was closer ideologically to the US than anywhere else in Europe, demonstrated just how different things were in Europe to things in the US. If Britain were not prepared to go down the kind of deregulation route that the US had proceeded along, then clearly whatever form of deregulation were crafted for Europe it would be different from what was happening in the US. It was widely felt that it was not enough to remove regulation to ensure competition. Dominant positions, distortions in the marketplace, and foreign government policies could compromise competition and adversely affect the interests of consumers and operators. Some thought that radical action, as had been proposed by the CAA, to reduce the dominance of major players, was necessary if true competition were to flourish. In other words competition needed to be managed by appropriate regulation if it were to be a reality that would benefit consumers and operators alike. One had to deregulate in order to re-regulate in a manner compatible with competition. And as time passed it was not just dominant positions, that worried new would-be competitors and those who promoted them, but availability of landing and take-off slots at congested airports, alliances, ownership and control regulations, frequent flyer programmes (FFPs), CRS operations, state subsidies, and obstacles to entry on foreign routes. All these concerns gradually began to take shape between 1974 and 1984 and tended to inhibit or at least give grounds for caution for the reformers. In addition, the early 1980s witnessed severe depression in the airline industry and that persuaded many, including the reformers in Britain, that the time was not right and to pedal slowly for reform. By 1983 things were beginning to change. The recession turned the corner into recovery and Ridley pushed for reform. That push had to be moderated because of considerations to do with BA and the reality that Britain alone could not liberalize the European aviation system unilaterally, but government policy continued to urge change to more competition so long as British airlines were not unfairly placed at a disadvantage. Ridley highlighted the problem of fare setting and the EC competition rules, and Britain in one respect at least made an approach similar to that of the US and began a policy of negotiating liberal ASAs in an attempt to spread deregulation, promote the fortunes of independent airlines such as BM, and nurture competition. The results of the latter tactic still had to be felt but they promised much.

The voices of aviation interests 1974–84

Because pressures are often exerted through informal channels or channels that lack transparency, direct causal links between the pressures interest groups and NGOs exert and policy outcomes favourable to their concerns cannot always be clearly established, and their significance and impact on policy developments are thus difficult to assess. The leading expert in the field of interest group activity in the EC concludes that the influence of interest groups tends generally to decline in power as issues rise in the institutional decision-making process, but can often help to set agendas and be influential in the early stages of development.[41] If these claims are correct then we should expect to find the various voices of aviation interests significant in the early stages of the development of momentum towards the SEAM, but this is only partly substantiated by the evidence at hand.

Interest group voices arguing for reform had little impact in the early days; however, during the late 1970s and early 1980s, things began to change. After the French Seamen's Case, because of developments in Brussels and in the UK and growing momentum in the marketplace, there was a flurry of activity. A number of lobbying organizations were established, for example in 1973 the CAA established the UK Air Transport Users Committee, and similarly FATUREC was established in 1982 with the support of the Commission; close cooperation between these lobby groups and their 'parent' organizations resulted in some benefits for supporting reform proposals, but these were very much cases of child to the father rather than father of the child. Other more broad-based interest groups contributed to the momentum for the development of the Single Market and that in turn helped the case for air transport regulatory reform, but the main effects of interest groups were not felt until after 1984 and then their proposals tended to be drawn along on the coattails of momentum for change already underway. As O'Reilly and Sweet observe, lobbying groups proliferated at the end of the 1970s and in early 1980s and also tended to become more supranational in their activities,[42] but generally their impact in favour of reform appears to have been pretty peripheral with the notable exception of Lord Bethell's Freedom of the Skies Campaign and the legal challenges that he mounted in the EC and in the UK, which affected the course of events in the development of the SEAM. It is also important to note that there was close collaboration between Bethell and Laker, and that it was not without effect in trying to proselytize to the more liberal dispensation. Laker and his Skytrain had wider resonance than just in the purely commercial domain. Laker was making a political point as well and he allied with Bethell to promote liberalization.

Countering developments favourable for reform, forces rallied in support of the status quo. For example, the AEA emerged in 1973 from the European Airlines Research Bureau and, as its Secretary General remarked in 1994,

> an underlying motivation behind the creation of the AEA was the awareness among EC airlines that, even though air transport policy was excluded from the field of application of the Rome Treaty, developments in the Common Market would, unavoidably, affect airline activities in many areas.[43]

Labour organizations were also fearful of change and opposed liberalization. One could argue that interest groups were very influential from the outset, but only in terms of trying to arrest the momentum for change and the creation of the SEAM. As the new economic theorists had highlighted, regulation tends to create strong and well embedded vested interests that strive to uphold the status quo even in the face of evidence that its operation is contrary to consumer and public interests. Consultant to Lord Bethell, John Loder, expounded on these dangers when he wrote in July 1988: 'Air travellers and their organizations are as vocal as the media and other parts of the system permit. There is a commercial conspiracy of censorship in which the cartel airlines and significant parts of the media system cooperate.'[44] Given Loder's lobbying for reform, his opinions were understandably not necessarily impartial; nevertheless, he painted a disturbing picture of industry and media collusion that verged on corruption involving payment in kind – free flights and hotel accommodation – and the placement of advertising in aviation journals. In return the media allegedly delivered anodyne criticisms of the status quo or merely refrained from any criticism of it.

> Add to that those journalists who have been bought by the AEA airlines and the cartel establishment and who simply put their name to any press release or opinion put out by the cartel, then the possibilities for the expression of public opinion become rather small and ineffective.[45]

The fact that someone associated with the most high profile lobbyist for reform should bemoan the impotence of those lobbying for change speaks reams about the role of interest groups in promoting liberalization and about interest groups trying to uphold the status quo. What came out of The Freedom of the Skies Campaign and matters that emerged from the ECAC struggled to make headway against such forces.

Bethell, looking back from the vantage point of 1995, summed up his ambitions in the 1980s in the following way.

> In the early 1980s I sought to outlaw the pooling arrangements and other restrictive practices of the national airlines by taking them to the courts: first to the European Court of Justice under Article 173; and then to the High Court in this country for violation of Articles 95 and 96 of the Treaty of Rome.[46]

Both he and Laker busied themselves in trying to raise the profile of, and to emphasize the need to bring about, regulatory reform. Laker, buoyed by his court success in retaining the transatlantic Skytrain and getting it under way, albeit in deteriorating economic circumstances, now tried to exploit the liberal policy of the CAA and applied for a host of routes operating from the UK to other states in Europe. In the spring of 1980 he was denied his request by the CAA: it was just too extreme for them. Laker now engaged with Lord Bethell to see if together they might overturn the status quo. Bethell launched his Freedom of the Skies Campaign in May 1980 with its programme of reform propagated in the *Business Traveller* magazine. The following year Bethell also turned to the law for help, hoping that he might exploit the ambiguity of the relationship between the European air transport system and the operation of the general provisions of the Treaty of Rome in order to move reform forward. He complained first to the Commission demanding that it discharge its responsibilities under Article 89 to ensure the application of the principles of Articles 85 and 86 concerning concerted practices and dominant positions and to do so by demanding information and explanations from the airlines about their cooperative practices. If the Commission did not act then he would complain to the European Court of Justice.

The Commission turned down Bethell's request. Its response was that 'in most cases the final fixing of air fares was the sole responsibility of the Member

States so that there was in principle no ground to scrutinize the activity of airline companies on the basis of Article 85' (i.e. concerted action). If that could indeed be sustained then the Commission had pronounced correctly because the remit of DG IV was restricted to private bodies and it had no authority over government actions. However, the response disguised serious differences between DG VII and the Commission's Legal Service which was more sceptical about the legality of fare fixing. Perhaps that uncertainty affected officials in DG VII as well and prompted them into action albeit falling short of what Bethell had wanted. The Commission undertook, in the light of the special relationship between airlines and government, to investigate matters further.[47] Bethell had not got what he wanted and now moved on to complain to the European Court of Justice, although he had already prompted action within the Commission, which was yet to bear fruit. The court case was less productive.

Bethell ran up against a general difficulty for interest groups seeking to take legal action to support their cause in the EC. Bethell brought his case under Article 173 or, failing that, under Article 175 of the Rome Treaty. In order for the case to succeed he needed to show that the issue he raised had 'direct and individual' concern for him. The Court found that 'the applicant is asking the Commission not to take a decision in respect of him, but to open an inquiry with regard to third parties and to take decisions in respect of them'.[48] In short, the issue was not of direct and individual concern to Bethell and as a result he lacked *locus standi*: the case was inadmissible. Bethell lost the battle, but as noted above he had, in fact, otherwise progressed in the war by encouraging the Commission into more activity. At the same time he had exposed a general problem for interest groups, which limited their effectiveness within the EC. It was difficult for them to establish *locus standi* in legal cases because of the direct and individual concern criteria. Many years later, in 2002 those principles were challenged, and it now seems possible that litigation by interest groups might have been made easier by reducing requirements solely to the establishment of direct concern.[49]

While Bethell's commitment to liberalization was clear, the role of ECAC is more difficult to assess. ECAC was a key institution for various technical aspects of European civil aviation, and it also made contributions to reform and did so in two guises. First, it negotiated a Memorandum of Understanding with the US on a fares' regime for the North Atlantic; and second, it produced the Report on Competition in Intra-European Air Services, hereafter referred to as the COMPAS Report, which laid out in great detail possibilities for reforming the air transport industry in Europe. In short ECAC helped to mediate change in pricing, which set a more liberal example, and it provided an important source of information about the shape a more liberal and competitive air transport market might take. Just how significant ECAC as an organization was in changing the North Atlantic fare regime and in proposing liberalization is, however, subject to rather differing views, which will need to be considered in some detail.

'ECAC being liberal ... is absolute nonsense.' This dismissive judgement, uttered by someone who has had first-hand experience of working with ECAC from both the national and Brussels perspective, makes its contributions to air transport reform rather difficult to explain.[50] In fact, it was not so much ECAC as an organization that promoted reform, rather individuals and circumstances conspired to produce liberal outcomes in spite of ECAC's innate conservatism. In the case of the North Atlantic fares regime, forces outside ECAC's control threatened to produce such a radical outcome that ECAC decided to shift ground and thereby try to keep the forces of reform under control. The change was US not ECAC led. ECAC played a similar role regarding intra-European tariff reform in the aftermath of the debate generated by the Commission's Memorandum 2 on civil aviation in 1984–86.

When CAB Chairman Cohen declared that anti-trust immunity would be extended to IATA fare fixing in February 1980, it looked as if the SCO had expired, but he entered an important caveat. The charter airlines, double designation on key routes and the operation of Laker's Skytrain had created more competition on the North Atlantic, and it was unlikely that the clock could be turned back to a rigidly controlled fares regime. Indeed, Cohen and the US government still wanted more competition, and so Cohen entered his caveat and announced the CAB's intention to deny anti-trust immunity to US airlines operating on the North Atlantic routes.[51] This turned out to be more a threat than a reality because the CAB never implemented the withdrawal of anti-trust immunity but, as a ploy to push the Europeans into negotiation for more liberal pricing, it worked. The SCO, after propelling IATA into reform, now performed a similar function with ECAC. Faced with the prospect of either the SCO totally preventing co-ordination of fares by airlines operating on the North Atlantic or of a compromise, ECAC chose the latter route. Over the following two years negotiations were conducted by ECAC and the USA in order to revise the 1967 'Multilateral Agreement on the Procedure for the Establishment of Tariffs for Scheduled Services'.[52] This agreement had essentially urged the members of ECAC to use IATA to set fares and provided dispute resolution procedures. ECAC now found itself under intense pressure to reform and move to a more liberal fares regime. The outcome was a compromise, but it embodied significant movement towards liberalization:

> no Party shall make participation in multilateral carrier coordination a condition for approval of any fare, nor shall any Party prevent or require participation by any carrier in such multilateral tariff coordination. ... Parties shall ... approve or, as the case may be, refrain from notifying dissatisfaction with, specified fares filed by the carrier of another Party ... within specified pricing zones.... Any fare filed above or below the zone ... shall continue to be subject to tariff arrangements under the applicable bilateral air service agreement.[53]

Collusion was neither required nor prohibited, but it was excluded from zones within which pricing could be more competitive. This was no revolution. There was no precipitate deregulation. However, rigid fare setting was now a practice under considerable pressure from a host of sources: institutional reforms in IATA and ECAC, market forces, Laker's Skytrain and US pressures through the SCO and its negotiation of liberal ASAs that permitted more competitive pricing. ECAC had played its part in all this but it was largely a part dictated by the necessity of circumstance.

The story of the ECAC's COMPAS Report and its contribution to air transport reform in Europe is even more complex. ECAC operates through committees which report to meetings of the Directors-General of Civil Aviation of the Member States, which can only make recommendations to their governments. It is a consultative and discussion body which largely concentrates on technical matters. Its members, with the exception of Britain and the Netherlands, reflected the conservative disposition of their governments' air transport policies in the 1980s. Brief flashes of liberal views lit up meetings from time to time, for example, the outgoing Dutch president of ECAC, Hans Raben, invited Fred Kahn to address his colleagues in 1979, but it was too little effect. More significantly, Raben was instrumental in setting up a new committee to look into European air transport policy. It became known as EURPOL, and he took the chair during 1980–82. From this there emerged a task force to explore competition issues in air services, the COMPAS group. Successively chaired by Gerry Lumsden of Ireland and Ronnie van der Maaten of the Netherlands, the group set to work to analyse the existing European airline system and explore possibilities for change.[54] What followed was the result of a curious combination of careful calculation by people like Raben and institutional benign neglect. The COMPAS group was able to proceed with a surprising amount of freedom. It was, in fact, hijacked by those who were well disposed towards reform and who wanted, at the very least, to spell out the possibilities for liberal change. One of the key actors in the group was John Loder. In retrospect he commented: 'Never before or since in international relations has any group of national representatives worked with such unrestrained candour and robustness.'[55] The global reach of this claim might be something of an over-exaggeration, but the group clearly produced something quite unusual. On the other hand, and possibly one of the reasons why it was possible to produce such a ruminatively liberal document, ECAC had no power to implement anything.

The brief for the COMPAS task force was to look at competition in scheduled intra-European airline operations. Much of the analysis was based on an ECAC questionnaire sent out to all of its twenty-two members. Of them, nineteen responded and the findings were pretty comprehensive. There were virtually no routes where more than one airline per state operated. Over 90 per cent of routes were governed by capacity regulations, and about 85 per cent of routes operated under pooling arrangements. Of the remaining 15 per cent, most could only sustain one airline so that there was no need for pooling. In 1981 the task force recommended to higher ECAC bodies that it should explore the concept of safety nets as a possible way to relax regulation: 'the "zone of freedom to compete/safety nets for tariffs, route entry and capacity" concept [should] be the subject of further study'.[56] In other words, within set parameters there should be more scope for competition in fares, capacity and route entry. The recommendation was approved in June and the task force moved on to produce its main report.

The final report with its eleven appendices ran to 115 pages in length and was a complex analysis that offered a series of even-handed possibilities for change. 'Competition was the main theme of the task force's work', but this was no radical American-style catechism for deregulation. The report recognized that any change would have to be 'evolutionary rather than revolutionary' and moreover, and here conservative caution prevailed, the changes would have to be implemented through a series of bilateral agreements and not multilaterally.[57] The tone of the report was as factual as possible. Each component of the air transport industry was meticulously surveyed and analysed and then varying scenarios were explored.

> It had a very honest way of putting its points across, ... it did go very systematically through the whole area of economic regulation, economic market situations. And [it] said, what if you do this? What if you do that? What are the pros and cons?[58]

Sensitive to the danger of overplaying their hand, the key players on the task force who favoured reform were careful not to resort to polemics. Thus, for example, the report observed that, while IATA fare fixing might result in cross-subsidization of adjacent routes, multilateral tariff setting might also avoid excessive subsidization. On interlining (the use of two different airlines to get to a single destination), while the task force noted that it was beneficial for some consumers and was greatly facilitated by multilateral fare fixing, nevertheless, direct route passengers ended up paying for a product feature that they did not require. This kind of even-handed analysis lent an overall air of blandness and modest conservatism to the report but there were some very important underpinning assumptions that held potential for liberal action.

The COMPAS Report presented a consistent position that competition depended upon three inextricably linked features of air transport: route entry; capacity and fares. Action in one area without action in the others would be ineffective. For competition to flourish, all three areas would need adjustment. Having established that, the group then addressed the strategic problem of trying to achieve such changes in an evolutionary way that would be likely to gain acceptance among a constituency that they knew to be highly conservative so far as regulatory reform was concerned. The group developed ideas that were already informing pricing deregulation in the US–ECAC talks, which resulted in the Memorandum of Understanding on North Atlantic fares, and generalized the idea of competitive price zones nested within a broader system of price regulation to produce zones of flexibility and safety nets.

> Its examination demonstrated to the task force's satisfaction that zones of freedom to compete for all three regulatory elements [route entry, capacity

and fares], coupled with appropriate safety nets, would open up potential for greater competition than exists in the present system, but it remained necessary to resolve many questions of detail.[59]

Those questions of detail would have to take a number of realities into consideration. A crucial factor, and one that became so telling among the Member States of the EC as they grudgingly moved towards the creation of the SEAM, was that 'the importance attached to each of the advantages and disadvantages [of possible reform spelt out in the COMPAS Report] will be different among Member States'.[60] Political decisions of Member States meant that unviable routes were often maintained by subsidies 'as a matter of policy, to maintain and expand their airlines' networks for prestige, cultural, or macroeconomic purposes'.[61] In short there were important constraints that would have to be taken into account for any liberalization regime successfully to be developed among ECAC or EC Member States:

a   It is inconceivable that any European government would accept the elimination of its flag carrier
b   There are differences of competitive ability amongst ECAC [and EC] Member States and the larger these differences are, the less likely it is that liberal arrangements could be introduced
c   The degree of liberalization that would be acceptable to governments is not the same on all routes.[62]

When the report came out in 1982, ECAC more or less disowned it. There was a disclaimer in the forward declaring that it did 'not necessarily represent ECAC policy'.[63] 'And there were quite a few in the Directorate-General trying to bury that report.'[64] In June 1982, ECAC tentatively suggested that its Member States might wish to experiment along lines set out in the COMPAS Report, but none had done so even four years later.[65] So, what exactly was its impact? Stevens believes that 'it is difficult to exaggerate the influence which it was to have on the practical content of the Commission's 1984 memorandum,' one of its first moves to start reform.[66] A senior official of the UK CAA, who was involved in the later stages of preparing the report

> thought it was rubbish ... it would have been used selectively, but in a largely ineffectual way by different people over a period and you know I think it wasn't long before most people had forgotten that it existed anyway.[67]

Barry Humphreys, sometime official in the CAA and later at Richard Branson's Virgin Atlantic, was also sceptical of its importance: 'it was not mentioned or used subsequently in negotiations'.[68] However, those within the EC who were later to draft the reform proposals, which led to the creation of the SEAM, held more sanguine views. Fennes thought that it was helpful generally and, along with Sorensen, particularly in setting a new intellectual framework.[69] Frederik Sorensen, the key player throughout the 1980s and 1990s and beyond in the Commission, thought that 'it had a tremendous influence'. In particular, the ideas in the COMPAS Report were influential in the process of modifying and developing the Commission's proposals for reform. Also, it had important tactical impact. It helped to mould the thinking of officials from the Member States of the EC in the middle management echelons and, as time went by and the momentum for reform grew, those officials often helped to mediate on proposals for reform between the Commission and the political leadership in their respective nation states.[70] A senior official in the UK Department of Transport did not have direct experience of the COMPAS Report but, interestingly, he observed, 'I think I would take what Frederik Sorensen says on the matter pretty seriously because he must be about the greatest authority on how all this came about.'[71]

What should we make of these conflicting views? The answer lies in the idea that where you sit determines what you see. It appeared to those outside the EC Commission that the COMPAS Report was insignificant in resonance and legacy. So far as officials in the UK were concerned, there was little direct relationship, if any at all, between the report and what came after. Part of the reason for their failure to perceive connections was that the COMPAS Report was not widely read, that ECAC was not seen as an important player by government and even Commission officials – it was a talking shop generally for highly technical matters – and that the report was not particularly original. Many of the ideas, that it expressed, were already immanent in the airline industry in the US or embodied in the compromises that had been forced upon IATA and ECAC by the US, or were being pursued by the more liberal EC Member States, Britain and the Netherlands. So, when these ideas appeared in proposals from the Commission over the following years, their origins were opaque, and it was impossible to ascribe their progeny to the COMPAS Report. However, from within the Commission there was a different perspective. If only officials like Sorensen had been asked, there is no doubt that he would have suitably answered and, in fact, he did declare that the report was influential in providing an intellectual framework, within which he and his colleagues operated over the following years, and that that framework helped to determine three important matters: change had to be evolutionary and not revolutionary; the movement would have to be towards a new regulatory framework that would promote competition; and that the three key competitive components of route entry, capacity and fares would require concerted action. That does not mean that the Commission always moved simultaneously on all three areas. The first draft of its Civil Aviation Memorandum 2 had no provisions for route entry because the Commission thought that such proposals were too politically ambitious. Other tactics, ideas and problems arose over time, but these were the contributions of ECAC's COMPAS Report to the liberalization movement in the European transport system.

Between 1974 and 1984 a variety of dynamics operated that raised the profile of the need for the reform of the EC air transport system. Traditional justifications for regulation were challenged by new economic theory. Regulatory reform in the US provided an example of what a deregulated market could achieve, although there was only a tiny minority in Europe who ever came to favour US-style deregulation for European civil aviation. The global impact of US deregulation soon began to be felt in Europe and the US government policy of negotiating liberal bilateral ASAs brought such effects directly into engagement with the Netherlands, Germany and Belgium. The new US mega-carriers posed serious challenges for European airlines and their governments which would be confronted with the prospect of injecting larger and larger subsidies into uncompetitive European flag carriers as they lost market share to the more competitive and efficient US carriers, if they did not move to reform the European air transport system. The SCO had unsettled fare coordination and pushed ECAC into a compromise with the US, which began the liberalization of the North Atlantic market. This was important because the European flag carriers made most of their profits on long-haul and particularly transatlantic routes. To change the North Atlantic regime was to change the key market and that would impinge on the thinking of many in the European airline industry.

While ideas and forces emanating from the global marketplace were the most significant developments to bear on the need for reform of the European airline system during this period, there were also some home-grown shoots of reform. Primarily in Britain, but also in the Netherlands, there were home-generated institutional and market reforms and gradual engagement with the idea that, for reform to work, it would have to be Europe-wide. As we have seen, many factors complicated Britain's commitment to liberal reform, but, after 1979, it moved clearly in that general direction. Britain's voice became more and more strident as the decade progressed in demanding reform. It did so not just at government and official levels but also by encouraging two influential figures, namely, Laker and Bethell, who promoted reform through their own private activities. And finally, ECAC, if rather unwittingly and begrudgingly, also contributed to the momentum for change through the COMPAS Report which painstakingly laid out possibilities for the European airline system.

All these dynamics from the market, the liberal Member States, interest groups and NGOs had impact on and among the institutions of the EC and, as time went by, key players emerged there, deeply committed to regulatory reform. Between 1974 and 1984 those players developed a sound platform from which to launch such reforms.

3 Tentative moves towards a common transport policy in aviation 1974–84

The European institutions

> Passengers should not pay for costs they do not incur and for services they do not want. At any rate they want to know what exactly they are paying for.[1]

How did the institutions of the EC, and most importantly the Commission, respond to the pressures that were beginning to grow for reform of regulation in the airline industry from the marketplace, the liberal Member States and NGOs and organized interests? It will take the rest of this chapter to answer that question fully, but one would have to say, in general terms, that the Commission responded rather erratically, changing its position, experiencing a very sharp learning curve, and accumulating expertise that led it, by 1984, to a clearer perspective on what was needed and how it might be achieved. But, along the way, it made serious miscalculations about what might be acceptable to the Member States, including those which wanted liberal reform. After they joined the Community in 1973, while the British worked closely with the Commission to advance the cause of regulatory reform, they were also, ironically, the most apprehensive about the possibility of the EC gaining more powers and encroaching further into state sovereignty.

The Council of Ministers was more consistent than the Commission in that it staunchly and generally opposed change, though there was some intermittent and gradual movement towards a more liberal position, detectable sometimes among the West German, Luxembourg and Belgian representatives, and Irish representatives turned out to be more liberal – or at least benignly neutral – than expected from time to time. Thus the possibility of a rather fragile liberal coalition, which might enable more radical change, was beginning to coalesce behind the vanguard of Britain and the Netherlands by 1984. After the Single European Act (SEA) brought transport liberalization under the aegis of qualified majority voting in the Council of Ministers in 1987, these shifts became more significant, and the potential for compromise, bargaining and accommodation increased. However, it should be noted that this change in voting only made things easier: it did not in and of itself construct working majorities.[2] Indeed, after three years of the Treaty of Rome coming into effect, according to Article 87, application of the competition rules could be effected by a qualified majority vote of the

Council after consultation with the European Parliament, but Britain and the Netherlands could not muster enough votes to meet the minimum requirements of the qualified majority principle. It is also important to note that the Commission's first package of reform in 1987 was adopted before the arrival of qualified majority voting authorized by the Single European Act. How did that happen? With only two out of the twelve Member States seeking reform how did the Council of Ministers come to endorse it? These questions will take a little time and several chapters to answer fully.

The European Parliament, particularly after the introduction of direct elections in 1979, became more vocal and significantly so about reform of the airline sector.[3] Nevertheless, the role of the Parliament at this point should not be overestimated because, of course, it did not have the strong legislative co-decision making powers that were later to empower it so significantly. Successive accretions of power, through the introduction of the cooperation procedure and the co-decision procedure as well as the expansion of the application of the co-decision procedure, were granted respectively by the SEA 1986, the Maastricht Treaty 1992 and the Amsterdam Treaty in 1997. The expansion of qualified majority voting in the Council of Ministers under the provisions of the SEA also opened up more opportunities for the influence of the Parliament to be brought to bear on policy developments. Such developments still lay well in the future, and thus between 1974 and 1984 the ability of the Parliament to influence the Council of Ministers was insignificant on civil aviation issues, though DG VII sometimes played a game of making suggestions to the Parliament, which were then embodied in its reports, and these were then in turn highlighted by the Commission to the Council as 'good ideas'.[4] The Parliament was not very influential, nor was it very liberal in its demands. While it called for reform, its actual position was highly conservative as its responses to both the Commission's First and Second Memorandum on Civil Aviation clearly demonstrate.[5]

As for the European Court of Justice, it continued to hand down several judgements, which seemed to suggest that the competition laws should be applied and that the regulation of the airline industry was at the very least contrary to the spirit of the general provisions of the Treaty of Rome; but nothing clear-cut enough to disperse the ambiguity that hung over these issues emerged until the *Nouvelles Frontières* Case was decided in 1986.

It is something of a platitude to state that institutional action to reform the system of regulation in the airline system, and to move towards an integrated market, had to happen in the European institutions themselves, but on their own they were incapable of delivering results. Only by harnessing and complementing the dynamics released by the marketplace, liberal Member States, NGOs and organized interests could the Commission hope to move things forward in the face of overwhelming opposition to change from the airline industry and the majority of the Member States with their veto power in the Council of Ministers. When considering the strength of the forces of opposition, one might say that between 1974 and 1984 the Commission played a constructive and an effective enabling role through a rather cautious approach to change. It made some serious mistakes in trying to advance the cause of regulatory reform, but generally its strategy was politically prudent. Its achievements included a Decision from the Council of Ministers in December 1979, which gave it powers of consultation. These were to prove vitally important when the Commission moved to try to establish exactly what kind of collusion was taking place on fare fixing and whether it in fact, amounted to illegal concerted action by the airlines rather than fares being fixed legally by 'autonomous' government decisions.[6] It also achieved progress on the development of regional air services.[7] The progress was not so much as the Commission or the British had wanted, but the new policy introduced ideas that were soon to become important. There were other minor successes with a Directive on the right of Member States to call for help in accident investigations and another on limiting noise emissions.[8] However, the side effects of the Commission's immediate failures were more important in the long run than some of its short term and limited successes.

The Commission failed to get any positive response from the Council of Ministers on its proposal in 1975 for a European air space managed on a Community basis, or on its proposal in 1981 for reforming tariffs, or on its proposal the same year to apply the competition rules to air transport. Furthermore, the only substantive action to emerge from its First Aviation Memorandum submitted to the Council in 1979 was a directive on regional services, and that did not appear in legislative form until 1983. Notwithstanding the failures, debate was enjoined and thinking in DG VII developed, sometimes on its own accord, but more often prompted by ideas from outside. These included the scenarios drawn up in the COMPAS Report, arguments developed by the Commission's Legal Service, the views of DG IV and policies developed in Britain and the Netherlands. Officials in the Commission also became increasingly sensitive to their own responsibility to act as guardians of the EC treaties and to perform their legal obligations. All this raised the profile of possibilities, and encouraged debate to spread out from the corridors of DG VII and DG IV. Most importantly of all, it resulted in the Commission's Second Memorandum on Civil Aviation in March 1984.

Initial moves and the presentation of the First Memorandum on Civil Aviation

The first indication of the Commission's attitude on reforming air transport came in a proposal to the Council that dealt primarily with the aeronautical manufacturing industry; but it also concluded that in the airline industry 'national intervention is no longer capable of ensuring the harmonious development of activities' and called for the 'creation of a European airspace to be managed on a Community basis'.[9] At this point the Commission had simply shown unrealistic and overblown ambition in trying to expand European as opposed to state powers. The fraught story of EUROCONTROL, the Europe-wide air traffic control agency, is ample testimony to that difficulty.[10] And in the broader context of creating the SEAM, expansion of Community competence was to be a perennial problem even among the Member States that sought liberalization of the airline market. They did indeed want deregulation, but baulked at the idea of the necessary re-regulation, for a more competitive dispensation, falling into the hands of the Commission. In 1975, there was not the slightest possibility that any of the Member States would consider delegating the kind of powers to a European body that would have been necessary to oversee a European airspace. The Council of Ministers took no action.

Elsewhere, however, things were moving. Most notably there was a groundswell of resentment against regulation in the US airline industry, which President Carter set about exploiting as soon as he came to office in January 1977, and within the EC, Roy Jenkins of Britain took over the Presidency of the Commission, while Richard Burke of Ireland took over from Carlo Mugnozza of Italy as Commissioner for Transport, reinvigorating things there; and the European Court of Justice handed down more judgements that same year, which further questioned the status of the then existing regulation.[11]

The accumulative impact of these developments resulted in the Commission's Presidency calling for the establishment of a special working party on air transport questions.[12] The COREPER duly complied, and a Working Party on Transport Questions was now charged with looking specifically at civil aviation matters. These developments also prompted the creation of a specialist air transport policy unit in DG VII. It recruited Frederik Sorensen, a soft spoken Dane, who was to prove to be the most important figure within the Commission for progress over the next twenty-five years towards the creation of the SEAM. He did not always get the ideas or the tactics right, but his dogged determination helped ensure that momentum once established was never allowed to dissipate entirely. Sorensen also appears to have managed to hold the centre ground between what were sometimes the more robust demands from DG IV for more emphasis on competition and the more cautious demands from within DG VII. At the same time, he managed to retain the respect of a broad spectrum both within and from outside the Commission. Furthermore, his general views very much reflect what gradually developed. This is how he expressed them in the spring of 1991, and it is probably one of the clearest expressions of the faith that prevailed in DG VII throughout the creation of the SEAM:

> air transport policy must on the one hand ensure a financially healthy industry providing a certain economic stability and reasonable conditions for employment and on the other hand ensure a market structure where air carriers can adapt their operations according to the growth and shifts in the market and provide sufficient choice of services to the consumer at reasonable prices. Experience has shown that a certain modicum of competition is desirable in order to avoid a stale cost plus system. However, a competitive market may lead to abuse or uncompetitive behaviour and we aim to avoid that through benign regulatory rules. The system of the past with the need for a-priori approval before an air carrier was allowed to do anything will be abolished. However, a certain monitoring of the market will be carried out

and if it is observed (directly or by complaint) that a company is using dirty tricks then it runs the risk of being penalised.[13]

Of course, both the die-hard supporters of the status quo, who only ever conceded a need for the most modest of reforms, and the liberalizers, who wanted to move more quickly than the Commission and sometimes differed about the agenda, all had problems with this position. How the Commission handled those differences largely determined the shape that the SEAM eventually took.

A year after its commission, the Working Party presented a nine-point list of priorities. These were approved by the Council of Ministers in June 1978 as areas where possible legislation might be drawn up, but most of the list covered technical matters such as application of uniform standards, reduction of noise, and mutual recognition of crew licences. When they touched on economic regulation, the proposals were simply a bland acknowledgment of the need for further work. There were no recommendations. The 'regulation of competition legislation and State aids ... [and] improvement of interregional air services' were the only issues connected with economic regulation that were mentioned. The three interlocking key components of a more competitive regime – route entry, capacity and pricing – were noticeable only by their absence.[14] Furthermore, approval of these priorities by the Council was not tantamount to action.

The establishment of the air transport policy unit in DG VII was an essential development, if regulatory reform and progress towards the SEAM were ever to have chances of success. However, DG VII was unsure of itself in the early days; it was certainly not robust in its calls for reform. In June 1978, in reviewing the condition of airline price competition, it held to the line that 'governments are ultimately responsible for setting fares', and, therefore. there was nothing that they or DG IV could do.[15] Such cautious complacency was soon to be ruffled by Bethell's complaints and the advice of the Commission's Legal Advice Service; but so far as developments went in 1977 and 1978, there was little sign of the more radical approach that was soon to develop.

Along the corridors of DG VII ideas were being formulated. The fact that the Council of Ministers had approved what was later rather comically misnamed as an 'action programme' in official publications at least encouraged further thought on new proposals.[16] There was a widespread belief that the competition rules should be applied to the air transport sector, but the means of doing so were lacking. The French Seamen's Case suggested that maybe there was a way forward towards reform and also stimulated thinking and hope. Le Goy wanted to see change, and an agenda was gradually generated within DG VII under the benign authority of the Irish Transport Commissioner Richard Burke. Sorensen was given the task of drawing up an analysis and recommendations for civil aviation that later became known as the Commission's First Memorandum on Civil Aviation. This was Sorensen's first major in-put into developing policy.[17] Its main purpose was to stimulate debate rather than make specific proposals for reform. At the same time as Memorandum 1 was submitted to the Council of

Ministers, the Commission also submitted an apparently anodyne 'draft Decision on consultation procedures'.

The introduction to the First Memorandum on Civil Aviation set the tone. The goal was to 'benefit consumers substantially, while keeping firmly to the need for airline viability and without disrupting the worldwide system'.[18] The phrase 'disrupting the worldwide system' in particular evinced conservatism regarding IATA fare fixing and reflected the hesitancy about interfering in pricing that the Commission had shown in its review of competition the year before. Not surprisingly, Memorandum 1 reflected many of the views communicated to the Council of Ministers in 1978, but there were now specific calls for more widespread cheap tariffs in the EC, for improved possibilities for both scheduled and non-scheduled services. It also called for compensation for passengers 'bumped' off flights, for a means to stabilize exchange rates for tariff setting, for regulations for competition, for criteria to govern both state subsidies and the right of establishment – something which had appeared in the 1978 list of priorities. The Memorandum nodded in acknowledgment towards US deregulation but called for a gradual, evolutionary course in Europe that would introduce greater flexibility. It backed away from the grand ambition expressed in 1975 for a European air space, and now spoke of gradual reform and removing national impediments to the efficient operation of a European airline market. Even with much toned down ambitions for itself, there were complaints from Britain, the most favourably disposed of the Member States to reform. It was fearful about the danger of the growth of power in the Commission. Norman Tebbit, Parliamentary Under Secretary for Trade, commented that Britain did not want to see the EC in control of air fares.[19] In fact, the Memorandum contained no specific policy recommendations, and it was heavily hedged around with a whole series of qualifying factors, which would complicate and, unless handled carefully, could compromise and constrain movement towards reform. Such problems were clearly illustrated in an official summary of the Commission's policy, which described its four broad objectives, some of which were either not easily reconciled to one another or else would at best complicate the development of a more integrated and competitive market. In their generality they begged questions rather than providing a strategy for progress.

> The first is to set up an efficient intra-Community network tailored to the interests of the passenger, unimpeded by national restrictions and offering moderate fares to all types of passenger. The second objective is to establish or restore the airlines' financial equilibrium by lowering costs and increased productivity. The third objective is to safeguard and improve social provisions for employees and to eliminate the remaining obstacles to the free exercise of an occupation throughout the Community. The fourth aim is to take account of general economic and social interests, including rationalizing energy consumption, improving protection of the environment, developing the aircraft industry and promoting regional policy.[20]

Scholars have varied views about Memorandum 1. Some see it as a cautious document that did little other than promote further debate,[21] while another opinion thought that what 'was proposed was ... so far reaching that it failed to gather political support'.[22] Part of the problem was that the Commission still did not have a clear framework within which to operate. It was a kind of Catch 22 situation: the Commission felt that it had an obligation to move forward and had a general mandate from the Treaty of Rome to do so regarding a common transport policy (CTP) for the airlines, but the means of doing so were not provided and when it tried to provide them, the Member States took little or no action. Regarding the crucial competition rules, 'there were no measures available for investigation and enforcement. The main objective was to adopt a regulation with procedures, decision-making powers and penalties to enable the Commission to apply the principles to the sector'.[23] In the absence of such powers of enforcement, one official from DG IV thought that Memorandum 1 'fell flat because no one was interested on our side'.[24] What was the point when nothing could be done?

The chief architect of Memorandum 1, in retrospect in 2000, expressed the view that:

> I still to this day think [it] was a very important event because it set out in detailed terms a very wide framework for what air transport ought to be ... it did present a view of what one could do with air transport.[25]

There is much truth in that claim, but, as Sorensen himself acknowledges, matters only came into clearer focus in recasting Memorandum 1 into Memorandum 2, and many of the ideas for that came from the COMPAS Report. In the meantime, the general response to Memorandum 1 divided along fairly predictable lines. The Council of Ministers referred everything back to COREPER for further consideration, with the sole exception of matters to do with interregional services. On that issue it asked for concrete policy proposals from the Commission. The European Parliament welcomed Memorandum 1 in general, but then proceeded to hedge that welcome with a whole series of conservative caveats. This type of conservatism was a largely unnoticed augury of things to come from the Parliament. The Economic and Social Committee, the AEA, IATA, the unions and the airlines were all critical. ACE and consumer groups came out in support. Concrete results from Memorandum 1 thus looked unlikely to materialize.

> Finally, in March 1981 the Council adopted the Commission drafts as a Decision laying down the new principal points for the 1981–83 programme. But it again refused to commit itself to adopting decisions on the Commission's priorities for those three years.[26]

This was dispiriting for the Commission, but in December 1979 the Council had adopted a Directive on consultation procedures, which was to have more important consequences than its rather dry bureaucratic title might suggest, and there was still the possibility of a result on inter-regional services. Finally, as an indirect result of Memorandum 1, there was also movement on pricing policy, though this was largely propelled forward by the British in the Council of Ministers and by Lord Bethell's allegations of illegal price fixing and culpable inaction regarding the implementation of a CTP.

Consultation procedures and inter-regional services

On 20 December 1979, at the same time as the Council acted on noise emissions, it also adopted a Directive on consultation procedures, which seemed a similarly technical matter. In fact, the latter was to have important consequences in the near future for the legal position of the airlines in relation to the Community's competition rules, which in turn in 1986 became an important element of leverage on recalcitrant Member States to force them out of the mind-set that was deeply embedded in cartel price-fixing.

The Directive established consultation procedures with the Commission, on relations between Member States, third countries and international organizations in the field of air transport.[27] This was actually the first substantial, albeit procedural, contribution that the EC made towards the creation of a CTP in the civil aviation sphere. The scope for consultations was broad with Article 1(b) providing pretty much a catch-all criterion, which could trigger consultations about 'various aspects of developments which have taken place in relations between the Member States and third countries in air transport, and on the functioning of the significant elements of bilateral or multilateral agreements concluded in this field'.[28] Having the means to gather information about the actual operation of the European airline system empowered the Commission. As its confidence grew and its views on tariff fixing became more critical, it took more vigorous action. In May 1985 it invoked the 1979 Directive on consultation procedures for the first time in order to investigate whether price fixing by European airlines in ECAC might be contrary to what was required by a European CTP in civil aviation.[29]

The Commission also made progress with the licensing of inter-regional European air services. This was one way of shifting the emphasis away from bilateral to a multilateral framework that was the logical requirement of the SEAM. More specifically, in the Regional Directive, DG VII sought to provide for the possibility of developing new routes with easy entry requirements, flexible pricing and without significant capacity restrictions, which would enable airlines to respond to market needs more effectively and provide consumers with cheaper and better services. The Commission worked closely with the British on the Directive as the latter were already busy pursuing liberal bilateral ASAs in Europe, and they believed that EC action would open up more opportunities for their airlines to penetrate further into the European market. Airports were categorized as 1, 2 or 3, in descending order of importance and size, with category 1 normally being national airports at capital cities. The proposed Directive excluded category 1 airports, which were already congested, and category 3 airports that could not handle international flights. Pricing and capacity were to be flexible and route entry easy. Airplanes larger than 130 seats were prohibited, and routes could not be shorter than 200 km, but these were generously permissive restrictions. The Commission sent its proposal to the Council at the end of 1980.[30]

The proposal ran into all kinds of difficulties. It was supported by the European Parliament, the Economic and Social Committee, the European Independent Airlines Association and its members, and consumer groups. Strong opposition came from the trade unions, the railways and the main scheduled airlines. Diversion effects, drawing traffic away from established routes and undermining their viability, and the fear of disrupting the system generally persuaded the Council of Ministers to water down the proposals. Category 1 airports were totally excluded from the Directive's scope, aircraft were limited to seventy seats not 130, minimum route length was raised from 200 to 400 km, the proposal to simplify procedures for obtaining traffic rights was abandoned and the grounds for refusing route entry were substantially increased. The Council removed all cargo operations from the Directive's ambit, and traffic covered by the Directive was restricted to routes between category 2 and 3 airports, which only embraced 2.6 per cent of air passenger traffic in the EC. By 1986, only fourteen new regional routes had appeared.[31]

DG VII had to wait until July 1983 before the watered-down Directive was promulgated but it was disappointing. Sorensen was not happy, but in the end felt that they still

> got a result on inter-regional air services and people tend to forget that, but when one goes back to it you see that it acts on market access, capacity, and fares ..., it is important that all those three areas were addressed.[32]

These principles that underpinned the regional services Directive had been discussed at length and agreed between the Commission and British officials who, like Sorensen, expected them to 'set a pattern for action in other sectors'.[33] This was precisely what the COMPAS Report had so forcefully and consistently maintained in 1982, that regulatory reform, in order to ensure a truly more competitive market, would have to move in concert on all three components of the market: route access, capacity, and fares. In the licensing of inter-regional air services in the EC, DG VII had actually achieved that objective, albeit not to the extent that it had originally desired, but it could provide a precedent, a model for further action. 'The European Commission does not intend to plot new air routes but to create a framework within which the airlines themselves can respond better to their customers' needs, wherever they can find a commercial interest.'[34] The picture of regulatory reform of civil aviation in the EC was slowly beginning to come into focus.

Pricing, dominant positions and concertations

In the previous chapter it was noted how Laker and Bethell, in particular, had stirred things up with regard to price fixing and the competition rules of the Community. The Commission's public stance in response was that the fixing of prices was the responsibility of the Member States and, as such, was not subject to correction by Article 85, which only applied to collusion between enterprises or private firms. However, the Commission was aware of, and concerned about, the fact that European cross-border fares were the highest in the world, and beneath the surface a far more complex situation was unfolding than the one that was publicly acknowledged.[35]

Bethell was not the only one to draw attention to uncompetitive pricing when he submitted his complaint to the Commission in May 1980. The US threat of brandishing a show cause order (SCO) over north Atlantic fares pushed ECAC into negotiation and eventually compromise, which produced a more liberal fares regime in 1982. Laker was also having impact with on his transatlantic Skytrain and, while his attempt to acquire routes in Europe failed, it at least highlighted the high prices that currently applied there. While recession encouraged caution, nevertheless, in the summer of 1980 the European Parliament expressed concerns about fares, and in the Council of Ministers in June the British pressed for and achieved agreement that the Commission should prepare a report on European scheduled air fares.[36] Twelve months later, when the Commission submitted its report, changes in personnel further encouraged reform action: Georges Contogeorgis from Greece as Transport Commissioner proved sympathetic, and John Steele from the UK replaced Le Goy as Director-General, and he soon made it clear that he wanted a new memorandum on civil aviation, which should propose specific reforms. So, DG VII not only presented its report but also submitted a draft Directive to apply the competition rules to transport, and in October 1981 followed up its report on tariffs with another draft Directive.

The Commission observed that, while tariffs did not yield excessive profits 'one might ask whether the efficiency is too low or in other words if costs are too high'. It thought that the fare structure was 'too much a result of the interest of the airlines' and echoed its 1979 findings that 'more opportunities should be given to airline initiatives', but seemed rather unsure about how changes could be effected.[37] In most cases price fixing was the sole responsibility of the Member States, and therefore it follows 'that the activity of Governments corresponds in general to an autonomous price fixing measure and not to a concertation between firms'. However, the Commission would 'continue to reflect' on these matters. At the heart of its pricing proposal was a modestly progressive recommendation for country of origin fares. While the Commission's position on pricing seemed cautious and conservative, to say the least, it blundered badly in its proposal to apply the competition rules. It over-reached itself by radically seeking their application to operations outside the EC. Such application would run up against Member States' bilateral agreements with non members, disrupting the web of ASAs upon which the international system was based, and it would mean acquiring authority for the Commission, which no Member State was willing to delegate away. In the Directive on scheduled fares, the Commission also sought extra-Community authority both as an arbitrator of disputes and as an observer at IATA fare conferences. These plays for power by the Commission were universally frowned upon by the Member States and helped to condemn its proposals to failure.[38]

Both Directives were debated in the European Parliament, which wanted to see some positive developments, but neither this nor pleas from the Commission and developments in the marketplace were enough to move the Council of Ministers. Britain held the Presidency of the Commission in the second half of 1981, and there were manoeuvres to try to by-pass the Working Party on Transport to see if the Directive on applying the competition rules might be actioned by more sympathetic officials, but it was all too controversial, particularly in its attempt to embrace ASAs with non-members of the EC.[39] Yet again on air transport, the Council refused to take action. The European Parliament, frustrated by lack of progress and egged on by John Steele directed its anger specifically at the Council. On 16 September 1982, it passed a resolution condemning the Council of Ministers' inaction, and then followed up with a formal complaint to the European Court of Justice that the Council was illegally refusing to act in accordance with the Treaty of Rome and to develop a CTP in air transport.[40] The Court's deliberations took until May 1985, but in the meantime there were important developments in the Commission in response to comments on Memorandum 1 and to the reaction to the challenge from Bethell on price fixing in the Community.

The judgement expressed by the Commission that price fixing was the sole responsibility of the Member States, and therefore was not subject to the competition laws, which only apply to enterprises or private entities, was by no means as secure as it first appeared. When Bethell wrote to the Commission on 13 May 1981, he raised the profile of a debate that was actually already ongoing within the Commission. For example, the Legal Service of the Commission had concluded in notes of the 27 February 1981 and 22 April 1981 that 'an agreement between air companies on the levels of tariffs, within the framework of the procedure leading to the fixing of those prices by Member States may be contrary to Article 85.1'.[41] In short, it very well could amount to a concertation between enterprises contrary to the competition rules. Officials in DG VII took exception to this, and Jurgen Erdmenger argued on their behalf that the position of the Legal Service divorced 'the method of fixation from the actual level of prices, leading to contradictions and arbitrary results, and neglects the aim of the competition rules which is to protect consumers'.[42] Van Der Esch and G.L. Close responded on behalf of the Legal Service that Article 85 adopted a broad approach to competition and simply outlawed concerted practices by enterprises and did not make that prohibition dependent on 'the level of prices of the agreements or practices concerned'.[43] Such prohibitions were only subject to exceptions under Article 85.3, i.e. in cases where agreements and concerted practices, without imposing unnecessary restrictions or eliminating competition in respect of a substantial part of the goods in question, contribute 'to improving the production or distribution of goods or to promoting technical or economic progress, while allowing consumers a fair share of the resulting benefit'. Their argument continued by questioning the 'fiction' that Member States acted autonomously in fixing prices. They suggested that one could imagine three different types of framework for price fixing: one, where airlines are asked to agree on fares and governments simply rubber stamp their decisions; two, where airlines are asked to agree on fares and then governments 'make a more or less independent assessment' before fixing them; and, three, where the airlines are asked to supply data independently of each other to governments in order that they can fix the fares autonomously.

The first case was clearly one of concertation outlawed by Article 85. The second gave 'rise to the suspicion that the Member State is not really acting autonomously' and, even if the Member State government had the last say on pricing, the procedure might still, in the opinion of the Legal Service, fall foul of Article 85, and furthermore DG VII had not provided a reasoned argument why exemptions under Article 85.3 might apply. In conclusion, therefore, the Legal Service held that the third alternative was the only one that provided a perfectly legal and workable system. And it was one that would still allow price fixing for approved policy objectives: for example, measures promulgated in pursuance of Article 84(2). Fares could still be fixed by the Member States acting autonomously, and they could balance the interests of users and providers as they did so within the legal framework of the Community.

Ironically, Van Der Esch represented the Commission in the preliminary hearing before the Court of Justice to hear Lord Bethell's allegation that it had failed to act with regard to the fixing of fares by the airlines. The views that he and Close had expressed in the spring and summer of 1981 were not evident in the letter of 17 July from the Director General for Competition to Bethell. It simply repeated the mantra expressed by the Commission publicly on several occasions, and most recently in its report to the Council of Ministers, that 'the final fixing of air fares was the sole responsibility of the Member States so that there was in principle no ground to scrutinize the activity of companies on the basis of Article 85'.[44] Further detailed examination of these matters was curtailed when the Court of Justice later ruled that Bethell lacked *locus standi* but maybe aware of the need to appease Bethell and his supporters, the Commission, while rejecting Bethell's claim, took an accommodating line, informed the Member States that tariffs must not be unfair and must not infringe Article 86 (concerning dominant positions), wrote to the airline companies requesting information about the various arrangements that they make, and expressed its intention to submit a draft directive to the Council to apply the competition rules to air transport.[45] In June the Council of Ministers agreed that the Commission should examine air fares in the Community and, as intimated in the letter from the Director General for Competition on 17 July, the Commission 'commenced an investigation on its own initiative under Article 89 into suspected infringements of Articles 85 and 86'.[46] Price fixing was not as secure as it appeared, and on 3 February 1982 the Council of Ministers was apprised of the view of the Commission's Legal Service. It was told on 9 December, when the Working Party on Transport Questions raised the issue of consultations between airlines, that the Legal Service 'indicated [there] could be problems'.[47] The Commission was gaining power and influence, confidence and expertise, and developing a clearer agenda.

Memorandum 2

John Steele's arrival in the Commission in 1981 brought new vigour to the task of regulatory reform, and he soon called for a new memorandum on civil aviation. Sorensen and his colleagues now set about re-thinking and reformulating the proposals of Memorandum 1 into recommendations for Memorandum 2. The outcome was intended to make the system more flexible and to deliver benefits to consumers. It sought to produce competitive pressures that would make the airlines more efficient, fares cheaper, and reduce the need for subsidies by bringing costs under better control. It also sought to bring the system, at least eventually, in line with the Community's competition rules. Unlike the proposed Directive to apply the competition rules sent to the Council in 1981, the scope of the proposals in Memorandum 2 were specifically restricted to intra-European services. Even so, that still left the regulators with a problem: for example, would any new fares regime be applied to non-Member States' fifth freedom services within the EC, for example, a US carrier picking up passengers in London and carrying them forward to Munich? The Commission also raised other ambitions it had for its role in external affairs, including representation on international bodies. The fiction that the SEAM could be created without addressing the problem of external commercial airline operations was a dangerous one and one that took a long time and much effort to address constructively. One of the surprising omissions from Memorandum 2 was any recommendation about route entry. This was particularly disappointing for the British who thought that the model they had agreed with the Commission for the Regional Services Directive, with its action on route entry, capacity and fares, would be followed by the Commission in its further recommendations.[48] They were far from content with this omission and worked hard over the following months to introduce provisions on route access.

It is somewhat puzzling that the Memorandum was silent on route entry, especially when Sorensen attributed many of the changes that were adopted between Memoranda 1 and 2, to the influence of the COMPAS Report and at the heart of that Report was the need for concerted action on all three components that determined the level of competition: route entry, capacity, and fares. However, the Commission saw liberalization as a process, in which reform would be achieved incrementally through negotiation and, if initial demands were too radical, it was feared that the process might be frozen and regulatory rigidity, which discriminated against passengers and efficiency, would be perpetuated. The idea of dual or multiple designation, implicit in more liberal route access provisions, was seen as too provocative by the Commission, given that many of the Member States simply did not have the airlines available to practice multiple designation. Well informed opinion at the time simply saw dual or multiple designation as just 'too controversial'.[49] Recommendations on liberal route entry could have jeopardized the chances of success of the moderate proposals on fares and capacity. Also, the recommendations were presented as a first package in an evolutionary process. The fact that there was a degree of opacity obscuring where the evolutionary process was destined to end up allowed for the possibility of action on route access later on, but the more ardent liberalizers still saw the silence on route access as a disappointing omission.[50]

An obviously important component of Memorandum 2 was the increased power that was envisaged for the Commission. Memorandum 2 was essentially to be implemented through adoption by the Council of draft Regulations to apply Articles 85 to 90, namely, the competition rules, to air transport for an initial period of seven years. They would be applied only to intra-European services, but there was to be the possibility of the Commission granting block exemptions from their scope. Such exemptions for tariff fixing would only be allowed, providing the fixing was not mandatory and that Commission observers could be present at tariff conferences. Exemptions would also be permitted for capacity and pooling arrangements, providing they did not involve transfers of revenue exceeding 1 per cent of the total. Something that was not apparent from these recommendations was the way the power of granting block exemptions might be exploited by the Commission. Once the competition rules were deemed to be applicable to air transport, either by the Council accepting the proposed Regulation or, as it actually happened, through a decision of the European Court of Justice, then the Commission could wield a powerful weapon to persuade recalcitrant Member States to fall in line and adopt more competitive practices. This became a very potent weapon once the Community agreed to the creation of the Single Market with its deadline set for the end of 1992. The weapon, simply, was the threat of refusing to grant block exemptions and taking those Member States to the European Court of Justice for not enforcing the competition rules against their own airlines unless they moved in an orderly fashion towards liberalization.

The Commission's recommendations for Directives on fares and capacity were modestly progressive. They proposed the removal of compulsion on airlines to consult over fares. Voluntary consultation was still permitted, but, even so, the proposal would effectively require both the disapplication of the 1967 ECAC Multilateral Fares Agreement and amendments to bilateral ASAs, including those with third parties, where internal EC fifth freedom routes were concerned. The Commission offered two types of pricing: one based on the country of origin, as put forward in its draft directive on tariffs in 1981, and the other based on 'zones of reasonableness', within which airlines would be free to decide what fares they wished to charge. The zones would be related to different base prices and different types of tickets, all agreed bilaterally, with the Council deciding on the minimum size for the zones, the criteria for both the reference prices and prices outside the zones. Proposals on capacity were much more adventurous, suggesting a move away from a 50/50 split to a possible split of 75/25, i.e. with a COMPAS-style safety net of 25 per cent. The Commission also sought to curb subsidies by requiring Member States to supply it with information, which was at least a step towards making the industry as a whole more transparent, and it also mentioned non-discriminatory access to airport facilities.[51]

From one perspective, what the Commission had done with Memorandum 2 was fairly modest and unadventurous. The recommendations on fares and capacity seemed inadequate and incomplete to those committed to the kind of reform that would deliver a more competitive market. The inadequacies lay in the danger that the permissive line on pooling and other forms of collusion would negate the effects of any momentum towards more competitive pricing and a loosening up of the 50/50 capacity controls. The incompleteness concerned the departure from the principle so forcibly expressed in the COMPAS Report that route entry, capacity and pricing needed concerted action otherwise progress with one or two of those components might easily be reversed by lack of attention to the third.

In March 1984 it was impossible to say how things might develop. The Commission was rapidly developing leadership resources and informational advantages. These were emerging as a result of setting up the air transport policy unit in DG VII, which now, among other things, acted as an intellectual clearing house for ideas such as those generated by the COMPAS Report. Those ideas were not only taken on board and bruited around by aviation specialists in the Commission, but they also had impact either directly or mediated through Commission officials, on many of the middle ranking officials of the Member States responsible for aviation policies. This was later to be helpful when the Commission came to urge reform more forcefully because such officials were often more receptive than their governments back home, and they played an important role in educating and persuading their superiors of the benefits of reform emanating from the Commission.[52] At the same time as the specialist air transport unit began to develop its expertise and gain respect, there was a growing interest in DG IV in applying the competition rules, there were important interventions by the Commission's Legal Service, and there was close cooperation with British expert officials who were committed to reform. All this enabled the Commission to carve out a privileged institutional position for itself in any negotiations about the reform of the civil aviation system in Europe. It is important to note that this was initially still very much to do with matters on the periphery of the industry, but the two memoranda on civil aviation, and the Directives on Consultation Procedures and Regional Services established the Commission as a more central player. With success came more respect and prestige. The negotiating position was becoming more and more complex, and the Commission was gradually acquiring the expertise to enable it to exploit that. However, while it had learnt a lot over the decade, it was still not so surefooted and knowledgeable as it was eventually to become. Air transport reform was highly technical, but the Commission still could not take full advantage of that with its limited resources and knowledge, nor was the low salience of the issue a particular advantage for promoting progress. The low profile leadership strategy of the Commission had only had fairly limited success. It was still highly doubtful that the Council would act even on the rather modest recommendations of Memorandum 2. Indeed, Member State preferences remained stubbornly pitched against reform, and it was still difficult to see how that obstacle to progress could be overcome.

The expertise and the authority of the Commission had developed during the decade since 1974, but it was not in a position to press changes upon a Council that had a substantial majority of members against regulatory reform. Pressure was building up from the liberal Member States, especially Britain and the Netherlands, now joined by Luxembourg. West Germany had also been notably supportive of the Regional Air Services Directive, but unanimity was needed for the development of a CTP for air services, and that seemed highly unlikely of achievement in 1984. Other pressures would have to be brought to bear to change things, and over the following two years those pressures did indeed emerge though not always from expected places. As Europe reactivated the drive towards economic integration in general, it helped to draw the design for the SEAM into clearer shape and provided additional fuel to drive it forward. Taking advantage of this new momentum, the Commission adopted a much more high profile leadership strategy and more confrontational and controversial tactics to try to advance the cause of regulatory reform, and these high risk plays were to prove successful in getting things well under way.

4 The single market and the reaction to Memorandum 2

> The Commission suggests that American-style deregulation would not work in the present European context.[1]

During the mid-1980s the forces that sought liberalization of the airline industry combined and recombined in changing strategic patterns. Sometimes they worked in harmony, at others they differed over tactical judgements about what was possible of achievement, or over how quickly reform should be implemented, or over how it might be achieved, or over how radical it should ideally be. The movement towards creating the SEAM was not straightforward. It was a messy process partly by design and partly because of the political landscape and institutional configurations within the EC. These two reasons for 'messiness' need some consideration. The design factor, the reaction it provoked in the guise of Memorandum 2 and the context of increased momentum towards the Single Market that emerged in the mid-1980s, will be dealt with here. Political and institutional features will be examined throughout the body of the next chapter as Memorandum 2 metamorphosed into the first package of reform.

The messiness by design aspect was to do with strategic thinking within the Commission. In view of the long embedded opposition to a more liberal market in both the scheduled airline industry and the overwhelming majority of the Member States, the Commission was fearful that a 'big bang' radical proposal would provoke stiff resistance and unite moderate and extreme opponents of change in such a way as to freeze the situation in its existing mould. In short, it would fail. In April 1985, Director-General John Steele warned his boss, the Transport Commissioner Clinton Davis, that even strong moves at the tactical level would be seen as extreme by the airlines and Member States, and would probably alienate the European Parliament, which 'is not necessarily in favour of drastic action.'[2] The latter observation was something of a British understatement. In addition, the Commission generated difficulties with Member States, and particularly with Britain, its main ally in trying to create the SEAM, because proposals for reform involved the expansion of Commission power through the spread of its competence over areas previously reserved for sovereign state control. Thatcherite Britain was only willing to see the bare minimum delegation of sovereignty necessary to consummate its single market objectives.

There was also another aspect to this, which aggravated relations between the Commission and those Member States in favour of reform. Because of the strength of opposition to reform, the Commission came to the view that a major strategic strength lay in developing the SEAM in a process of gradual change and in the changing light of what might be possible: ' the First Package came about because that was what was possible at the time.'[3] In the end this strategy delivered the full blown SEAM, at least to the general satisfaction of the Commission, in the form of three packages of reform between 1987 and 1992. However, this strategy necessarily entailed uncertainty throughout the process as to where the vision of a SEAM would eventually lead. Member States like Britain often saw this as frustrating and rather dangerous in the sense that it placed much power of initiative, discretion and control in the hands of the Commission and, as noted before, the British were deeply suspicious about the loss of sovereign state powers to Brussels. And others, most significantly the Danes, shared those fears.

So far as Commission officials were concerned, their strategy made eminent sense. They feared that setting out the details of the destination would be too provocative, and that it were better to travel hopefully without knowledge of final destination than not to travel at all. This avoided the danger of an early and detailed articulation of what the SEAM should be, which would have provoked ideological confrontation and the kind of opposition that would have frozen the existing regulatory dispensation as it was. The Commission's strategy avoided those dangers and at the same time set things in motion, which eventually led to a more liberal market, harmonized throughout the EC and under the guiding regulatory hand of the Commission. This process enabled the Commission gradually to foster its expertise in aviation and establish its credibility and power over developments, as it engaged in negotiation, compromise and accommodation to drive the agenda of reform forward. Its view at the time was that this strategy would progressively achieve the achievable at each stage of the process and build on past achievements as the momentum for reform gathered pace and as faith in a more liberal market gained more disciples. Needless to say, the conservative majority among the Member States saw the process as far too radical and the liberal minority saw it as inadequately market-driven and as leading down a dangerous route that would establish a new regulatory system, which would fall under the authority of the Commission. Whichever way it looked, the Commission was in for a difficult time.

As the next chapter will demonstrate, the second reason for 'messiness' was the unique political and institutional character of the EC, but rather paradoxically there also arose, from its morass of shifting political alliances and changing institutional positions, a strong underlying movement, which brought some over-arching order to the process of developing the EC Single Market. As the 1980s progressed the EC gradually emerged from the doldrums that had afflicted it since the 1960s, and the period from 1984 to 1987 proved to be a crucial one for the development of the EC and for the renewal of impetus towards completing the Single Market. This had benefits for the specific airline sector as well and influenced both the reaction to Memorandum 2 and the eventual outcome of the debate that it provoked.

Moving towards the single market

With some notable exceptions, such as in regional policy and the introduction of the European Council, the EC had rather trodden water since the completion of its customs union in 1968 in terms of its structures, policies, and deepening integration. However, the EC had broadened with the admission of Britain, Ireland, and Denmark in 1973 and Greece in 1981. This increased size, and prospective further growth after entry talks began with Portugal and Spain respectively in 1978 and 1979, raised concern over whether or not the unanimity principle, generally used for decision-making, would allow the EC to respond effectively to the challenges that now confronted it. In effect, this meant addressing the individual nation-state veto power, which had been institutionalized by the Luxembourg Compromise of 1966, promulgated to meet French concerns about threats to national sovereignty. In retrospect, Dinan and others have identified a broad causal reason that supposedly drove things forward, namely, globalization. 'Rapid technological change and fierce competition forced Western European countries to deepen integration.'[4] At a very general level these two dynamics of globalization were undoubtedly important, but forward momentum on integration was not so inevitable as the bi-causality of technological change and fierce competition might suggest. Among other things, it is important to explain how the impetus for change was mediated and given voice within important EC constituencies, which determined whether, how, and in what direction change would, in fact, take place. Interestingly, actors who called for the development of the Single Market did so for different reasons, and envisaged different versions of integration. Some political leaders, most notably Margaret Thatcher of Britain, lobbyists for reform such as Lord Bethell, independent scheduled airlines and organizations like the ERTI were primarily motivated by self-interest and a commitment to the free market as a good in itself as well as something that would deliver efficiency, profits and better goods and services for the consumer. As Thatcher later put it: 'The Single Market – which Britain pioneered – was intended to give real substance to the Treaty of Rome and to revive its liberal, free trade, deregulatory purpose.'[5] Other political actors within the EC institutions and among the Member States agreed on the desirability of a Single Market as a means to respond to the competitive forces released by globalization, but their vision of what the Single Market should be was not always so free-market oriented as Thatcher's. For them the achievement of a Single Market, while valuable in and of itself was also seen as a vehicle to drive European integration forward on political cooperation and a common foreign and security policy as well as on economic issues such as a single currency, which also had enormous political implications. This kind of deepening of integration and the bureaucratic empowerment of the Commission in some of the less market-oriented visions for the Single Market were anathema to Thatcher.

Notwithstanding the 'anathema', these different positions had to undergo some degree of reconciliation before a Single Market could be achieved, but even after some accommodation had been made the broad political support for the Single Market still constituted an unstable compound that could easily have self-combusted and destroyed the project: the situation regarding the SEAM was not dissimilar. As we have seen, the airline market was often an exception to market developments elsewhere, and the European system that existed in the 1980s was well embedded and defended by powerful interests in the industry and in national governments and among many parts of EC institutions. It is easy to imagine that something much closer to the status quo could have developed than the SEAM scenario and the deepening integration of the sector that actually unfolded. It is beyond the scope of this study to consider why the Single Market project did not self-combust, but, with respect to the alliance that worked for liberalization of the airline system, one can identify the prudent strategy of the Commission as at least partly responsible for helping to stabilize the compound that supported reform until the SEAM was realized.

The concerns about the need to develop the EC further had become widespread in the late 1970s, and they began to converge into a concerted drive by 1984. In the European Parliament cross-party action was brought together in the Kangaroo Group, which agitated for a Single Market, and the eminent parliamentarian and staunch Europeanist, Altiero Spinelli, led a group of like-minded reformers in the Crocodile Club, founded in July 1980 and named after the restaurant in which they originally came together. Over the next four years the Crocodile Club did much to raise the profile and spread the word on reform, and by 1984 its members had produced a Draft Treaty Establishing the European Union. In a momentous vote in February, the European Parliament approved the draft treaty. While it only had bland provisions concerning transport, overall it was far too politically radical to be accepted by the Council of Ministers in 1984, but it was symbolically very important for furthering the cause of integration and anticipated much of what eventually went into the Treaty on European Union at Maastricht in 1992.[6]

The European Parliament was not alone in its conviction that the institutional operation of the EC needed overhauling to facilitate further developments, and in particular to advance the agenda of the Single Market. In the summer of 1983 West German Foreign Minister, Hans Dietrich Genscher and his Italian counterpart Emilio Colombo drew up proposals for reforming the EC, which were incorporated into the Solemn Declaration on European Unity at the EC Summit in Stuttgart on 19 June 1983. It called for deepening integration and gave emphasis to developing foreign and security policy. The EC leaders approved the declaration, and there was a visible convergence of policy objectives taking place. Thatcher called for a deepening of integration in order to achieve the Single Market and also for more foreign policy coordination. President Mitterand of France and Chancellor Kohl of West Germany argued for reform as well, including an expansion of qualified majority voting in the Council of Ministers, which was widely seen as necessary for implementing the Single Market and for making the EC work more effectively. Convergence was palpable, even though different motivations were driving things forward, but, until the Fontainbleau Summit in 1984, arguments about Greece's position within the EC and Thatcher's demand for a rebate on Britain's contribution to the EC budget forestalled any progress. But then at Fontainbleau both issues were resolved and reforming the EC became possible. The Member States set up the Dooge Committee on institutional affairs. Named after its Irish chairman, James Dooge, the committee was charged with examining the EC and how it might develop in the future. It reported in March 1985 and, among other things, identified completion of the Single Market as a key priority.

Simultaneously, in the Commission there was a flurry of activity stirred up by Jacques Delors, its new president, 1985–95. Delors raised morale and reinvigorated action. Since the late 1970s, the Commission had been lobbying as best as it could for the completion of the Single Market; and, even though its morale was low, it still notched up some successes at least in sensitizing Member States to some of the potential that the EC held for helping them to respond to the challenges of globalization. The skilful Belgian, Etienne Dauvignon, Commissioner responsible for industrial affairs, took vigorous action in the early 1980s to try to mobilize Community resources and power to help rationalize ailing industries such as steel, and to promote education, and research and development. In 1984 he launched the First Framework Programme for Research and Development, and it had impact across the EC. These initiatives attracted the support of the ERTI, which became active and the leading lobby group for the completion of the Single Market. Dauvignon was an important and impressive figure within the Commission, but his notable achievements were soon overshadowed by those of Delors.

The use of terms like 'important dynamics' should not mislead us into thinking that developments in the Single Market generally and the airline sector, specifically, were primarily to do with impersonal market, institutional or state forces. Certainly, with regard to states and institutions, individuals were often more influential than standardized procedures, practices and policy traditions, and nowhere was this truer than in the Commission and in the case of Jacques Delors and his creative work therein. Delors was president-designate of the Commission in 1984, and he began to prepare the ground for what he wanted to be a period of renewal and development for the EC. In the second half of 1984 he toured the Member States in an attempt to assess what might be a practical Commission-driven agenda. Ideally, he wanted progress on political cooperation, monetary union and movement towards a common foreign and security policy. The reality proved disappointing, at least initially. He realized that none of these ambitions was achievable. However, he was pleasantly surprised with the widespread support for completing the Single Market. This now became his target, but he also hoped that it would lead on to monetary union and deepening of political cooperation.[7] Unlike Thatcher, he did not see or want the Single

Market to be an end in itself. He envisaged a different type of market emerging, and for him it was just as much a means to the end of deeper political union as it was a means to greater economic efficiency and competitiveness. The potential to move forward generated at the Fontainbleau Summit and by the admonitions of the Dooge Report in early 1985 were important, but Delors had also set in motion parallel action in the Commission by lobbying for a White Paper on the completion of the Single Market. In March 1985 the task of producing that fell to Lord Arthur Cockfield, Commissioner for the Internal Market 1985–88. An ex-member of Thatcher's government and someone she had insisted should be given the Internal Market brief, Cockfield, much to Thatcher's expressed dismay, now appeared to go native.

Superficially Delors and Cockfield hardly looked compatible. Cockfield came from a highly privileged background, Delors did not; Delors was a socialist, Cockfield a conservative; Cockfield came from a business and industry background, Delors was a professional politician. Nevertheless, they worked closely and well on the Single Market.[8] In fact, Cockfield was not a disciple of the Thatcherite free-market. While his natural disposition led him towards liberalization, he also saw the need for safeguarding regulations, and the logic of creating a Single European Market seemed to indicate that those regulations should be implemented at an EC level. Needless to say, this did not please Thatcher:

> He [Cockfield] tended to disregard the larger questions of politics – constitutional sovereignty, national sentiment, and the promptings of liberty. He was the prisoner as well as the master of his subject. It was all too easy for him therefore, to go native and to move from deregulating the market, to re-regulating it under the rubric of harmonization.[9]

However, one might ask how far would Cockfield have got with the Single Market if he had not bowed to demands for what seemed to most as inevitable regulatory accompaniments to the Single Market and a degree of harmonization? Cockfield did not so much go native as recognize that if it were in Britain's interests to have a Single European Market then the reality of the situation dictated certain types of accommodations if it were to ever have a chance of becoming a reality. Among those developments were more power for the Commission and an expansion of qualified majority voting. Thatcher also recognized the need for these developments as well. Did she really believe that the Commission could be further empowered and qualified majority voting expanded without some inevitable loss of British sovereignty? Or, like Cockfield did she recognize the reality of what had to be done to realize the Single Market, but found it politically inexpedient for her to admit that Britain's economic wellbeing was now so inextricably linked with the EC's that Britain had to make sovereignty concessions to Brussels?[10] If one accepts the latter proposition then Thatcher was ironically just as guilty and indeed more responsible for any 'going native' than Cockfield. It was after all her government that signed up for the Single Market.

The Cockfield White Paper identified 279 specific actions that were needed to bring the Single Market into being and among other things it specified the need for urgent progress in air transport as one of the areas needing reform and called for action on fares by 1985, on bilateral agreements, memoranda of understandings between Member States and other items by 1986, and on application of the competition rules to aviation by 1987.[11] It suggested the end of 1992 as the target date for the completion of the Single Market and specifically

> warned the Council that if no action was taken concerning the application of the competition rules to air transport, it would have to take note of infringements and authorize Member States to take measures determined by it in accordance with Article 89.[12]

This amounted to a much more supportive context for developing the SEAM, with its threat of legal drivers and time limits. At the EC Milan Summit, 28–9 June 1985, the White Paper was accepted. The Member States were now committed to the achievement of a Single Market by the end of 1992 and air transport was specifically included in that objective. This added momentum to the impetus already created by the reception of the Dooge Report and a majority at Milan supported an Italian proposal for an intergovernmental conference (IGC) to action progress. Britain, Denmark and Greece opposed the idea, but, as all that was required was a simple majority vote the IGC opened in Luxembourg on 9 September 1985 and ran through until its closure at the Hague on 28 February 1986. The outcome was the single European act (SEA), which was the result of a convergence of views, albeit informed by different reasons, about the growing need for the EC to move forward and to respond more effectively to the competitive challenges of globalization. There were three significant components of the SEA. The first was the 1992 deadline for the completion of the Single Market. The second was the expansion of the powers of the European Parliament to include the right to a second reading of certain types of legislation – the co-operation procedure – and rights of assent regarding both new membership and association agreements. The third and most significant was the expansion of the use of qualified majority voting, which drastically curtailed the scope of the unanimous decision-making of the Luxembourg Compromise. There was widespread acknowledgement that it would not be possible to consummate the Single Market without utilizing the majoritarian principle more broadly.

These developments on the broader plane of the Single Market as a whole had important consequences for the SEAM. The expansion of qualified majority voting did not take effect until the SEA came into force in July 1987, so it had only an indirect effect on the first package of aviation reform but symbolically it was important. It was a sign of the potential for change and that obstructing the development of a more liberal airline market would soon become more difficult. The fact that all Member States were now committed to the creation of the Single Market made the position of the defenders of the status quo in the airline sector more vulnerable. They could no longer complacently hold to their default position that changes were not necessary or desirable. The working assumption now had to be that the airline sector must follow the general policy for the broader marketplace and within a specified time-frame. A SEAM was now no longer a hobby horse for a few bureaucrats, independent airlines, consumer groups and one or two of the Member States: it was assumed that it would have to come about in one form or another in order to meet the requirements laid down in the SEA. As a senior Commission official put it:

> the decision, the political decision to finalise the internal market, that made it imperative for difficult sectors like the aviation sector, to achieve – establish – the internal market before a certain cut off date, before [the end of] 1992. If that wouldn't have happened, I don't think we would have had an internal policy, maybe not even now [2000].[13]

Whether or not there would have been a SEAM by 2000 without the SEA and the Single Market is impossible to say. Other developments, particularly after the *Novelles Frontières* Case was handed down by the European Court of Justice in 1986, drove things forward, but there is no denying that the objective of, and political commitment to, a Single Market provided a more supportive context for those who wanted to promote the SEAM. Given the initial reaction to the Commission's Second Memorandum on air transport, it became clear that the Commission would need all the help and support it could get.

Reaction to Memorandum 2

When Memorandum 2 was published on 15 March 1984, it was not warmly received. Even in Britain, the leader of reform among the Member States, the reaction was a mixture of disappointment, anger and suspicion. Analysis in the Department of Transport was scathing. There was fear that permissiveness regarding pooling and inter-airline fares agreements 'could be used to negate the effects of the loosening of government regulation' and could produce less rather than more competition. 'The scheme involves EC rules on only certain aspects of the regulatory system. It does not, for example, cover any aspect of route entry and wholly departs from the philosophies and objectives agreed between Her Majesty's government (HMG) and the Commission as the basis for the Regional Services Directive – which it was foreseen would set the pattern for action in other sectors.'[14] The principles of the COMPAS Report had been ignored. and it was feared that lack of concerted action in all three areas of pricing, capacity and route entry would subvert any potential for greater competition. Memorandum 2 restricted itself specifically to intra-European airline services, but 'there may obviously be some repercussions for other countries' and the Commission noted its cooperation agreements with ECAC and EUROCONTROL, its ambition to have observer status in ICAO and stressed the importance of its intention to continue dialogue with third party states.[15] As a result, fears about its ambitions in external relations abided among the Member

States. There was worry about the Commission grasping competence over matters in ASAs between Member States *inter se* and between Member States and non-members of the EC: 'The Commission's present proposals for action under Article 84.2 will create permanent Community Competence over States' bilateral agreements in relation to capacity provisions, fares approvals, airline pools and JV [joint venture] operation of routes.' 'Once conceded this Competence would be irreversible.'[16] A real dilemma was emerging. The state, best positioned to work with the Commission to promote liberalization and more competition in the airline industry, was being alienated by its tactics and by fears about the growth of its power at the expense of the nation state.

> The Commission is getting very ambitious and expansive on International Relations and States have already clashed with it over relations with ICAO. The Commission should not be encouraged in this area and we shall certainly need to maintain preventative action in order to ensure that it does not obtain observer status in ICAO.[17]

There was now a real danger of a break in the ranks of those wanting reform. On 10 May 1984, when the Second Memorandum was first considered by the Transport Council, the UK Secretary of Transport, Nicholas Ridley, and his Dutch colleague expressed disappointment with the timidity of the proposals, and Ridley went on to declare his government's opposition to price fixing. He announced that Britain no longer felt able to await Council action and would proceed under its own understanding of the Treaty of Rome's competition rules, and unilaterally allow airlines to file fares without consulting with other airlines. Like the provisions proposed in the Second Memorandum, Ridley was in effect challenging the legality of the ECAC Multilateral Tariffs Agreement and, by direct implication, the legality of IATA tariff conferences. However, while his stance was more uncompromising than that embodied in Memorandum 2, the announcement, in fact, wrought little change to the substance of British policy.

The situation for the British was complex and two factors in particular constrained what they could do. Ridley's declaration was dramatic and had impact as yet another notice of general intent to liberalize the airline industry, but specifically it did not result in Britain withdrawing from the ECAC Multilateral Tariffs Agreement with its recommendation to work through IATA tariff conferences. The British Government took no action to prohibit its airlines from undertaking fare consultations with their notional competitors: concerted practices in setting fares continued. Indeed it would have been near impossible for it to prohibit fare agreements because apart from the soon-to-be exception of the bilateral agreement with the Netherlands, all other ASAs with Member States of the EC required airlines to agree fares. In practice this continued to be the case between BA and KLM even after their governments concluded a liberal ASA with easy route entry, no capacity restrictions and country of origin pricing, which a year later became a double disapproval fare regime. The Anglo-Dutch ASA was accompanied with a flurry of publicity and with British airlines such as Air UK, B.Cal. and BM all lining up to take advantage of the new more liberal dispensation. Perhaps most significant, as was noted in Chapter 2, was the launch of the BM service from Heathrow to Amsterdam in June 1986. But all this was still more image than reality. The fact was that price fixing continued unabated throughout the EC, and the British knew, that they could only successfully change that by action at the EC level, and that in turn meant working with the Commission. So, although there was clear water between what the British ideally wanted and what the Commission had currently proposed, the need for both of them to work together to achieve any kind of progress would soon lead them to bridge the gap.

The second factor constraining the British was national interest in their own airlines and in particular in BA. As noted previously, 1984 was a crucial year for BA because of the Laker law suit and Lord King's tussle with those in the CAA and elsewhere, who wanted to redistribute some 8 per cent of BA's routes to B.Cal. Lord King routed his opponents with the help of a dominant group in government, which included Prime Minister Thatcher. Those who supported King were sensitive to the complexities of liberalization and to the imperative of making BA's flotation a success, which it finally was when it came in 1987. They were aware that, if Britain liberalized out of line with its European counterparts that could disadvantage British airlines very seriously. As a result, considerations of both national interest in British airlines and caution about moving ahead of others and exposing British airlines generally to commercial disadvantages were evident in British actions and in the wording of the White Paper in October 1984 on 'Airline Competition Policy'. It reiterated commitment to a more liberal, deregulated and competitive market but also recognized the harsh realities of the situation.

> Governments have to be persuaded that they do a disservice to the traveller by insisting on highly protectionist regimes. The long term goal must be to liberalise air services wherever possible – where foreign competition is fair and Britain's interests are not prejudiced.[18]

If Britain and the Commission were going to keep in step and mutually support each other in the struggle for reform, there would have to be changes in the Commission's proposals, but the British also realized that, to attain their ultimate goal, they too would have to compromise along the way, just as they had done in the domestic context over BA. For the British a key issue that would have to be addressed in the re-working of Memorandum 2 was that of route entry. The British were forthright about this. As Sorensen recalls, they simply 'came in and said, we must have market access legislation.'[19] As we shall see there were several changes that the Commission and the British together designed for route entry, but, while the British wanted more reform, the Commission also had to deal with the majority of the Member States, which remained staunchly opposed, or at best pursued only cosmetic change in attempts to draw the sting of criticism, and it had therefore to present a stance that would appeal to more moderate states and steer them away from the more radical camp. For the time being the forces of regulatory conservatism seemed to prevail, and the Council of Ministers looked content not to take action.

The Commission might have expected support from the European Parliament. It had been critical of the Council's inaction on the CTP, and in January 1983 its frustrations had boiled over; it took the Council to the European Court of Justice alleging it had failed to carry out its mandated duties. A court decision was not handed down until May 1985, but, in the meantime, there was widespread belief that the European Parliament was one of the key supporters of transport reform and particularly of the airline sector. It certainly produced the most detailed and thorough response to Memorandum 2, but, in fact, the European Parliament had an agenda rather different to that of the Commission and the British, which included principles that implied more intervention in the marketplace and emphasized harmonization at the expense of competition:

> Among those principles were better services for users, the establishment of rational framework conditions for viable and well-run airlines, job security, improved safety, a reduction of the damage caused to the environment by this type of transport, and energy savings.[20]

The Parliamentary Klinkenborg Report that emerged in March 1985 made all this very clear. The European Parliament feared radical reform and unacceptable growth in Commission competence and power. It was far more critical than supportive of the Commission's proposals.

It is worth considering the Klinkenborg Report at length because, in fact, its views largely reflected those of the regulatory conservative Member States. It rehearsed the arguments of those, who either wanted to preserve the status quo, or who only favoured the very minimum of reform. The European Parliament, consisting of directly elected members since 1979, was gradually growing in terms of its influence. Direct elections gave it a measure of popular legitimacy that it had previously lacked, and it became an important mouthpiece for a number of lobby groups and organizations, including trade unions, which found a powerful voice among the large ranks of socialist and left-leaning parties in the Parliament. Their concerns in particular were influential in helping to cast the Parliament's position and to distance it considerably from that of the Commission and, even more so, from that of the radical reformers. Here is a clear instance of the influence of a pressure group, mediated through an EC institution that supported the status quo: the trade unions had a conservative restraining influence on the momentum for reform. Other important factors for the Parliament were a sense of social justice in the round and regional development, and these also connected with traditional trade union concerns. Members of the European Parliament placed great value on regional development, and this was one of the main reasons why it had agitated for change, but it did not amount to a particularly ambitious agenda, which certainly fell far short of that of the Commission and indeed the requirements of the Treaty of Rome read literally. The European Parliament was driven by the belief that

> the European Community is ... directly required to act on the basis of Article 2 of the EEC Treaty which specifies that the Community shall ensure a harmonious development of economic activities and closer relations between the Member States. The Community must take the appropriate measures to ensure that structurally weaker regions can take part in economic development and to promote exchanges between them across internal borders.[21]

The Parliament had thrown its weight behind the Regional Air Services Directive in 1983 for those very reasons, and that led many to conceive of the Parliament as a strong supporter of reform. It was, and it was not. It wanted to nurture a CTP, but not of the kind favoured by the Commission, but one that in the airline sector would only differ modestly from the existing regime. In fact, a close examination of the Parliament's position even on regional services discloses conservatism largely untouched by new thinking about generating new customers, increasing competition and efficiency, creating community airlines and lowering fares. Among other things it was obsessed with the so-called problem of siphoning off passengers from existing routes to new regional routes. This type of thinking, certainly so far as the reformers were concerned, was positioned in the mind-set of a low-growth market with the necessity of division of spoils that prevailed in the AEA and IATA cartels.[22] Furthermore, members of the Parliament shared the anxious suspicion of some of the Member States that the Commission had power ambitions above its station, and that grasping competence over large areas of airline operations was a chosen strategy for advancing them.

On 9 April 1984 the Council of Ministers asked the Parliament to deliver an opinion on Memorandum 2. Between then and March 1985 that request was intermittently acted on, and thus after a rather tortuous progress through the Parliamentary labyrinth of procedures, consultations with interested parties and deliberations, the draft Klinkenborg Report finally emerged. It was deeply influenced by two important inputs: one from an analysis by the Dutch academic and specialist in air law and the airlines, P.P.C. Haanappel, commissioned for the Committee for Economic Affairs and Development, and the other from statements of US officials at hearings about the impact of deregulation in the US.

Haanappel's analysis should have dispelled some fears about the consequences of liberalization. For example he thought that there would be little problem for small communities, which were thought to be disadvantaged by freer competition, i.e. commercially unviable routes would be abandoned. He observed that in Europe such communities were well serviced by ground transportation and could be provided with air services through public service routes.[23] He also spoke favourably about the Commission's tariff reform proposals, though like others he felt that they were somewhat complicated. However, on three key issues he provided grounds for either upholding the status quo, or at best for effecting only modest and gradual change. On pooling, he commented that:

> it should be kept in mind that pooling is deeply embedded in intra-European scheduled air transport and that changes should come gradually. Too sudden changes might mean a severe financial blow to some small and/or weaker carriers, and might also lead to carriers asking Governments for state-aid to cover operating losses.[24]

He highlighted possible problems in labour relations and mused that as hub-and-spoke configurations already exist in Europe: 'One wonders whether hub-and-spoke operations can be made more efficient for intra-European scheduled international air transport.'[25]

Some rather inconsistent assumptions seem to have been in play in this analysis. Underlying the warning about labour relations was the assumption that a US-style deregulated market might come into existence, but this was never on the Commission's agenda and was specifically disavowed in Memorandum 2. Even after the impact of the *Nouvelles Frontières* case, which determined that the competition laws applied to air transport, *Flight International* wrote in May 1986: 'In a month's time the nations of the European Economic Community will know exactly what airline deregulation in the Community means, and it is nothing remotely like deregulation in the USA.'[26] On hub-and-spoke configurations, while the author noted national constraints on such a system's operation, he also claimed that a hub-and-spoke system already existed in Europe. While the European system might indeed *look* like a US hub-and-spoke system from the outside, it certainly did not operate with the kind of commercial freedom on the inside, which was the crucial factor. Maybe unwittingly the analysis thus undermined one of the key arguments in favour of reform. And finally, while talking positively about the need for more competition and liberalization, the analysis emphasized the importance of continued airline collusion and pooling, the very things that made competition and liberalization so difficult to achieve.

The effect of the Haanappel analysis and evidence given in hearings about the negative consequences of US-style deregulation promoted both fear of change and suspicion of the Commission's true objectives. This led the Klinkenborg Report actually to question the Commission's integrity.[27]

> The Commission, by referring to the lack of a real internal market, raises the suspicion that they first want to wait for the internal market to be created and in the meantime develop their anti-cartel control instruments so that once this development is complete, deregulation of air transport can be introduced into the Community. ... this must be excluded from the outset.[28]

Reinforcing the caution of the Haanappel analysis came evidence from hearings organized by the Parliament on 21–22 February 1985 with Matthew Scocozza,

Assistant Secretary for Policy and International Affairs at the US Department of Transportation and William Scheri, representative of the US airline workers' union.

> Various contributions to this hearing make it clear that deregulation of air transport in the United States has had effects which were severely detrimental to workers, led to major changes in flight organization such that the number of flights on the well frequented routes over large distances became better and cheaper whereas the services on little-frequented short routes became worse and more expensive. The level of accidents per kilometer flown has fallen; the trade unions point out, however, that the number of critical situations grew because workers were put under pressure from certain companies, particularly where collective agreements did not exist.[29]

Specifically the Klinkenborg Report argued that there were four reasons why US-style deregulation had to be ruled out in Europe. The first, which actually ignored the conclusion of Haanappel, argued that regional routes could not be left to the vagaries of the market when the pursuit of profit would lead to concentration on major routes and the withering away of poorly frequented routes. Such results would be in direct contradiction of Article 2 of the Rome Treaty in its call for harmonized and closer relations within the Community. Second, reform of the transport system 'should not be solely at the expense of the workers'.[30] The report asserted the widespread value held in the Community of balancing social justice and competition; and 'deregulation ... gives absolute priority to the principle of free competition and is unacceptable in Europe because of the enormous social conflict it would involve'.[31] Towards the end of the report the language used was positively scathing: 'It is absolutely irresponsible of the Commission ... to ignore ... the problems of industrial and social legislation' when it 'cannot forecast the effects of its measures on the number of jobs in civil aviation, .'[32] Third, geography counted. The larger continental land mass and longer distances for routes held intrinsic benefits for US deregulation, which could not be replicated in Europe. And fourth, there were considerations of state. The report observed that an airline going out of business in the US was of little significance but in Europe it was unlikely 'that even one Member State would ever allow its 'national' airline to be pushed out of the market.'[33]

In its general assessment of the Commission's proposal, the Klinkenborg Report welcomed the momentum it had established towards creating a CTP in aviation, and specifically noted renewed multilateral activity in IATA, AEA and ECAC and, at the bilateral level, the liberalization agreements between Britain on the one hand and the Netherlands and West Germany on the other. However, it then recommended a more critical examination to see whether Memorandum 2 met the 'basic criteria which the European Parliament has set for aviation policy'[34] and proceeded to set out a whole series of points that amounted, in fact, to a wholesale rejection of the Commission's position.

While paying some lip-service to increasing competition, the Report insisted that civil aviation was not simply a commercial operation. It was also a 'means of fulfilling purposes of state and is held by many Member States to be an instrument of national policy.'[35] This conviction and assumptions about its unalterability led the Parliament to its claim that no national airline would be allowed to go into liquidation. This also then led on to emphasis on the need for a balance between competition and maintaining the financial strength of the airlines; otherwise governments would be burdened with the pay-out of large subsidies if their airlines, as a result of increased competition, started to fail. Subsidies were a very real problem, but the Report was not sanguine about the ability of the Commission to be effective because any controls introduced for the Commission to police subsidies would hit the political buffers once the life of a national airline was at stake. In those circumstances it would be better to have the political power of Parliament behind limiting subsidies, rather than Commission bureaucrats trying to enforce subsidy rules in the face of a Member State's political opposition. The Commission was not the only institution in the game of making plays for power.

Civil aviation should thus operate under a carefully crafted system, according to the report, that took all consumer, airline and national government interests into account, along with the need for integration with other modes of transport. 'However, reform in this area must not lead to the creation of new supranational administrative powers or even of a European transport authority.' 'it is totally unrealistic to suppose that the Member States would relinquish a foreign policy instrument as important as the negotiation and conclusion of air transport agreements with third countries.'[36] In the Parliament's view broad discretionary powers for the Commission were 'hardly advisable', nor was the prospect, suggested by Memorandum 2, that the Commission would develop a regulatory bureaucracy to oversee the SEAM. In those fears it was at one with the radical reformers in Britain. A gradual relaxation of bilateral agreements with no European Commission-run multilateral overlay was as radical as the Parliament could get at this stage.

The issue that separated the Parliament and the Commission most clearly was on what the Parliament called 'splitting the market', in other words, creating competitive fares, for example, in Europe, which were at odds with practice elsewhere governed by IATA fare setting. The Report categorically announced that 'the Community's initiatives must not, under any circumstances, provoke a split in Western Europe's air transport system.'[37] The US-prompted liberalization of the north transatlantic fare regime was not seen in a positive light, but as a severe disturbance that had to be solved by the US–ECAC Memorandum of Understanding. The positive effects of the SCO in moving IATA and ECAC towards what was seen by many as beneficial, if modest, liberalization went unmentioned. What the Parliament saw as positive in a united market, the advocates of reform, including some in the Commission, but more commonly in the UK and the Netherlands, saw as negative cartelization practices. The Report's position, when translated into direct comments on routes, rates, capacity and agreements between airlines, also made for varying degrees of conservative reading.

On route access, while the Report spoke of the long-term aim of the right of aircraft of any Member State to operate to any point in another state, if it so wished, they were restricted to operations from country of origin; there was no concept of a community airline operating freely throughout the EC, something which the establishment rules of the Treaty of Rome clearly implied; and once created would undermine the political importance of national flag carriers. It also noted the possible positive developments that might arise from the liberal bilaterals negotiated by the British, but then qualified that by emphasizing needs for a rational and controllable tariff system and for safeguards against the danger of siphoning off traffic and suggested the use of small aircraft as a means of achieving that, or very small aircraft, if the application of the Regional Air Services Directive were ever expanded to include category 1 airports. On capacity, the Report was unhappy with the Commission's proposal for a safety net of 25 per cent, and declared that it was 'important to ensure that the airlines can continue to conclude without restriction those agreements which they believe economically useful as part of their cooperation'.[38] On tariffs, the Report rejected the Commission's proposals on pricing zones of flexibility as too complicated, and it spoke of the danger of chaos in the event of substantial changes being made that allowed more scope for market forces. In contrast it spoke favourably of efforts under way in ECAC to modify the existing price-setting system. Only if the ECAC negotiations failed would there be a need for a Community Directive. Furthermore, pending the conclusion of the ECAC negotiations the Report recommended that 'the Council could temporarily exempt the forms of cooperation in the air transport sector, which are currently standard practice from the ban on cartels.'[39]

The reasoning behind that suggestion was immanent throughout the Report, which in fact was not hostile to the existing condition of civil aviation in Europe and only wanted minor reform of both the bilateral and multilateral parts of the airline system. When the Report appeared to use the rhetoric of more radical reform, it was soon hemmed in with so many qualifications as to become meaningless. Nowhere did this become more apparent than in paragraph 73:

> In air transport close cooperation between the companies active in the field is essential to a proper transport service. The various types of cooperation which have developed in the air transport sector are therefore not opposed to competition although strictly speaking they are agreements between companies as defined in Article 85 of the EEC Treaty. They ensure a comprehensive range of services and as a result tend to promote rather than hinder intra-Community trade.[40]

The 'strictly speaking' is the give away. The Commission's Legal Service and the Commission went with the 'strictly speaking' interpretation. They felt that they were mandated to do so by the legal requirements of the Treaty of Rome. And they wanted to use the power of granting or withholding exemptions from the application of the competition rules to the airlines as a means of pushing the entire system down the liberalization route.

The Report concluded that Memorandum 2 was fundamentally flawed in two respects. First, 'the underlying policy is not clearly and honestly defined', and the Parliament thought that the Commission was trying to turn itself into a European air transport authority. Second, the Report claimed that the Memorandum was driven largely by a tendency to meet the position of a small group of Community citizens, namely, air travellers, articulated by FATUREC, which, the Report waspishly noted, had only come into being with the help of the Commission. Somewhat incredibly, the Report ended with the observation: 'If these two cardinal errors are removed and their effects on individual programmes corrected, the second memorandum on civil aviation would be an excellent document which would represent a milestone in the development of a common transport policy.'[41]

Not surprisingly the Dutch and British members of the committee refused to endorse the Klinkenborg Report and issued a dissenting minority report.[42] Lord Bethell, who, as well as running his Freedom of the Skies Campaign, was a British member of the European parliament (MEP), declared the report to be 'one of the most shocking ever to have been put before this House.'[43] Nevertheless, it was approved by the Parliament with an overwhelming majority of 198 votes to sixty-six, with eight abstentions. This clearly indicated the weakness of the forces in favour of substantial reform in the Parliament and the strength of the conservative disposition in favour of only a modestly modified status quo.

The European Parliament's thinking, as represented in the Klinkenborg Report, was seriously at odds with the position slowly developing in DG VII, DG IV and among members of the Commission's Legal Service. It was even further removed from the stance of the British, except insofar as they both opposed the idea of the Commission acquiring substantial power and authority over a new European civil aviation bureaucracy. The report ignored the possibilities of passenger growth on regional routes that were operated efficiently, with lower prices and using appropriately-sized aircraft, and simply concentrated on how to safeguard against the siphoning off of traffic from the established flag carriers. It set up deregulation as a straw man to knock down: deregulation 'gives absolute priority to the principle of free competition'. But no one in the Commission ever countenanced such a policy. Similarly, geographical conditions did vary between the US and Europe, but such an observation needed to be used as an invitation to construct an appropriate European system of a freer market, rather than using it as a full-stop to close debate. A new system of interregional services could very well cope with Europe's geography as suggested above and in the European context, so far as the Commission was concerned, this would be under effective control of dominant positions and cartel practices and with provisions for those community services that might not be lifted by the new market changes into viability. On matters of nation-state political interest in airlines, the Commission, like the Parliament, recognized that there were huge problems here, but saw them as challenges and not unalterable conditions of life.

And in Britain notice had already been given that things were at least to change there with the privatization of BA. There were all kinds of difficulties fraught with interests of state, but the Parliament seemed to be unwilling to get out of the national box, even though its members were supposed to represent Europe.

The Commission on the other hand saw the logic of the Rome Treaty and its competition rules as leading on to a SEAM that would require the concept of community airlines in accordance with the Treaty's establishment rules, run on a commercial basis, subject to bankruptcy just like any other enterprise, with oversight from a benign regulatory regime. This is not to suggest that there were not differences of opinion and policy within the Commission. There were between the DG IV and DG VII and between colleagues within the Transport Commission, for example, between Steele and Clinton Davis, and over the years the Commission had to compromise and accommodate with a variety of forces, but its logic generally ran along the lines of gradual, but substantial reform with appropriate safeguards. This Commission position was derived from what was required by the Treaty of Rome whereas rather mysteriously and rather arrogantly the Klinkenborg Report spoke of the European Parliament setting the 'basic criteria' for the aviation market. So far as the Commission was concerned, this was a case of Parliamentary *ultra vires*. Neither the Parliament nor the Commission had the right to set the basic criteria. Those had been set by the Treaty of Rome and had to be implemented by the Council of Ministers, possibly with recommendations from the Commission.

The two most important general differences between the Commission and the Parliament, one strategic and one tactical, were over the danger of splitting, or fragmenting the market, and over the power to grant or withhold exemptions for practices contrary to Article 85's prohibition of collusion by enterprises and circumstances contrary to safeguards against the abuse of dominant positions provided for in Article 86. The introduction of more competition inevitably involved a more adversarial type of system: that is what competition means. The Klinkenborg Report's insistence that the market must not be fragmented and that airline cooperation agreements must be allowed to continue clearly placed it in the same camp as the AEA, IATA and ECAC, the scheduled national airlines and the regulatory conservative majority among the Member States. This obsession with maintaining order in the marketplace was totally at odds with any framework that would promote serious competition. As Richard Branson of Virgin Atlantic put it:

> IATA-standardised fares and seats and food and excess baggage charges delivered by IATA standardised airlines with what look like IATA-standardised plastic smiles are certainly 'orderly', but they prevent competition by depriving passengers of any freedom of choice, whether one airline flies the route or ten.[44]

Finally, the Report's proposal, that there should be a general exemption from Article 85 for the airlines, until discussions proceeding in ECAC on tariff reform were completed, in effect reiterated sympathy for only the most modest kind of change, but more importantly also threatened to take away what would become the Commission's main lever for moving recalcitrant Member States along the road to more substantial reform.

One of the interesting and instructive features that gradually emerged in the debate prompted by Memorandum 2, was how the American experience of deregulation was treated and what lessons were drawn from it for liberalization in Europe. There was a spate of studies comparing the actualities and possibilities of the two markets. The problem for policy-makers in the Commission and elsewhere was that the verdicts were often totally at odds with each other. Not surprisingly Alfred Kahn wrote in 1983: 'Although the experience of the airline industry in the very few years since deregulation has been turbulent and dominated by the doubling of fuel prices, worldwide recession, and the effects of the flight controllers strike [in 1981 in the US], it already abundantly documents the wisdom of this national preference for competition.'[45] Richard Pryke in Britain held a similar view. He was sensitive to the problems that Kahn indicated had plagued the industry, but he also strongly believed that deregulation in some form was not only beneficial but inevitable.[46] Peter Forsyth, while noting significant differences in the two markets, drew important lessons from the US experience for Europe, and several years later Sean D. Barrett demonstrated the benefits of liberalization on the London–Dublin route as a consequence of the 1988 UK–Ireland liberal bilateral ASA. Passenger numbers grew from under one million a year to over 2.3 million and prices dropped 37 per cent out of Dublin and 42 per cent out of London.[47] And finally the recollection from a senior official in DG IV was that, at the time of Memorandum 2, 'in terms of drivers from the consumer perspective, the US example showed that air transport could be done more cheaply than it had been done traditionally.' It took some time for 'the airlines [in Europe] to realise that this translated to volume growth, that they could really obtain very high growth rates by adopting a more dynamic approach to markets'.[48]

By 1988 the dynamism of deregulation had admittedly thrown up some problems, but not insurmountable ones according to Matthew Scocozza. He pointed out that since 1978 passenger traffic in the US had risen from 275 million to 450 million, markets served had risen from 4,900 to 5,300, and prices had dropped on average by 13 per cent.[49] Juxtaposed in opposition to such views were those expressed by the Klinkenborg Report, which despite disclaimers to the contrary by the Commission, raised the spectre of US-style deregulation for Europe with all kinds of adverse consequences for labour, disruptions in the European airline system in fares and services, bankruptcies for smaller airlines and ever larger subsidies for the national flag carriers. As late as 1987, when some improvements in services for customers were becoming apparent in Europe because of the liberal bilaterals that Britain had concluded with several Member States, the AEA remained adamant in its opposition to anything but the most modest kind of change. It insisted on the folly of what it called local change, which would fragment the market, and continued to reiterate the claim that US-style deregulation should not be implemented in Europe, even when Commission proposals by that time were clearly miles away from that kind of reform. 'The AEA concluded that the fundamental differences between the two continents make the application of their respective market principles non-transferable when related to air transport.'[50] It even suggested that the European airline system was superior to that in the US. The AEA study compared

> the operating ratio – the revenue over costs after net interest – in both regions. For European operations, the AEA ratio averaged 103 compared with 101 for U.S. domestic carriers. This suggests that by 1985, the European carriers were doing better in Europe than their U.S. counterparts were doing in America.[51]

From the perspective of the airlines, this was probably true. Unfortunately, it did not take efficiency and productivity into account or the problems that the European system 'was uniform and expensive and made no variations in the nature of demand'. Nevertheless, it was effective propaganda about why Europe did not need to liberalize.[52] Both BA and B.Cal. temporarily left AEA in protest at its response to Memorandum 2, and Clinton Davis, who was no radical reformer, dubbed AEA's response a 'no-change package.'[53]

Sorensen was undoubtedly right when he commented that 'everything in those days was influenced by what happened in the United States,'[54] but he did not mean to imply that everything that the US had done should be replicated in Europe, and if one listened carefully, one might have heard that no one in a position of power in Europe was suggesting that. The Commission, for example, was always in favour of a much more robust line on dominant positions in Europe than the laisser-faire attitude in the US (or so it seemed in Brussels). Repeated denials that the European agenda was US-style deregulation fell on deaf ears among the opponents of liberalization, who persisted in using the spectre of full-blown US-style deregulation to rouse opposition to any form of liberalization. This was either because they were protecting the cartelized privileged positions, that were at the heart of Kahn's attack on regulation, or else it was because of sincerely held ideological beliefs, though of course those two positions are not mutually exclusive. Ideology helps to explain why two radically different views about deregulation were bruited about in the field of debate about what to do in Europe. Ideology turns the old adage of seeing is believing on its head: the ideologue's beliefs largely determine what she or he sees. It was the values that rigid proponents and opponents carried in their heads that provided them with such radically different views of what change in the airline system had or might produce.

Riding on the back of the rejections of full-blown US-style deregulation were conservative proposals for change from IATA, and then from a joint IATA/AEA initiative and finally from ECAC. These proposals came in response to growing pressures for greater liberalization, and epitomized what the forces of conservative regulation felt were necessary to contain the movement for reform. Just how conservative this all was will be assessed in some detail in the next chapter. The Commission had to find a way of dealing with this strategic attack on their proposals, which threatened to gain support from the Parliament and from those who were perhaps unhappy with the existing system, but were not prepared to embrace more radical reform. At the same time it did not want to alienate allies such as Britain, or lobby groups like ACE and BEUC, which favoured going further than Memorandum 2 suggested. For example, the Association of Independent Air Carriers criticized the Commission for not going far enough and contemptuously dismissed the Klinkenborg Report as a 'whitewash of the present system'.[55]

The Commission thus had to deal with a whole range of difficulties thrown up by Memorandum 2. The difficulties were not just with the die-hard defenders of the status quo but also with the reformers ranging from the radical to the moderate. There was also the almost universal problem of the growth of Commission power, which from within the Commission looked a necessary pre-requisite for developing and effectively policing the SEAM; from outside it looked like an unacceptable power-play from the perspective of both the pro and anti-reform groups. The only group that seemed content with the Commission was the lobby group FATUREC, which it itself had fostered.

How was the Commission to overcome or sidestep opposition to its proposals from the die-hard defenders of the existing regulatory system? How was it to dispel the view, propagated by regulatory conservatives, that US-style deregulation was intended for Europe? Even those most vociferous about reform knew deregulation was not the solution. 'The need was not for simplistic DE-regulation, but for the replacement of the old ANTI-competitive regulation by PRO-competitive rules.'[56] How was the Commission to handle what appeared to be reform proposals, but which were in fact simply tactics calculated to keep the essentials of the existing system intact? And how was it to deal with the British and re-engage with them effectively as their main ally in the drive for reform when the British were suspicious of Commission power ambitions and felt that Memorandum 2 was hardly satisfactory? Fortunately for the reform movement there soon emerged a signal that the British Government recognized that the only way forward was in partnership. 'The European Community offers the best chance for further liberalisation.' As the 1984 White Paper put it: 'The Government is seeking to persuade other member states that the Community should rapidly move to a liberal aviation market.'[57] Collaboration between Britain and the Commission turned out to be effective and that in combination with a dramatic ruling by the European Court of Justice were the two key dynamics that pushed liberalization forward and helped the Commission successfully cope with the host of challenges that had arisen, or at least had developed clearer form, as a result of Memorandum 2.

5 Achieving the first package of reform

> 1 January 1988 was ... a red letter day in the history of European air transport[1]

Perceptions of how far progress had been made with liberalization of the European airline market by the delivery of the first package of reform in 1987 depended on the perspective of individuals, often determined by judgments about what might come next, by strong ideological convictions and by the weight of vested national and commercial interests. While the Commission officially dubbed the arrival of Package 1 as a 'red letter day', others made very different judgements about the message it sent out. Its main architect, Frederik Sorensen, admitted that it 'may not move liberalization that far, but it is done in a reasonable way'.[2] Those like Lord Bethell and his associates, who were more openly and radically opposed to the regulatory system in Europe, thought:

> The December package may represent political progress to those who wish to pretend to themselves or others that something real has been achieved. For the most part it has not. The December package is cosmetic in most aspects as we predicted and publicly warned.[3]

From the ranks of those marshalled in support of the status quo, when it was clear what was going to emerge in Package 1, came caustic criticism from a different perspective. Karl-Heinz Neumeister of the AEA, in an attempt yet again to evoke US deregulation as a bogeyman to scare people in Europe, ridiculed the idea of applying US practice in the EC: 'Just because Americans drive on the same side of the road as most of us doesn't mean they are better drivers. The mistake most commentators make is in assuming the roads and driving conditions are the same in both regions.'[4] Rather ironically, it was the British, who did not drive on the same side of the road, who were more familiar with driving conditions in the US than any other nationality in Europe, and who were in the forefront of advocating reform that came closest to the US model.

Given all these differing views about what the provisions of Package 1 actually meant in practice, it is not surprising that twenty years on controversy still abounds not only in terms of what it actually achieved, but also about how it came about. The simple fact is that Package 1 was more important for its promise than for its delivery of substantial reform. How one explains that nuance in and the genesis of the new provisions for European civil aviation is highly complicated. They were wrought by the changing interplay of impersonal market forces with inputs from the Member States, institutions, lobbyists and influential individuals. Explanation rests on adducing a lot of detailed evidence so it would be rather inappropriate to anticipate the findings here, but a number of important factors and developments might be usefully identified as signposts for the direction in which the more detailed explanation progresses.

The initial reaction to Memorandum 2 indicated the breadth and strength of hostility that was harboured by the regulatory conservatives towards liberalizing the European aviation market. Nevertheless, the reformers managed to transform Memorandum 2 into Package 1 between 1987 and 1988, added market access provisions, set deadlines for change, implemented enabling legislation specifically to apply the competition rules to air transport and, perhaps most importantly, achieved commitment to a further reform package. The actual substance of Package 1 at the end of the day was still slight and that caused many reformers disappointment; they remained sceptical about the prospects for further reform for much of the negotiation of Package 2. But Package 1 promised more than they realized. In particular it provided a crucial weapon – the offer of temporary exemption from the application of the competition rules in return for gradual and orderly liberalization.

While the prospects for substantial liberalization still hung in the balance, the negative views about what had been achieved in Package 1 were a little uncharitable, given the fact that progress had been made in the face of well-entrenched positions and what appeared initially as an unmovable, strong coalition in support of the status quo. In achieving those successes, reformers had had to contain demands for harmonization prior to liberalization, and to deflect strategies that offered some change, but whose main aim was to curb, not promote, reform. They also began to apply pressure to lever the majority of the Member States out of well-embedded anti-competitive positions on fare setting, pooling arrangements, restrictions on capacity and their insistence on single designation and a strictly limited number of routes.

The development of the Single Market project nurtured and propelled forward by Delors was probably a necessary prerequisite for the advances that were made in Package 1, but this was not a sufficient condition for what materialized. From within the institutional framework of the EC came strong attacks upon commercial collusion from both DG IV under the leadership of Commissioner Peter Sutherland and from the European Court of Justice with its decision in the *Nouvelles Frontières* case. From DG VII came a forceful exposition of the growing need for reform but also expressions of willingness to compromise with and accommodate the forces of both radical reform and regulatory conservatism, and that facilitated progress. In support of their case for reform, officials from

DG VII were able to cite growing public demands for change and to argue that action was legally required by Community law. The latter provided a crucial threat strategy for the Commission for pushing recalcitrant Member States into compliance with at least a modicum of reform in Package 1, and this threat was robustly used by DG IV.

From Britain and the Netherlands came continuing pressures and support for reform, including the negotiation of liberal ASAs with some of their European partners. However, immediate national interests sometimes tempered their enthusiasm for reform, and occasionally their tactics diverged. In particular, a serious dispute arose about capacity reform, with the British prepared to accept far more modest measures than the Dutch were willing initially to countenance. This type of flexibility, evinced on more than one occasion by the British, led one analyst at the time to note the following suspicions about their positioning during the development of Package 1:

> whilst the U.K. paraded an enthusiasm for more competition in European air travel, when the chips were down and the possibility existed that Member States ... might do something, the U.K. is said to have reneged ... due to concern about the selling price of British Airways.[5]

There were important calculations made in the British Government about the interests of BA, but, like the Commission, it was also driven by a genuine commitment to liberalization. That conviction abided even though pragmatic compromises were often made. Underpinning the position of both the Commission and the British was the belief that once liberalization was initiated, it would develop an ineluctable momentum that would drive forward to a much more liberal position than the forces of regulatory conservatism ever wanted. The British were in fact often more impatient about this process than the Commission, but in the end the results proved them both correct.

Favourable public opinion and arguments from lobby groups, while often invoked by the British and the Commission, do not appear to have brought a great deal of pressure to bear directly on the process of advancing reform. Expressions of opinion that were negative about reform, in fact often had more impact. For example, the European Parliament with its direct elections was now the most obvious medium for the expression of public concerns on EC-wide issues, but the Parliament's Klinkenborg Report was critical even of the Commission's modest proposals, and its views were endorsed by an overwhelming majority in the House. Lord Bethell continued to worry away at the establishment and to keep regulatory issues in the news; and in November 1984 he considered trying his luck in the British courts after his disappointment in the European Court of Justice. On 25 November he was advised:

> The object of the claim would be to establish the application of the Treaty of Rome to UK air transport. A favourable judgment would also establish the illegality of all similar airline behaviour in respect of fares agreements

and, by analogue, capacity on routes between the UK and the territories of the other EC Member States.[6]

In the end, the cost of action in British courts proved prohibitive, but fortunately for Bethell, in April 1986 the European Court of Justice ruled precisely in the way that he wanted when it decided *Nouvelles Frontières*. At best, the arousal of public opinion for reform only added to the more favourable context created by the Single Market project. Far more important than public opinion and lobbying pressures was the political happenstance of a series of Council presidencies from 1985–86, which were all well disposed to reform. The tenacity of Transport Secretary, John Moore, during the British presidency, July–December 1986, proved to be an important component in developments at intergovernmental level. In particular a compromise he struck on capacity provisions with France and Germany in October 1986 was significant in luring the conservative majority into modest liberalization.

Controversy may remain about just how much progress was made by Package 1, but no one disputes that progress of a sort was achieved. Movement towards the final approval of the package came in stages. The first stage was the work of the high-level group (HLG) established to examine the proposals in Memorandum 2, its recommendations in December 1984 and its further deliberations during the first part of 1985. The second phase began with the impact of the new Commission that came into office in 1985. Among the new commissioners was Peter Sutherland at DG IV, who 'from the very first ... used the competition rules as a lever. He attacked the pool agreements between airlines'.[7] The third phase came with the *Nouvelles Frontières* case, more aggressive pressures from the Commission, and the work of the British presidency from June to December 1986. The final phase came in 1987 as remaining issues were resolved, including a six-month delay in the acceptance of Package 1 because of an Anglo-Spanish dispute over airline access to Gibraltar.

The HLG from May 1984 and on into 1985

On 22 February 1984 the Commission approved Memorandum 2 for transmission to the Council. It was received under a French presidency that was strongly opposed to reform. In May that year the Council had an 'initial exchange of views on the Commission's memorandum on air transport; it recognised the need to adjust the present system and decided to set up a working party to report by the end of the year'.[8] The working party took the form of a HLG, composed of Directors General of Aviation from the Member States and officials from the Commission. The French tactic was to try to talk the issue of airline liberalization into the ground, or at least hedge any proposals for reform with so many conditions about workers' rights and social policy that they would be ineffective. They tried to sideline any consideration of market reform by proposing that the primary focus should be on the possible social consequences of reform, thus prioritizing harmonization issues over market liberalization measures. In support of this they were able to invoke the scare stories about the impact of US-style deregulation both on pay and conditions, and of disrupting the market, and to draw on negative views commonly held in the European Parliament. Fortunately for the reform agenda, the British delegate on the HLG, Handley Stevens, was able to intervene with a counter-proposal, namely that the sequence of attention for the HLG should be the three key features of commercial airline operations – route access, capacity, and fares, followed by consideration of the role of the Community's competition rules and the proposal for temporary bloc exemptions from their application, and then, and only then, should the HLG concern itself with the possible social consequences of reform. Somewhat to Stevens' surprise his proposal garnered sufficient support to be accepted.[9]

In July Ireland succeeded to the Council presidency, and under Donal O'Mahony the HLG met frequently, on average at least once a month, between July and November 1984. Even so, progress was difficult, slow and, in fact, barely perceptible. Generally there emerged a reluctance to disrupt the existing market and a commitment to ensuring that harmonization should go hand in hand with gradual and progressive liberalization. But, 'progressive liberalization' so far did not amount to much. The HLG agreed to move away from 50/50 capacity sharing, but was unable to reach any consensus on how large the departure would be. It was abundantly clear that the Commission's proposal for a 25 per cent safety net, where one side could mount three times the capacity of the other, was totally unacceptable. This was going to be a serious and difficult issue to resolve. Both the British and, even more so, the Dutch were determined to liberalize capacity controls, which not only limited competition directly, but also had important secondary consequential effects for market access. On fares there was some movement towards the kind of regime that the Commission had proposed for non-mandatory consultations, country of origin fares and zones of flexibility; but the fact that IATA, AEA and ECAC were soon to champion similar proposals gives an indication of just how timid and useful they were as a way of containing the reform movement. IATA's initial tariff proposal never engaged wide support, but it did once reincarnated as an IATA–AEA proposal and then in slightly more liberal form as an ECAC proposal in June 1985. This attracted broad support from the regulatory conservative Member States, and became an important strategy for trying to head off more radical proposals emerging from within the EC.[10] On route access, the HLG indicated a willingness to consider a more liberal approach to regional operations and to accept some degree of multiple designation, even on some individual routes, providing traffic conditions warranted it. The British had demanded and pushed vigorously for more liberal route access provisions, but even the very modest measures countenanced by the HLG made the Council of Ministers feel uneasy. The HLG also commented on the competition rules and decided that their application and bloc exemptions should be left in the hands of the Council, at the time a sound strategy for conserving the status quo. Finally, on the need for the control of state aids, there was a call for a clear Directive from the Council.

Handley Stevens later described these outcomes in moderately optimistic terms, claiming that 'the outline of a liberal consensus was beginning to take shape', with Britain and the Netherlands in the vanguard, Italy and Greece manning the ramparts of the status quo and the remaining six Member States falling into a new category that was grudgingly prepared to accept some liberalization. In particular, he claimed that this new configuration of national forces had managed to get route access and a more liberal fares regime firmly on the agenda.[11] Such views are not entirely warranted by the evidence. While there may have been some slight movement towards liberalization among the Member States, it was more grudging and achieved less than Stevens has suggested. The Dutch representative on the HLG, Hans Raben, saw developments slightly differently with a liberal group composed of Britain, the Netherlands and Luxembourg ranged against the rest in a conservative majority. And Wheatcroft and Lipman in their analysis in 1986 were less impressed by the liberal credentials of the outcome of the HLG than Stevens. In fact, the HLG's proposals were all a little feeble and even then the reaction of the Council to them could hardly be described as sanguine.[12]

The Council took note of the Report from the HLG in November, and then on 11 December 1984, after accepting the report's guidelines, referred them back for further consideration and for definite proposals to be drafted during the course of 1985. However, while the Council endorsed the guidelines, it did so with some cautionary comments:

> The Council endorsed the guidelines annexed to the report but said that access to the market could be considered when the Council comes to review the Directive on interregional air services, which must be before 1 July 1986. It felt that particular attention would have to be paid to capacity, fares and competition.[13]

The Council had simply authorized further talking, cautioned care on fares, capacity and competition issues, and tried to contain market access matters to a review of the Regional Air Services Directive of 1983, which had to be reviewed in any case before the summer of 1986. The Council did set the end of 1985 as the deadline for specific proposals to be submitted to itself, but over the next five months the HLG only met four times and little progress was made. Fifteen months of work on the Commission's proposals did not result in a great deal of substance. Intergovernmentalism, in the form of the HLG and the Transport Council, seemed to be going nowhere with Memorandum 2, but things began to change, and pressures built up during the early months of 1985 and came to something of a head in May.

The impact of the new Commission from 1985 to April 1986

The new Commission in 1985 brought the Irishman Peter Sutherland into contention, and he was strongly committed to applying the competition rules in the transport sector and to the airlines in particular. It did not take long for his impact to be felt. At the same time, his influence was somewhat counterbalanced by that of Stanley Clinton Davis, who took over as Transport Commissioner in DG VII from Georges Contogeorgis of Greece. Clinton Davis had been Peter Shore's Parliamentary Secretary in the 1970s and could hardly be labelled as a liberal so far as civil aviation regulation was concerned. He soon found himself unable to work with his more robustly liberal Director-General John Steele and he replaced him in 1986 with Eduardo Peña.[14] Another possible setback for the liberal camp was the work of ECAC in developing proposals into more palatable but dangerous form so far as the liberal agenda was concerned. By June 1985 ECAC was about to issue a policy statement on intra-European air transport. The overlap of personnel between the HLG and national representatives at ECAC meant that the proposals they both developed were not all that dissimilar, but there were fears among members of DG IV and in Britain and the Netherlands that proposals from ECAC might deflect EC proposals away from real liberalization into very modest changes, primarily designed to uphold as much of the status quo as possible. There was also a danger that ECAC might seize much of the airline agenda from the EC, arguing that the integrity of the market would be better served by applying changes in the wider European context, which it represented. That, however, held within it a serious problem for the regulatory conservative members of the EC because ECAC did not have the power to grant exemptions from EC competition rules, which would be contravened by the collusion involved in the application of its proposals. This was something that haunted the defenders of the status quo over the following months and was the Achilles heel of their strategy.

For the time being, these developments in ECAC and the widespread negative response to Memorandum 2 were partly offset by the increased momentum, generated for the Single Market project, and particularly by the Cockfield White Paper with its exhortations about the Single Market in general and the SEAM in particular. This had influence and began to shift the balance away from inaction to the need for at least action of some kind. Then also in May, the European Court of Justice delivered its verdict on the case brought by the European Parliament against the Council for its inaction on the CTP. The Court deemed the Council culpable in that it had not developed the CTP, but found that its failings were not sufficient to warrant further legal proceedings at that time. Once again, while there was a considerable degree of ambiguity in the decision that was handed down, nevertheless the judgement was regarded as helpful in 'increasing the pressure for a common transport policy'.[15]

Emboldened by growing criticisms of the Council's failure to take action on the CTP, the Commission now made a stiff statement of intent on 23 May 1985 and added its own criticisms of Council inaction to those of the European Parliament and the Court. The Commission declared itself 'profoundly disappointed with the lack of progress' on Memorandum 2 and urged the Council to give the civil aviation dossier more attention and greater priority. Then came the most robust announcement of intent that the Commission had yet made. It declared that it should be made clear that:

> The Commission is in no way prepared to sacrifice its objective of creating more competition in the air transport sector. To do so would be to fail in our obligations under the Treaty and to fail our duty to the European citizen. If the negotiating process does not work, we shall have no option but to use other weapons.[16]

This dramatic statement came after careful consideration of tactics within DG VII, and in the knowledge that Sutherland had made it publicly clear that DG IV would use the competition rules and bring cases before the European Court of Justice as a last resort if satisfactory progress could not be achieved on Memorandum 2. At the end of April 1985 the Director General of Transport, John Steele, prepared a note for Clinton Davis on the tactical considerations involved in the then current negotiations about aviation policy.

Steele explained that it was important to think of the Commission's proposals as a package because they involved measures for both the commercial airlines and the governments of the Member States, which had so much say in how the airlines operated. He argued that to introduce flexibility into the airline industry 'we have to change it at both levels'. In other words the Member States must be prodded into introducing appropriate measures in the Council by taking action under Article 84(2), and the competition rules of Articles 85 to 90 needed to be applied to the airlines. However, Memorandum 2 offered a pact with the devil: providing 'the total system is sufficiently changed to ensure that the benefits pass through to the consumer' then 'current practices can be condoned', at least for a while. The airlines subject to certain conditions being met would be exempted from the application of the competition articles, and the Member State governments would have to accept Council provisions that would 'allow up to a point commercial competition to operate'.[17]

The 'pact' was conceived of by Steele as being flexible and dynamic. Given that the majority of the Member States preferred no change – or only slight change – things had to be handled deftly:

> Our main leverage is the offer of exemptions to their airlines, which they badly want. It follows from this that the final decision on our competition proposals should come at the end of the process of negotiation. Any decision taken earlier, whether favourable to the airlines or not, removes this leverage.[18]

Steele offered several reasons why he thought that a court case should not form part of immediate tactics and that instead the Commission should adopt the less glamorous approach of a hard-slog with a detailed set of negotiations, backed up by the threat of *not granting* block exemptions. He argued that Memorandum 2 had ignited a debate and that there was now discernible movement in the industry's thinking. July 1985 was also going to inaugurate a succession of the most favourable presidencies possible in the Council – successively till the end of 1986 – Luxembourg, the Netherlands and the UK. If drastic action were taken now, moderate opinion might be driven into the arms of the conservatives. In short, he felt that a productive process was currently in train. On the other hand:

> A court case by the commission would freeze this process. Both sides would dig in; their lawyers would prevent them from taking any initiative which prejudiced their legal position. It is our ultimate weapon; the promise of exemptions, or the threat of no exemptions, is at this stage a more potent persuader.[19]

For public consumption things were put in a softer way, holding out the prospect of gradual change, but the clenched fist remained visible beneath the silken glove.

> It [Court action] is our weapon of last resort and before we use it we must be sure that we have exercised to the full the process of negotiation and political persuasion that can best ensure that we do not risk losing the benefits of the present system in our attempts to improve it.[20]

It was Steele's reasoning that lay behind the May exhortations to the Council and the strategy of threatening, but trying to avoid the use of legal action. The Council was reminded that the Commission had already taken action under Article 69 against seven Member States for failing to help obtain information about commercial collusion and pooling agreements and that the Commission would not 'hesitate to take similar steps in the future'.[21] Then for the first time the Commission played its card under the authority of the 1979 Council Decision, and invoked its right of consultation regarding the forthcoming policy statement and discussions in ECAC. The Commission frankly and pointedly explained that it suspected that the ECAC meeting might be used to reach anti-competitive agreements through collusion, which were contrary to the Treaty of Rome. Thus, it insisted on invoking its powers under the 1979 Decision:

> We do so because we sense the danger that conflicts may arise between what Member States must do to build a common aviation policy and what they agree in these international *fora*. We are not prepared to let this happen
>
> [The Commission] would not hesitate to use this mechanism in future where items affecting Community interests are being discussed.[22]

The Commission was clearly laying the ground for the possibility of legal action against the airlines for anti-competitive practices. That tactic fed off the problem that hung in the air, namely, if and when the competition rules were applied to air transport, the Member States and the airlines would need exemptions for a transition to the new and more competitive dispensation – the type of exemptions that were offered in Memorandum 2. The danger of the competition rules for European airlines had still not fully materialized even after the verdict in the *European Parliament* v. *Council of Ministers* case and was not to do so until the

Nouvelles Frontierères case a year later. However, in 1985, particularly with the increased momentum towards creating the Single Market, it was becoming ever more likely that the competition laws would be applied to air transport. So, even if agreement were reached in ECAC, there would still be a problem because it did not have the power to grant exemptions from EC law, and whatever agreements were made could not be screened off from Commission view. If collusion of an anti-competitive nature were to take place, then the Commission would know and airlines would become vulnerable to legal action as soon as the competition laws became applicable to air transport. The Commission was thus showing a robustness that it had not demonstrated before, but, as Steele had indicated, legal action was to be reserved as a potential but real threat as they progressed along the preferred route of negotiation. In accordance with that strategy, after the threats came expression of a willingness to cooperate: 'the work so far shows that there is common ground between us and that a breakthrough is possible'. But the political will to go forward and meet the December 1985 deadline for proposals needed to be demonstrated because the Commission 'insists that we work to this end'.[23]

Over the next months between June 1985 and April 1986 when the *Nouvelles Frontières* case hit the system and caused a dramatic shock-wave to pass through the states and the airlines that had set their faces against liberalization, there was only marginal progress made with the reform agenda. The robust line that the Commission had taken with the Council in May and early June appeared to have had little immediate effect. This was largely because of the entrenched position of commanding forces well-disposed towards the existing system of regulation, and because of the fact that there was still ambiguity about the role of the competition rules in air transport. It has also been suggested that DG IV was restrained by the caution of DG VII, and there is some truth in that.[24] British and Dutch Transport Ministers Malcolm Ridley and Neelie Smit Kroes urged Sutherland and DG IV on to legal action, but the reluctance of DG VII to go down that route had nothing to do with lack of enthusiasm for liberalization, at least not so far as Steele was concerned. There is more of a question mark over the motivation and liberalization credentials of Clinton Davis, but Steele made it clear in his May 1985 note that it was indeed tactical considerations, not lack of temerity to pursue the liberalization agenda, that led him to the conclusion that it was better to keep the legal route in reserve. It was not that DG VII was holding Sutherland back because it was more cautious: it was holding back on the legal route because colleagues there thought that it would have negative and not positive outcomes for liberalization. When the European Parliament gave its overwhelmingly negative opinion on Memorandum 2 on 10 September 1985, it unavoidably raised questions in some minds about just how effective DG VII's strategy was likely to be. Would it be robust enough to shift the kind of views expressed formally by the Parliament's Klinkenborg Report, which favoured 'extremely cautious liberalization' of the conditions governing the operation of air transport?[25] DG VII continued to hope so, and when Clinton Davis told the press the next day that he still favoured a balanced approach, preferred other weapons to a legal case and that 'trying to achieve our objective through the Court is only second-best solution', he was simply reiterating what Steele had argued four months earlier.[26] Nevertheless, lack of progress was frustrating, and in November the Council was still 'unable to reach agreement regarding ... air transport'.[27] This created an opening for the conservative majority to deploy their strategy of minimal reform in order to conserve as much as possible of the existing regulatory regime.

Appended to the Klinkenborg Report were the June proposals from ECAC, which were generally favoured by the conservative Member States and the scheduled airlines. In particular, the proposals argued that the EC market should not be broken off from the wider European one covered by ECAC and that through ECAC it would also remain connected to the international framework, represented by IATA. ECAC's proposals drew on previous work by IATA and the AEA, and substantially overlapped with the majority position on the HLG. As Stevens put it, its provisions were 'liberal in tone but cautious in substance'.[28] The liberal tone was to attract conservative moderates and the substance was to preserve the status quo. The policy statement was largely a re-tread of general ideas set forth in the COMPAS Report, but with closure on some of its more liberal possibilities. The rhetoric sounded progressive – recognizing the need for more flexibility in pricing, market access, and capacity and more choice and voice for the consumer – but the devil was in the detail. It favoured abandoning rigid 50/50 capacity arrangements, but failed to suggest by how much and pledged support for non-mandatory pooling and even transfers of revenue providing not too much was involved. On tariffs, it favoured reviewing the 1967 Tariff Agreement, offered an ECAC tariff zone of flexibility, quicker arbitration of fare disputes and supported upholding non-mandatory airline collusion on pricing. On market access, it spoke of easier entry, but this only amounted to trifles: more scope for small aircraft (with up to thirty seats) and for developing regional routes and multiple designation at least on a country to country basis (i.e. more than one airline should be allowed to operate between two countries, not necessarily on the same route!). And overlaying all were considerations of harmonization and the impact on social conditions and labour.[29] Even after all this, some states felt that there was not enough provision for protecting their national airlines. On the other hand the British and the Dutch saw this clearly for what it was – a ploy to side-track the drive for liberalization.

There were dangers here for the Commission. In particular the initiative could be taken from them by ECAC, and the result would undoubtedly be a more conservative regulatory framework than they wanted and which they believed was required by Community law. Sutherland had taken steps in the summer of 1985 to try to deal with this by invoking the power of the 1979 Decision on consultation procedures that would at least allow the Commission to know precisely what was going on in ECAC. In January the Commission felt it needed to move again regarding developments and sent a communication to the Council urging that the Member States should adopt a common position in the ECAC negotiations on fares and capacity. For the Commission, while it recognized, that there were some parallels in the negotiations on Memorandum 2 and what was going on in both the HLG and ECAC, it was imperative that it should retain control, and ensure that any outcome in ECAC would not pre-empt a successful outcome within the EC on Memorandum 2. EC policy had to be paramount here, if for no other reason than the Commission felt that EC law demanded it.[30] ECAC could not be allowed to reach more anti-competitive agreements.

The Dutch presidency during the first half of 1986 proved to be something of a disappointment. The regulatory conservative states took the more significant initiatives, particularly through ECAC. In March it looked a little like there was some progress achieved on fares, but, in fact, it only amounted to the Council accepting the kind of thing that had been worked out in ECAC. On capacity nothing had changed and market access was not even mentioned.

> Progress was made on fare setting in the air transport sector, with a number of broad principles being agreed (defining areas in which rules are automatically approved and introduction of a procedure of accelerated arbitration for rates outside those areas).
>
> Pressure will have to be applied by the Commission to ensure agreement on capacity (where there has been little progress so far) and the application of competition to air transport.[31]

While the situation with the competition laws still remained indeterminate, the conservative majority sought to exploit that in their attempts to contain liberalization through their ECAC strategy, or simply refused to budge on some issues, but once the situation with the competition laws was clarified, the initiative ineluctably moved more and more into the hands of the Commission. In April 1986 the European Court of Justice came to the aid of the Commission when it pronounced, without any leeway for misinterpretation, that the competition laws applied to the air transport sector. Among other things, the clarification made the offer of block exemptions from the competition laws in return for movement within a specified period of time towards liberalization a more powerful weapon for the Commission to wield.

Nouvelles Frontières and its aftermath: April 1985 to December 1986

The Court in the *Nouvelles Frontières* case demanded that the competition rules should be applied to the airline industry.[32] Ambiguity any longer, there was not. Furthermore, if anyone were so disposed as to try to reintroduce any sense of ambiguity, the Commission's Legal Service made it very clear that that would be most difficult.

> The main point at which the judgement breaks new ground is its finding that the competition rules do apply to air transport.

Under Article 89, the Court said the Commission may, on application by a Member State or on its own initiative, investigate 'cases of suspected infringement' of Articles 85 and 86, and if it finds that there has been infringement it may propose 'appropriate measures to bring it to an end.' If the infringement is not brought to an end, the Commission has power to record that infringement 'in a reasoned decision,' and to authorise Member States to take the measures needed to remedy the situation.[33]

In other words, although the Council had not introduced regulations to implement the competition principles laid out in Articles 85 and 86 in the air transport sector, nevertheless the Commission still had implementation powers under Article 89. This honed the Commission's legal weapon. It now had a clear mandate: it could apply the competition rules as required by EC law and throw the existing system into convulsions. Alternatively, it could urge the Member States to take action through the Council to make provision for a SEAM and offer the inducement of temporary block exemptions from the competition rules in return for gradual movement into a more liberal regime. The attraction of this was that it would facilitate a smooth and incremental transition from the current regulatory system, which now clearly fell foul of the competition rules, to a new and more liberal dispensation that would eventually come into line with those rules. In theory, the way forward looked clear: the regulatory conservative Member States would be foolish not to accept the modicum of reform embodied in Package 1, but in practice much hinged on the credibility of the Commission's threat of tipping the air transport system into chaos if they did not. Things thus still remained complicated and an intricate period of negotiation, bluff, counter-bluff and manoeuvre lay ahead for those working for reform.

The immediate reaction to the *Nouvelles Frontières* case verged on the ecstatically optimistic among the reform-minded. But, as April passed into May, and the June Council meeting approached, pessimism took over, and the chances of Memorandum 2 becoming the basis for reform continued to be dismissed by those in favour of the status quo. Just days before the Council convened, Kees Veenstra, general manager for aero-political affairs at AEA, was confident enough to say, when asked if Memorandum 2 had any chance of being accepted by the Council, 'No, I don't really think so. Too much time has passed since Memo 2 was drawn up.'[34] Veenstra was confident that the focus had shifted away from the EC to ECAC, where multilateral flexible tariff zones were now under consideration. On the surface, these appeared more progressive than the Commission's proposal for bilateral negotiations for tariff zones and country of origin fares in the EC, but the reality was that the preponderance of states within ECAC were conservative, well disposed towards the existing system and would only agree to the most modest of changes. Furthermore, they could be confident about limiting the extent of change because, unlike within the EC, those in favour of liberalization had no legal levers to pull in ECAC. So, while flexible multilateral tariff zones sounded reasonable and liberal, the reality was that they would not deliver enough flexibility for cheaper fares to be widely implemented.

Veenstra further commented that he believed that both the Commission and ECAC had moved away from Memorandum 2 towards 'the multilateralism needed to keep international scheduled air transport coherent'.[35] This was a code which anyone knowledgeable about the airlines at the time could easily decrypt. Scheduled transport coherence meant airline collusion to fix rates and capacity and to restrict route access in order to avoid what the regulatory conservatives regarded as disruptive and therefore excessive competition.

The reformers were dispirited. ACE, which had consistently advocated reform and was often critical of the Commission's lack of radicalism, was depressed, and even Sorensen was subdued and pessimistic about achieving much in the forthcoming Council meeting. He thought that there would be lively debate with at best agreement on some principles, but any substantive developments would have to await the British presidency that was due to begin on 1 July.[36]

The Council met on 18, 19 and 30 June, but yet again, despite developments favourable to reform and the pro-liberalization Dutch presidency, it was 'unable to reach agreement on the Commission's civil aviation proposals'.[37] The Commission had tried to beef up its position on 20 June when it sent revised proposals to the Council, which took into consideration the added weight that *Nouvelles Frontières* provided for their case, but to little immediate effect.[38] Nevertheless, the broader movement towards the Single Market and appreciation of the role that transport would have to play in that resulted in strong expressions of political support for more vigorous developments in the transport sector. Even the European Parliament was keen to see its own rather conservative vision of reform actioned. Rapporteur Anastassopoulos of the Transport Committee declared in June that it was 'high time the Council assumed its responsibilities in the field of civil aviation and acted more promptly on the Commission's proposals ....'[39] The Transport Council was coming under considerable pressures from outside, including statements from the heads-of-government European Council Meeting at the Hague held between 26 and 27 June. It called for speedy action in the light of the *Nouvelles Frontières* case on tariffs, capacity and market access. Thus, although the Transport Council made no decisions of real substance, it did issue, as Sorensen had predicted, a statement of principles, which proved to be a lot more significant than has generally been acknowledged. They confirmed:

i the need for a coherent Community air transport system based on a balanced set of instruments promoting increased competition in intra-Community air services as regards tariffs, capacity and market entry, in conformity with the competition rules of the Treaty;
ii in this context ... such a system should be established gradually. To that end, the Council agrees on an initial period of application of three years, during which the Council will review developments and take decisions on further steps in order to achieve the objective of the completion of the internal market by the year 1992.[40]

In effect the Council had reiterated the findings of *Nouvelles Frontières*, set a three year period for the first phase of development, and established clearly that further reform would follow on at the end of that period in order to consummate the SEAM by the end of 1992. There was a real commitment here, driven by the legal mandate of having to apply the competition rules throughout the transport sector. However, just how it was to be accomplished still remained in question, and both the proponents and the opponents of reform could extract some comfort from the June Council. The conservative majority was pleased that specific decisions had not been taken on the proposals that the Commission had tabled, and still sought to move down the ECAC route to contain the reform movement. The reformers were disappointed at the lack of substantive progress on implementing reform, but John Moore, who had succeeded Ridley as British Transport Minister, attempted to maintain the pressure on the Council and to force it to take effective action. He made it known that the British Government was reviewing the machinery and procedure necessary to enable it to apply the competition rules between the UK and other Member States, and that action would follow particularly if there were no movement in the Council of Ministers. Unfortunately this was no more of an effective threat than Ridley's in May 1984, when Memorandum 2 was first considered by the Council. Unilateral action in an attempt to craft a multilateral system could only have limited effects and could damage the commercial interests of British airlines.

At the end of June, before Moore assumed the presidency, the French and the Germans had urged members of the Council to adopt an agenda for the upcoming session based on proposals that had been worked up in ECAC. These were hardly radical, with detailed provisions on fares, that applied rigid conditions for discount and deep discount fares, capacity rules that offered only a 5 per cent departure from the existing 50/50 split, and little except the possibility of minor developments for regional routes.[41] The latter was a major priority for the British, and they pressed the Commission into action and helped them with market access proposals to try to fill the vacuum here. Moore had no intention of letting the French and the Germans dictate policy through the ECAC ploy. Even though the Luxembourg and Dutch presidencies had been disappointing on balance, John Moore was optimistic. After all, he assumed the presidency of the Transport Council with the added weapon provided by *Nouvelles Frontières*. All this augured well for reform, even though it took a little longer than Moore had expected and was not as liberal as he wanted.

Moore's initial optimism was soon challenged: it was not going to be fourth time lucky for Memorandum 2 in the 19 July Council Meeting. Virtually unchanged from the original submission back in March 1984, from the perspective of those who wanted reform, it was still very modest in its demands. It called for flexibility and more competition in bilateral agreements, controls over negotiations with bloc exemptions from the competition rules, a 25 per cent capacity safety net, allowing pooling, but only with transfers of up to 1 per cent of revenue, and allowing voluntary price negotiations with flexible pricing zones and country of origin fares.[42] So far little mention had been made of market access and then only in the context of regional developments. Lack of progress in Council on this modest package of reform caused frustration and anger among officials, and finally propelled the Commission into confrontation with the Member States and the majority of their airlines.

The Commission decided to push ahead with their main weapon: the threat of not granting exemption from the competition rules. In order to make that a more imminent and realistic threat, DG IV drafted letters for Peter Sutherland to dispatch on 18 July to ten airlines including BA, KLM, Sabena, Air France and SAS. In prologue the letters explained that the Commission was acting in accordance with the conclusions of the European Council at the Hague 26–27 June and under its obligations to apply the competition rules of the Treaty under the auspices of Article 89(1), an obligation which was made clear for civil aviation by the *Nouvelles Frontières* case. The letter to BA then proceeded to state.

> In proceeding under Article 89, the Commission wishes to open a formal dialogue with your company with a view to ensuring that your agreements and practices are brought into conformity with the competition rules of the Treaty as soon as possible.... The Commission considers having examined the information currently available to it, that there are good grounds for finding that British Airways has infringed the provisions of Article 85 of the EEC Treaty.[43]

This was the tactic that Steele had spoken of with such optimism back in May 1985. It was now a reality. All that remained was to see how effective the threat of not granting exemptions from the competition rules in return for movement towards reform would be.

DG VII acted in concert with DG IV. It recommended further liberalization for regional routes, by extending services to category 1 airports, something which the Commission had originally had in the draft of the Regional Air Services Directive of 1983. It also proposed the introduction of fifth freedom rights for regional operators and some liberalization of the 400-km-route restriction. These measures were sent to the Council on 19 August in the form of a draft Directive.[44] At this stage neither the French nor the Germans were prepared to buy into even this kind of modest reform, and they continued to lead the regulatory conservative states along a path with ECAC. Over the following months it became clear that this strategy to limit reform to as modest a scope as possible still had life and some way to run.

On 21 May 1991, Rifkind in a speech at the Aviation Club retrospectively claimed that the British 'gave the EC's first liberalization package its shape in our presidency in 1986'. That may indeed be the case, but what Rifkind did not emphasize was the fact that Moore had to make some major concessions to the regulatory conservative Member States to move liberalization forward; they also 'shaped' the package. Although the failure of the 19 July Council Meeting had prompted the Commission into vigorous action, Moore gradually became convinced during the course of the summer that he would have to compromise over the Commission's most radical proposal, namely, the move to 75/25 capacity divisions. Such a compromise was fraught with danger because capacity freedom was the top priority for their allies, the Dutch. Nevertheless, Moore and his officials engaged with their French counterparts in an effort to reach agreement. By the autumn it looked as if a deal were within Moore's grasp. On 3 October he convened an informal meeting of the Transport Council in London to finalize it. The Dutch, aware of what was to be conceded, were so angry that they boycotted the meeting. The British, in a compromise in which they gave more than they received, agreed to limit the range of permissible capacity divisions to a 55/45 split for two years, but they also insisted that the range had then to be widened in the third year to a 60/40 split. This was at least an improvement on the capacity proposal currently favoured in ECAC. In addition the British insisted on introducing market access provisions, namely, for multiple designation, not just between Member States, but also on specific routes where traffic could justify it. Agreement emerged on slightly more liberal pricing, and there was endorsement of the June Council's statement that there should be follow-on measures after Package 1.[45]

Moore was delighted with the outcome, and although the Dutch were angry they soon returned to support whatever liberalization could be achieved. They were sorely needed because at the Council Meeting on 11–12 November Italy, Spain, Portugal, Denmark, Greece and France – despite all the hard work the British had put in over the late summer and early autumn to entice them into modest reform – blocked Moore's proposals. The capacity deal held, but the Member States could not agree on conditions for deep discount fares, and problems remained over market access. Moore explained the reason why agreement had eluded them: 'I and the Commission made it clear that the measures had to be adopted as a package, and that any watering down of the key elements would not be acceptable.'[46] Discernible here were the shades of the COMPAS Report which had given such emphasis for the need for coordinated action on fares, capacity and market access in any reform of the airline market.

Once again the regulatory conservative majority seemed to have resisted pressures and avoided the temptation to compromise beyond minimal concessions. However, pressures continued to bear down on them. Replies to Sutherland's letter to the airlines about allegations of anti-competitive practices were due by 20 November; and in 1987 unanimity would change to qualified majority voting on the Transport Council. There was still not enough of the Member States to push liberalization through even with qualified majority voting, but it would, nevertheless, open up more opportunities for negotiation and compromise. Also, some states had already seen possible benefits for their airlines from liberalization. Ireland was notable in this respect with regard to gaining fifth freedom rights out of the UK. Other Member States had important divisions within their own domestic politics and in their airline sectors with respect to liberalization, and these divisions offered opportunities that the reformers could exploit in negotiations. These considerations added to the pressures on the regulatory conservative states. More important still was the threat of legal action.

Some still cavalierly dismissed such possibilities. Umberto Nordio, head of Alitalia, at the autumn IATA conference in Montreux declared that 'he would not do as the EC says, but as his own government tells him',[47] but the reality was

> If some airlines do not reply (to Sutherland's letter), or fail to respond in a manner suggesting they will cease anti-competitive behaviour, which some will almost certainly do, then the Commission may be moved to take court action.[48]

Soon after the failure at the November Council meeting, the French representative Jacques Douffiagues, said he thought that progress had been made and that things could probably be finalized at the December meeting. In particular, he said that the French would drop their objection to removing the Saturday night stopover provision in order to provide more flexibility and cheaper fares for business people.[49] In the event, the result of the Council Meeting on 15–16 December was that:

> All Member States are now in a position, in the context of an overall package, to subscribe to the minimum capacity sharing range of 55:45 in the first two years and 60:40 in the third year unless the Council decides otherwise. There was also some progress on fares and multiple designation, though there is still no agreement on the specific conditions to be attached to cheap fares nor on some aspects of access to the market.[50]

Moore was not to get his package through. He ended his presidency by squarely laying the responsibility for finalizing matters on the incoming Belgian presidency. He claimed that there was 'an irreversible basis on which Mr. Herman De Croo ... would be able to build and thus secure the adoption of measures after taking over as Council President in January'.[51] The problem was that Belgium was not in favour of liberalization.

1987: the final phase for Package 1

Continued failure to reach agreement on Package 1 delivered one final chance to the regulatory conservative states to move the EC airline system into the cul desac of ECAC sponsored reform. Since the June policy statement the counter-reform movement had been busy on fares and capacity proposals, which were now tendered to the members of ECAC as memoranda of understanding. The British prompted the Commission's Legal Service to warn would-be signatories that they were legally obliged to avoid commitments that might jeopardize the aims of the Treaty of Rome. Nevertheless, several Member States signed up despite that warning and in the knowledge that any such provisions could not take precedence over Community law.[52] Over the following months several of the regulatory conservative Member States, including France and Germany, continued along this route, and developed the memoranda of understanding into

100   Achieving the first package of reform

full-blown internationally binding agreements, but in the end these developments were overtaken and their significance negated by developments in the EC. Fortunately for Package 1, the new Belgian presidency, under Herman De Croo, displayed considerable loyalty to the legal requirements of the Treaty of Rome. Belgium did not sign up for the ECAC programme, and Package 1 continued to make progress albeit slowly. Although Belgium was not in the liberal camp, De Croo was a member of the Liberal Party and naturally inclined towards reform.

In March the Council edged further towards a package agreement. A 'consensus was reached' on fares, and the capacity arrangements reached in December were confirmed. Two out of the three commercial components of the airline sector had now been agreed. Only certain aspects of market access, multiple designation and fifth freedom rights remained contentious. The Council agreed to reconvene on 9 June to try to finalize those issues. The Commission, determined to keep the pressure on, 'decided to continue the action' initiated by Peter Sutherland in July 1986 against airlines suspected of contravening the competition rules.[53]

The final breakthrough, when it came in three Council sessions in June 1987, seemed rather inevitable in the end. Increasingly there appeared nowhere for the regulatory conservative states to go. Something had to be given up, especially when one rationally weighed up the costs of not accepting reform against the costs for the regulatory conservatives of accepting the modest reforms tabled in Council. With the clear declaration that the competition rules applied to air transport, the Commission was able to exert immense pressure through the threat of legal action. If it were forced into actually bringing legal actions, and if it succeeded in them, the whole European airline system would have been pitched into real turmoil. This was an expense which even those firmly opposed to reform were not prepared to pay in the end. After all, much of their defence of the status quo was based on maintaining order and coherence in the marketplace. This proved to be the determining factor. The ECAC strategy was always deeply flawed because it did not have the power to offer block exemptions from Community legislation and never provided a realistic alternative to the EC's treaty obligation to develop a SEAM. Furthermore, as time went by, compromises were made to appease the regulatory conservatives, most notably Moore's deal on capacity sharing, and opportunities arose that attracted the cautious into firmer support for liberalization, for example, fifth freedom rights in the UK for Ireland. Finally, there was the moving backdrop of the development of the Single Market, the imminent change to qualified majority voting in the Transport Council, the market impact of US and UK liberalization, and the increasing background noise from public opinion and pro-liberalization lobby groups, which also emphasized the case in favour of reform.

The June Council approved Package 1. It took the final form of two Directives, one on air fares and the other on capacity and market access, and two enabling Regulations on the application of the competition rules and on agreements and cartel practices.[54]

On fares, the new regime still looked rather like the old one. There was still double approval required, but that was modified by the caveat that fares must be approved if they were reasonably related to long-term, fully allocated costs. Furthermore, if such fares were not approved, then they would become subject to a new and speedy arbitration process that could overcome Member State objections. There was also a zone of flexibility within which fares were to be automatically approved, in the discount zone between 90 and 65 per cent of normal economy fare, and in the deep discount zone between 65 and 45 per cent of the normal economy fare. The conditions governing such fares were relaxed to allow them to operate in off-peak periods. All this did not amount to a great deal. As one analysis put it: 'Where liberal arrangements already exist, the new latitude will have little effect ... but it will oblige hitherto less liberal states to approve a wider range of promotional fares.'[55]

Capacity and market access, being closely linked, were appropriately dealt with under the same Directive. Moore's compromise on 45/55 split moving to a capacity share of 40/60 in the third year carried through into the final agreement. There was also acceptance of multiple designation, fifth freedom rights and the extension of third and fourth freedom rights on regional routes to include category 1 airports. These measures all impacted on capacity as well as market access, but there were many qualifying conditions. Multiple designation was only allowed on individual routes providing passenger numbers exceeded 250,000 in 1987, 200,000 in 1988, and 180,000 in 1989. Several airports in Denmark, Greece, Italy, Portugal, and Spain were specifically excluded from the more liberal regional route regime, and fifth freedom rights were restricted to 30 per cent of route capacity. Fifth freedom rights could only be extensions from existing services and one of the airports involved had to be a category 2 airport. So, for example, BA could not operate fifths out of Schiphol to Rome; instead it was restricted to smaller, category 2 airports where passenger numbers would be unlikely to make fifth freedom right operations attractive. Spanish airlines and airports and other airports deemed to have insufficient facilities or navigational aids were totally excluded from the new provisions for fifth freedom rights.

The enabling regulations allowed the application of the competition rules and made provision for block exemptions in three areas: capacity sharing, revenue sharing, fare consultations, scheduling and take-off and landing slot allocations; the use of CRSs; ground handling and in-flight catering services. These exemptions would not, however, last for ever. Pressure on the airlines would continue. They would have to move towards behaviour in conformity with the competition rules. The Commission now had broad powers of investigation and the authority to impose substantial fines on airlines if they did not comply with the conditions of the developing and more liberal regime. Furthermore, it was made plain that Package 1 was only temporary. The Council would revise it no later than 30 June 1990 into a second package, and that would lead on to a fully fledged SEAM by the end of 1992 as part of the wider agenda involved in creating the Single Market.[56]

An article in *Flight International* aptly summarized what Package 1 achieved: 'A true common market in air transport services will only exist when airlines from one state can operate freely in and between other states. The first, very tentative, steps towards this end have now been taken.'[57] However, although Package 1 was agreed in June, it could not be formally adopted until a dispute between Britain and Spain had been resolved over Gibraltar. That was accomplished by December, and on 14 December the Council formally adopted Package 1. The Council view, rather like commentary elsewhere, was modestly cautious about the achievement of Package 1.

> These measures represent a first step in implementing a common air transport policy in Europe. Its aims will include greater liberalization, a continuing very high level of safety, and a common approach in relations with non-community countries.[58]

Although that statement was generally cautious and measured, the third point about relations with non-community countries indicated something that was eventually to become one of the most difficult and complex can of worms for the SEAM. When the Commission had raised the issue of applying the competition rules to operations between Member States and non-members, it had been severely criticized, and thus specifically restricted itself in Memorandum 2 to intra-EC airline operations, though fifths remained an anomaly and the broader issue of the need for uniformity among the Member States' ASAs with third parties remained as an obvious challenge. These external relations issues could not be ignored for ever. There would be little point in designing a level competitive playing field within the EC if the airlines of the Member States still had discriminatory advantages vis-à-vis one another in the way that they operated outside. This was particularly so as the national flag carriers made most of their profits on long-haul routes outside the EC and mainly across the Atlantic. For the time being this continued to be a major problem in waiting.

Package 1 was the first substantially significant development in the integration of the Community's airline sector. Deregulation in the US and liberalization promoted in the bilateral ASAs of Britain and the Netherlands had begun to unsettle the market by the mid 1980s, and people were becoming increasingly aware of the benefits for both the consumer and of the increased efficiency of the industry that liberalization could offer. As US, British and Dutch airlines became more competitive, pressures gradually seeped out into the wider European and international airline system. These pressures raised the spectre of increasing state subsidies for uncompetitive airlines that failed to move away from the sclerosis-inducing system of tight regulation and the complacent comfort of the cartel. Deregulation in the US was by no means a universal success story, and airline consolidations, CRSs and alliances soon posed their own threats of dominant positions and anti-competitive practices; but it had shown that economies of scale could be reaped, greater efficiency achieved, and lower cost and better services delivered to a much larger consumer market. These market pressures were silent partners in the drive for liberalization of the

European airline market. Their silent presence was more effective than the rising clamour for reform from consumer and lobby groups. In part, that was the case because the clamour had counterpoint from organizations such as the AEA and from the main representative forum in the Community, the European Parliament. This is not to say that pro-reform consumer and lobby groups did not provide important background noise. They did, particularly Laker, Bethell and the Freedom of the Skies Campaign, but that in the end was all it was – supportive background noise.

Intergovernmental agreement at the end of the day was essential. The Council had to make decisions on reform to initiate the liberalization of the airline sector. However, the absence of a majority of regulatory liberal states and inability to reach a consensus on a common denominator that would reflect the minimum the reformers would accept, and the maximum the defenders of the status quo were willing to concede, resulted in a long-standing stalemate that was extremely difficult to shake down. The HLG made only minor progress in 1984 and early 1985, and even then much of it, as reflected in the proposals that emanated from ECAC, was designed to contain the drive for reform within the tightest parameters feasible. If it had not been for both vigorous action by the Commission in threatening legal action and the unequivocal decision in the *Nouvelles Frontières* case that the Community's competition laws applied to air transport, the Council would, in all likelihood, have continued to procrastinate and to prevaricate over reform. As it was, the Commission was empowered by the European Court of Justice's ruling and was able to raise the spectre of legal cases. They would have tipped the European airline system into turmoil because the law would have required immediate abandonment of price fixing and pooling arrangements, and it would have highlighted many difficulties with regard to possible abuse of dominant positions. Much, of course, depended on the credibility of Sutherland's threat to take airlines to court as a last resort if progress on liberalization were not achieved. Initially it looked as if some airlines such as Alitalia and organizations such as the AEA did not take the threat seriously. However, other airlines and governments did, and furthermore, in the developing context of the Single Market and the legal framework provided by the Community, it looked increasingly difficult not to take some movement towards a SEAM. Once that became more widely acknowledged, than it had been in the past, the initiative clearly moved in favour of the Commission and the reform states. Their willingness to negotiate and compromise and come forward with a package that implemented reform in what Sorensen described as a 'reasonable way' eventually broke the stalemate in the Council and a first tentative step towards liberalization became a reality.

In terms of the dynamics at play in this integration move, close scrutiny of what actually happened demonstrates just how intertwined and mutually dependent they were and that claim applies to the role of key individuals such as Sutherland and Sorensen, the supportive background noise from lobby and consumer groups and the interplay of NGOs, the actions of Member States, the role of market forces, and the in-puts from EC institutions, especially DGs IV and

104 *Achieving the first package of reform*

VII and the European Court of Justice. However, during this period 1984–88, at the heart of things, the combination which provided the motor to move things along was the dynamic interplay between the forces of intergovernmentalism in the HLG and in the Council and those of supranationalism emanating from the Commission and the Court, which in cooperation with the liberal Member States did so much to craft strategy and implement it through a series of pragmatic compromises underpinned by the need to meet the legal requirements of the Treaty of Rome. At the end of the day, this combination of forces in favour of liberalizing the airline market manoeuvred in such a way that it became clear that to obstruct liberalization any further would be tantamount to challenging the very fabric of the EC itself. This also was a powerful element in the gradual retreat of the regulatory conservative states.

The first significant breach in the regulatory wall had been achieved, and a clear commitment to further reform had been made. It was now important for the Commission and the regulatory liberal Member States to continue to drive things forward. Package 1 was as much a package of symbolic significance and promise as of substance, and as such much hinged on what would come next. One of the key symbolic developments was the way Package 1 had chipped away at the conservative mantra of the need for coherence in the airline system. The airline system had always been a rather curious and contradictory mixture of fragmentation and coherence. The fragmentation arose because of the mosaic of nation states and their cabotage rights, which imposed a complex network of barriers in the marketplace. The regulatory conservatives argued that such fragmentation needed to be overlaid with a form of coherence that would enable the airline system to operate effectively. That coherence came from cartel practices on fare setting, pooling capacity, and controlling schedules. In addition nation states were complicit in such practices and strengthened them by often subsidizing their flag carriers and by restrictive route licensing policies. The defenders of the status quo warned of the chaos that could result from a freer market, with volatile pricing, predatory behaviour, a disruptive sequence of start-up airlines and failures, falling safety standards and deteriorating employment conditions. They also lauded the merits of the existing system and in particular were always keen to point out the benefits of consultations and agreements between airlines which facilitated interlining. This allowed passengers to embark on a complex journey from A to B on a single ticket, via several flights on different airlines and with flexibility on how the ticket might be used. What the regulatory conservatives failed to recognize was that the market could be more competitive and still avoid chaos with a lighter regulatory system. They also failed to acknowledge that the EC offered the possibility of overcoming the problems posed by the mosaic of nation states. The mosaic would continue outside, but within the EC, the argument that national barriers and national interests required the overlay of a coherence provided by cartel practices was now clearly flawed. Package 1 provided some actual, if modest, recognition of that and the broad dynamics for change that flowed from the Single Market project added further support for more progress in this direction.

Achieving the first package of reform 105

The Commission would still have to proceed cautiously, but could now afford to do so with vigour as well. This was not an easy combination. The regulatory conservative forces may have over-exaggerated the dangers of disrupting the system and played down the possible benefits of liberalization, but there was no denying that dangers did indeed exist. US experience, from a European perspective, rang alarm bells about dangers that could arise from airline consolidation, alliances, and dominant positions and those would have to be warded off in Europe by more interventionist practices. There were also complex problems ranging from external aviation relations to state aids, and from CRS operations to the allocation of landing and take-off slots. All these and more would involve the Commission in a process of bureaucratic growth that was unpalatable to many Member States and in particular to Britain. How these regulatory problems were to be dealt with and the market liberalized further were to exercise many in the Commission and among the Member States during the two years that it took to stitch Package 2 together.

6 Receiving Package 1
Delivering Package 2

> ... too many restrictions and too many exceptions were agreed by the 12 Member States in the process of constructing a political compromise [for Package 1].
> Leon Brittan Commissioner for Competition, IATA Conference, Marrakesh 1–3 June 1989[1]

The effects of Package 1 need to be seen in terms of its substance, its symbolic importance, its procedural impact, and the competition issues that it now drove into prominence.

Reactions about the substance of its likely impact ranged from the smug contentment among the regulatory conservatives to the outrage of Bethell and his supporters, who saw it as a sell-out. Commission, British and Dutch officials acknowledged the severe limitations on progress made by Package 1, and there was quiet resignation and a determination that next time they would have to do better. Experience over the following two years gradually made clear exactly what Package 1 had done, and what it had failed to touch.

In terms of its symbolism, Package 1 was more threatening for the regulatory conservatives and heartening for the reformers. The ramparts of regulatory conservatism were still heavily manned, but defections were growing in number, minor breaches had been made, and structural weaknesses were exposed. The latter emerged due to the impact of both global and regional competitive forces and because of the changing political architecture of the Community. The symbolic importance of all this was not without consequence. The comfort zone of the regulatory conservatives gradually eroded away, and they were confronted then with the reality that change was coming. Most of them slowly adjusted to that reality and over the following years begrudgingly gave way.

Package 1 may not have achieved much of substance, but it was a start, and it established important procedural pathways for the future. The most obvious of these was the formal and binding commitment that more changes would follow. However, that commitment in itself also had further consequences for how matters would proceed. Package 1 formulated a concrete agenda that now clearly fell within the competence of the Commission, and demanded action from the Member States. Pressures from interest and lobby groups and NGOs, market forces and input from key individuals would all continue to play a part; but the civil aviation agenda had by now become primarily a matter for the Commission and inter-governmental decision-making in the Council of Ministers. After Package 1, it was the inter-play between the Commission and the Member States acting through the Council that would have the greatest say on how the SEAM would develop, in what manner and how swiftly. The combined forces of the Commission and the Council of Ministers eventually produced a regulatory framework in which adventurous entrepreneurs and market forces could later drive things forward, to make a competitive SEAM a reality.

Once Package 1 indicated the direction for the future, a number of areas, that had not been problematic under a conservative regulatory regime, became so once there was a real prospect of more competition. Effectively dealing with these problems would determine whether or not the SEAM would ever be a reality. Member States' external civil aviation relations, common criteria for community airline and route licensing, the operation of CRSs, the allocation of airport take-off and landing slots and how the major airlines – the dominant national flag carriers – would behave, all belonged to those competition issues that now attracted more attention. Among other things, this plethora of issues demonstrated just how complex the business of crafting a new and more liberal regime would be. It was not simply a matter of taking away the old corset of regulation. To make competition a reality the old would have to be replaced with new regulation supportive of competition.

Although forces for change were gathering momentum, practice in the European airline industry changed little for the time being, and the Regulations granting block exemptions from the competition rules introduced in 1988, in fact, temporarily strengthened the forces of anti-competitive behaviour. As a clear picture of the impact of Package 1 on the state of play in the European airline system gradually emerged, it presented two major problems for the reformers. Actual developments confirmed suspicions that Package 1 would not make major inroads into the well-embedded network of regulatory conservatism; the only exception was the way new regional routes proliferated. Secondly, national flag carriers not only continued to exhibit anti-competitive behaviour, but they also abused the modestly liberal changes that had been introduced. This problem was compounded by the fact that the Commission, for longer-term strategic reasons, was reluctant to bring them to task. In short, the old system was only modestly amended, and the new system was ineffectually enforced.

All this gave the reformers some idea of the heights that still had to be scaled and impressed upon them the need to be more robust about the measures for Package 2. Their hopes for reform were given some sustenance by movement towards the Single Market, the increasing intensity of globalization, and institutional reform that widened the application of qualified majority voting. These developments had impact eventually on the French Government, the leader of regulatory conservatism, and as we shall see, it shifted its stance to one of accepting modest reform in Package 2. But, that shift did not come quickly, and in many ways modest reform still seemed to be the message about what was achievable when the debate on Package 2 began. For example, the strength of the proposals that the Commission initially tendered to the Council of Ministers for Package 2 were substantially diluted, largely by French doings. However, at the end of the day, the Commissioner for Competition, Leon Brittan, who was strongly and ideologically committed to liberalization across the board, was less unhappy with the compromises that had to be made for Package 2 than with those made for Package 1.[2] This was partly because Package 2, in addition to immediately activated provisions, also promised to deliver more in the near future.

There were thus several important developments between agreement on Package 1 and the delivery of Package 2. First, there were assessments of what Package 1 had actually delivered. Most of them were highly critical and much emphasis was given to continuing competitive abuses in the marketplace. Second, the Commission responded to some of the competition problems, highlighted by the early transitional process towards a freer market. Those problems generated concern and drew out of the Commission various proposals for dealing with them: the most charitable assessment could only describe them as having mixed fortunes. And third, the Commission formulated ambitious proposals for Package 2, which were the subject of fraught negotiations. Package 2 could only be agreed upon after substantial compromise and some outright rejections of the Commission's proposals had been made.

Assessing the marketplace after Package 1: problems and prospects

After the agreement on the substance of Package 1 came the block exemptions that would temporarily permit the old evils of collusion to continue. Capacity and revenue sharing, interlining agreements, collusion on tariff setting, and take-off and landing slot allocations could all proceed immune to the competition rules, providing the airlines abided by the rules promulgated by Package 1.[3] Similarly, exemptions were granted for all ground-handling services and in-flight catering and for the operation of CRSs.[4]

To those in favour of radical reform like Bethell and Loder, the block exemptions from the competition rules seemed particularly retrograde and compromised what Package 1 might otherwise have done to help the small start-up airlines compete with the well-established national flag carriers. Loder expounded on these problems, in a lengthy note to Bethell in July 1988. Part of the difficulty was that the smaller airlines, which stood to benefit from more competition, were generally too afraid to challenge anti-competitive practices of the national flag carriers like BA and Air France, but there was a solitary exception to this. 'London European is the only one which has actually laid a complaint to the Commission under Competition Regulation 17/62. The Commission immediately raided SABENA and London European got what it needed and was entitled to.'[5] This was heartening for Loder especially, as he decried the Commission's general unwillingness to initiate enforcement of even the mildly reformist system, it had brought into being: 'The Commission has not, and seemingly will not, act on its own.'[6] However, much worse than Commission inaction was the effect of its proposals for block exemptions, which would soon remove the possibility of the kind of action that London European had taken against Sabena. It was in this sense that the block exemption provisions were literally retrograde.

In November 1962, while Regulation 141 had held Regulation 17, and hence the competition rules, inapplicable to sea and air transport, it still applied to other commercial practices. However, in July 1988 the block exemption regulations broadened the scope of the inapplicability of Regulation 17. With hardly suppressed fury, Loder wrote:

> One of the most distressing elements of that situation is that Regulation 17 of 1962 (which applies to all other commercial sectors) has also always applied to air transport – except for the direct provision of air transport i.e. it applies to CRSs and everything which is ancillary to the provision of air transport such as CRSs, ground handling etc. etc. The Block Exemption Regulations to be adopted as a result of the December Package will apply retrospectively to Regulation 17 and liberate the AEA cartel airlines from the Community Rules and the Council Regulation to which they have been subject ever since 1962. It was Regulation 17 under which the Commission raided SABENA on the complaint of London European![7]

There is little doubt that the Commission had provided more of a smoke screen, under which the 'AEA cartel airlines' could continue to flout the spirit and the letter of competition requirements of Package 1 than they had intended. Loder was right to point out the problems for bringing the large powerful airlines to task, and there was a whole range of abuses that they continued to practice, which, to him at least, seemed indicative of an absence of change to the well-established system of conservative regulation.

It was not only that the Commission appeared reluctant to enforce the regulations it had introduced, but there was also an ongoing problem with the lack of clear information upon which complaints may be brought against airlines abusing the system. So far as Bethell and Loder were concerned this was a real problem. Airlines were effectively screening off their illegal pricing behaviour by invoking the need for commercial confidentiality. In February 1988 Bethell wrote to Christopher Tugendhat, recently returned from the Commission in Brussels and now Chairman of the UK CAA. He complained about the cost of air fares from London to Paris, Brussels and Amsterdam, arguing that according to Package 1 they were supposed to be cost related: in his view they clearly were not. Tugendhat's reply embodied the catch-22 that so infuriated the reformers. 'I am afraid that we are unable to disclose the figures we get from the airlines in support of their tariff filings. The information is supplied to us under the Civil Aviation Act, and the Act guarantees confidentiality.'[8]

Loder's response to that was:

> Tugenhadt's [sic] statement on confidentiality reflects the old, old attitude that governments, civil aviation administrations, airlines and international civil aviation organisations (i.e. the totality of civil air transport) can conduct affairs in secret for the benefit of the airlines and governments' regulators and in exploitation of the public which finances the system and the travellers who use it. In Europe and the UK, very little has changed.[9]

Tugendhat also cautioned Bethell that it would be a mistake 'to look for too much too soon in terms of price competition' and that Package 1 was more designed to create alternative lower priced products rather than effect a reduction in the price of existing products. When Loder saw this he exploded: 'In the light of such outrageous humbug it is difficult to know where to begin. The statement is obviously a justification for the advice which led to HMG's sell-out in the EC Council on the December Package.'[10]

Notwithstanding his anger at most of what Tugendhat wrote, Loder observed that elsewhere in his letter he, Tugendhat, had been a little indiscreet and that he appeared to be encouraging Bethell 'to stir up the matter'.[11] Loder was right. The UK CAA was supportive of reform, but sensitive to the political complexities of the situation in a manner similar to calculations made in the Commission. The CAA continued to be supportive even after what was seen by many as a major blow to nurturing more competition in the UK – the takeover of B.Cal. by BA. B.Cal. had originally been conceived of as an essential competitor in Britain's multi-airline policy. The response of the CAA to the takeover was to define a robust competition policy in February 1988, with Raymond Colegate, the CAA's Economic Policy Chief, promising to regulate fares where competition was muffled and to give preference to other airlines over BA where possible.[12] Nurturing competition was not easy, and political realities could often compromise good intentions. The CAA was not the only organization well disposed to competition, to recognize these truths; the Commission with its brief experience of regulatory reform of the aviation industry had also come to the same conclusion. The CAA, however, no matter how robust a line it might take, could not by itself solve the problem of 'commercial confidentiality', which provided a screen behind which anti-competitive practices could continue. Transparency in the European aviation market would not come overnight. This was yet another issue that appeared in a particular form in 1988, but which posed a broader challenge for the Commission. Over the years it gradually tried to implement more and more transparent procedures and practices.

Other competitive abuses also demanded attention. The use of CRSs to gain unfair commercial advantages posed a particularly difficult challenge because their use was highly technical with legal and commercial complexities. However, they demanded attention because their use threatened to increase the dominant position of airlines that were already market leaders. The abuse of CRSs had emerged as a problem in the US as early as 1984 and had received some attention and partial remedy there. Large CRSs, such as Sabre and Apollo, owned respectively by AA and UA, could be used in a commercially discriminating way to the advantage of the airlines that owned them. When a travel agent was asked for a flight, the Sabre and Apollo CRS displays would respectively favour AA and UA flights. Smaller airlines could not afford their own costly CRSs and thus had to buy in to their larger competitors' systems, often with exorbitant charges being applied for a display that discriminated against their own operations. In Europe the cost of CRSs caused a further problem in that airlines colluded together to share costs and to develop jointly owned systems. The initiative for this began with an AEA study in 1986 with the intention of creating a Europe-wide CRS, but in the event the airlines divided into two camps forming Galileo (by BA, Covia, KLM and Swissair) and Amadeus (by Air France, Iberia, Lufthansa and SAS). These systems were prima facie in breach of the competition rules prohibiting cooperation and collusion between enterprises and soon prompted action by the Commission.

In the US, action to bring a form of governance to CRSs was taken in November 1984 with rules promulgated by the Department of Transportation to try to ensure non-discriminatory displays of flight options and non-discriminatory charges.[13] These measures, however, were not entirely successful, and problems continued, in particular because of differing practices in the US and Europe, which affected transatlantic flights. As a result, a serious row broke out in 1987 between AA and BA, when each of them alleged that the other's CRSs were discriminatory. For example BA's Business System (BABS), developed as a temporary stop-gap before Galileo came on line, when asked to display London–Dallas flights, failed to show AA's Gatwick to Dallas non-stop service.[14] On the US side, CRSs were allowed to show code sharing as a continuous flight. Code-sharing was where a single ticket with a single flight code was issued for a journey that involved travel on two different airlines. For example, a US domestic feeder service from a regional airport to a transatlantic gateway by one airline and the transatlantic flight of another airline would appear as a non-stop single airline operation and as such come high on the CRS display screen, much to the disadvantage of European airlines offering transatlantic flights.[15] Legal action ensued in 1988, but eventually BA and AA settled matters out of court with a company-to-company arrangement in which the European approach to CRSs was more in evidence than American practice. After this, several other US airlines voluntarily followed in AA's wake in offering European-style displays.[16] These developments brought focus to bear in Europe on the competitive implications of CRS misuse, but if one had cared to look closely, there was already plenty of evidence within Europe of unfair CRS operations.

The British independent airline Air Europe ran into all kinds of difficulties with European national flag carriers, which displayed its fares on their CRS screens at the same price as their own, even though Air Europe's were in fact lower. Alternatively, they refused to show them at all. Similarly the Portuguese airline Air Portugal (TAP) declined to show Dan Air's fares to Lisbon, and British Air Ferries route between Rotterdam and Southend soon failed because

KLM refused to display their fares on its CRS, Corda. Even more devious was a ploy by BA and SAS in collusion with IATA to have Southend airport's designation changed so that it could no longer be described as serving London. That conveniently left Maersk Air high and dry. Its Billund-Southend route could no longer be marketed as a service to London. Effectively it now had no chance of competing with SAS and BA flying Copenhagen to Heathrow and Gatwick. The Maersk Billund–Southend route was the first to be set up under the aegis of the Regional Air Services Directive[17] and, much to the dismay of reformers, it was among the first casualties as well. However, the Commission was not blind to the imperfections of the system or to the danger of perpetuating potential for abuses. On CRSs, in particular, they took a robust line and presented proposals to the Council in October 1988 for a compulsory code of practice for their use.[18]

A host of other problems afflicted those who wanted to try to compete. A particularly serious one was fear of predatory actions by the large airlines.

> Regional Airlines ... pointed out that they are scared of victimisation if they institute legal complaints in the national courts or the Commission. The trunk [national flag carrier] airlines (who are also the CRS operators) exercise considerable power over the smaller carriers who are obliged to use all sorts of facilities and services which are provided by the trunk carriers at airports – either because they are the only ones with the resources to set up the systems or because the government or airport authority has given them monopoly or oligopolistic privileges.[19]

This was clearly a problem, and one that did not lend itself to easy remedy. The nature of things was that the powerful were in embedded positions, which favoured their interests. The weak were trying to assail those positions, but if they did so, before effective governance measures to protect them were in place, then they confronted the danger of being penalized and punished and driven off routes, or into bankruptcy, by the large airlines. These dangers were not conjured up by the over-active imagination of paranoid reformers: Laker had gone bust in 1982, and he alleged that the cause was collusion on predatory pricing and other commercial matters by BA, Pan Am., TWA, McDonnell Douglas and others. After years of legal wrangling, BA eventually settled out of court with Laker and paid him £33 million. There was a real difficulty here for the smaller airlines and for their part the Commission was reluctant to initiate enforcing actions itself for fear of endangering further reforms to which it had extracted a binding commitment in Package 1. For the time being at least, it looked as if the pain that these imperfections in the Community's airline system produced would have to be endured without much remedy for the sake of not endangering the larger and more comprehensive goal of completing the SEAM.

Another issue to engage Commission attention was slot allocations for landing and take-off at airports, which was not unrelated to problems associated with CRSs. At one level the problem was simple: the well established national flag carriers had de facto dominant positions at the major national airports. They had accumulated over the years the vast majority of slots available and, more importantly, those that were at the key traffic times. All this was well established and had been firmly buttressed since 1947 by IATA with its twice yearly International Schedules Coordination Conferences and its concept of grandfathered rights: past use guarantees future use. To take slots away from national flag carriers would severely weaken their positions and with regard to privatized airlines, it would reduce their share value. All this proved to be a fraught, complicated and enduring problem, especially at Heathrow. Dell's traffic distribution rules introduced in 1977, and periodically updated thereafter, had more or less frozen the state of affairs between the airlines at Heathrow, with no new international operators allowed entry to the airport, US airlines restricted to Pan Am. and TWA or their corporate successors,[20] and with BA sitting in a position that was often referred to as *Fortress Heathrow* because of its overwhelmingly strong position there.[21] With the status quo as it was, it was difficult to see how effective competition could be mounted against BA at Heathrow. Start-up airlines could not get operating rights for Heathrow at all, and established airlines at Heathrow that wanted to compete more strongly, such as BM, could not get the slots they wanted. Similar, if less acute, problems afflicted other major airports throughout the EC.

There were three possible strategic solutions to this problem. The first was to expand capacity, but that was difficult because of both cost and environmental objections. And the other two, if they were to be effective, would both be too radical in their commercial implications for the national flag carriers to have any immediate or even long-term chance of success. One of these strategies was to redistribute slots, with the situation eased for incumbent slot holders by simultaneously improving the efficiency of the system, thereby creating additional slots and reducing the number that might have to be forcibly prised out of the grip of the national flag carriers.[22] However, increased efficiency would only ease the situation on the margins, redistribution would still be essential and there were two possible ways of doing this. One way, favoured by the UK CAA in the mid 1990s, was to offer slots for sale. This would have been acceptable to BA and other national flag carriers, especially as they already owned so many of such assets. However, they would also be able to outbid smaller airlines with fewer resources for any slots that came up for sale, and that was not acceptable to most reformers as there would thus be little de facto re-distribution. The alternative way would be to take slots from one player and hand them to another on the *diktat* of government or by rules promulgated by the EC Commission, which was favoured by the smaller airlines, but was not acceptable to national flag carriers because it would take away valuable assets needed by them to operate successfully. It would also have eroded BA's value as a private sector company, and it was not just Lord King with his responsibility to shareholders, but also the British Government, who were wary of such actions.[23] Nevertheless, this, as we shall see, was the route that the Commission initially chose to take. The other strategy was even more radical in some ways because rather than redistributing slots the plan would be to redistribute flights through sectorization. Under this concept, airlines would be allocated slots, for example, around the London airports – Heathrow, Gatwick, Luton, Stansted – in accordance with the direction the flight was to take.

Whichever strategy for slot allocation was adopted and in whatever form, if it resulted in effective redistribution of slots, it would weaken the dominance of national flag carriers at major airports and that was simply unacceptable to them. This was a real dilemma. On one hand without some strategy for providing more slots for new entrants at major airports, it seemed difficult to see how else there could be effective competition; on the other hand, from the perspective of the likes of BA, arguments for the reallocation of slots seemed 'half-baked ideas about competition'.[24] Much depended on where one wanted to compete. Taking slots away from BA might help nurture competition in Europe, but it would make BA a less potent competitor globally. Slot re-allocation was a major problem throughout the Community and was to remain intractably so long after the SEAM became fully operational.

Before looking at the Commission's own official assessment of the workings of the airline system under Package 1, one further problem, a particularly ironic abuse of the competitive market, deserves attention. The scheduled airlines, IATA and the AEA, in defending the existing system, had always spoken strongly of both the need for maintaining a coherent market and, in particular, of the benefits of interlining for customers. The latter benefit was used by Community law to justify block exemptions from the competition rules. Under interlining, passengers could travel with ease between destinations using two or more different airlines if that is what were necessary. Furthermore, tickets issued by one airline would be accepted by another if connections were missed, or last minute changes had to be made. How wonderful the system seemed – smooth and seamless in its operation, overcoming national boundaries and complex travel routes that traversed several countries and involved various changes of aircraft and airline. The reality was somewhat different. To airlines prepared to compete and trying to grow in the EC, the benefits of interlining were not extended. The seamless flow became seamed: the coherence cracked. The system was compromised in order to disadvantage cheaper competitors. Loder was able to offer Harry Goodman, head of the low cost airline, Air Europe, an *ad hominem* story to illustrate these problems.

After his retirement from government service in 1984, Loder had set up a private aviation consultancy agency, and worked vigorously for the liberalization of the European airline system. In 1988–89 he was busy formulating complaints against Air France and Sabena for the abuse of interlining practices. As fate would have it, Loder was to gain unwanted personal experience of this. On 28 May 1989, he wrote to Goodman about an ill-fated trip to Paris.

> Because of a broken leg I could not get to Gatwick therefore, at my request, Air Europe endorsed my ticket to Brymon – with Brymon's agreement. Stickers were attached by Brymon for London City Airport to Paris and for the return sector – Paris to London City Airport.

At check-in in Paris, Air France said they do not accept Air Europe tickets even though my ticket was accepted by their Joint Venture partner – Brymon, and was issued by an IATA travel agent on IATA ticket stock at the fully flexible IATA fare[25]

Loder had to buy a one-way ticket from Air France to get back to London. Not surprisingly, given his personal experience and his professional knowledge of the shortcomings of Air France's behaviour, he added the incident to his growing catalogue of complaints against national airlines like Air France, Sabena, BA, SAS and Lufthansa. Their shortcomings were compounded by their duplicity in arguing the benefits of interlining and then denying them to their low cost competitors' customers. This was clearly contrary to the provisions of Package 1 and the exemptions that were granted from the application of the competition rules. Directive 87/601 and Regulation 3975/87 allowed consultations on fares for interlining agreements and were accorded block exemptions from Article 85(3) of the Treaty of Rome by Regulation 2671/88, but only on the grounds of consumer benefit. Article 85(3) only authorizes exemption from agreements and concerted practices if consumers get 'a fair share of the resulting benefit'. But Air France and others were doing just the opposite. They denied the benefits of interlining to customers who bought tickets from lower priced competitors and in doing so both abused their dominant positions on routes and breached the conditions on which block exemptions from the competition rules had been granted for agreements and concertations.

Throughout 1988 and 1989 Bethell and Loder were only too keen to bring the above shortcomings of the system, as it operated under the aegis of Package 1, to the attention of officials in DG IV and DG VII. With their emotionally fuelled crusade to overturn what they saw as the evils of the AEA/scheduled airlines' cartel, they sometimes over-exaggerated the abuses, disregarded the prudence of the political compromises of the Commission (and their own government), and, even in terms of the evidence available at the time, they were overly pessimistic about future developments. The Commission itself was certainly not blind or insensitive to the existing shortcomings of the system or to the size of the task that still lay ahead. If anyone had thought that it were, then the report it issued on the first year of the operation of Package 1 should have disabused them.

In January 1989, the Commission sent out a questionnaire to all Member States, seeking information and opinion from them on the workings and impact of Package 1. All states except Denmark responded, and those responses provided the basis for the Commission's report.[26] The report, with the sole exception of the introduction of new regional operations, was disappointing for the reformers and seemed to endorse the view of Bethell that Package 1 had been a sell-out to the forces of conservative regulation. The conditions in the industry were generally healthy and had been so since the recovery from recession beginning in 1983–84, but there was little evidence that these conditions had been exploited to develop the system towards a significantly more liberal practice. Fares generally had risen in accordance with inflation. Only in a few cases, where new airlines entered the marketplace, had significant fare reductions of up to 15 per cent been achieved. Otherwise there was little change. The zonal scheme had hardly been used at all, and in any case it was redundant, where more liberal regimes had been introduced into ASAs bilaterally, as in the cases of British agreements with Belgium, Germany, Ireland, Luxembourg and the Netherlands. On the possibility of cheaper fares, one Member State observed in its feedback to the Commission, 'The conditions attached to discount and deep discount zones are unrealistic and therefore not widely accepted and used by the airlines.'[27] On capacity, there were similar findings. Where liberal bilaterals applied, developments were promising, where they did not and Package 1 set the framework there was still a 'restrictive effect on mutual developments'.[28] Perhaps the most telling aspect of the report on the impact of the capacity reforms of Package 1 was that no Member State had availed itself of the right of temporary exemption from them. As they say, there is no gain without pain, and here there was clearly no pain.

Only on market access was there any significant and clear improvement, but even here the story was not straightforward. The one unqualified success attributable to Package 1 was the increase in routes between regional airports and between regional airports and hubs. Even the Commission allowed itself to comment that this aspect of Package 1 'has developed favourably'. Some operators had run into problems, for example Maersk Air on the Billund-Southend route, but overall there had been a net increase of 114 new regional routes (127 launched and thirteen later withdrawn). Multiple designation was less of a success, rising from twenty-two routes in 1987 to thirty-three in 1989, but these routes only involved five of the twelve Member States, and there seemed to be a distinct reluctance to allow multiple designation on busy routes, where they could have flourished best and would have brought most benefit through competition. Fifth freedoms were 'used in only a few instances', but the Commission celebrated them as 'the re-emergence of fifth freedom air services by Community air carriers'.[29] Here were more substantial effects from Package 1. Or were there? In fact the renewal of much of the fifth freedom activity was a result of Britain's liberal bilaterals with other Member States. The only success stories from Package 1 were Portuguese and Irish fifth freedom operations into and out of Britain. Aer Lingus traffic, for example, rose by over 33per cent between 1986 and 1988. But these developments posed as many problems as they appeared to solve. There was always awareness in Britain that there could be commercial disadvantages from liberalizing one's own civil aviation market in advance of other countries and this now appeared to some to be what had happened.

> The UK has lost enormously through the weakness of the civil servants and the government in making these arrangements. They give other nations benefits of access to the UK traffic generation and market for NO reciproca-

tion of any practical use to UK airlines. Aer Lingus and Air Portugal are irrelevant in international aviation terms yet they are benefiting from British traffic. Their home traffic generating markets are tiny but they have access to ours – the largest in the free world after the USA, including opportunistic consequential access to long haul traffic. The final rub in all this is that since 1978 the Irish Republic and Aer Lingus have in all *fora* been jointly amongst the most vehement opponents of change, liberalization and competition. The Portuguese government and TAP (Air Portugal) still are – yet they are the beneficiaries.[30]

There is no doubt that a real problem had been identified here. British aviation interests would suffer, and Package 1 did not offer other types of opportunity, with the possible exception of the opening up of the regional route market, for gaining compensation. Suffering damage to its aviation interests in the course of the liberalization process could have alienated Britain from the cause and that would have endangered the chances of eventually creating the SEAM. Fortunately for the reformers that did not happen; but it was a danger that had to be carefully handled and partly accounts for the manifestation of British timidity on some aspects of reform. This was no more evident than in external relations where the British departed company with those in the Commission. Somewhat ironically, while Package 1 placed restrictions on the operation of fifth freedom rights exercised between Member States, there were no restrictions on new fifth freedom rights negotiated between two Member States and a third party outside the EC. For example there could be agreement between the US and the UK for fifth freedom rights out of London to Munich and if the West German government acquiesced, then that could be a more liberal fifth than those possible solely between Member States. This was clearly negative discrimination against Member States, and it was something that was soon seized on by the Commission, and used by it to argue for external competence; in other words competence over ASAs between Member States and countries outside the EC. If such powers were to be granted, however, it would have meant a significant delegation of sovereignty to Brussels and a major increase in the power of the Commission. As we have already noted, such developments were highly unpalatable for the British. Here again were problems that might divide those in favour of regulatory reform.

Package 1 thus created a highly complex context, within which the Commission, in conjunction with its allies among the Member States, would have to draft new proposals for carrying the SEAM project forward. This was a real and difficult challenge. While Package 1 was symbolically important and indicated that further liberalization would come, it also further emphasized just how complex and complicated achieving a more competitive market would be.

New proposals from the Commission

The proposals that emerged from the Commission in the months after acceptance of Package 1 fell roughly into two categories: those that were included in Package 2 and those that were not, such as CRSs; airport slot allocations; and all-cargo operations. It is also important to note that some of the original proposals for Package 2 failed. The most significant of these were to do with external relations. Package 2 concentrated on the usual triumvirate of issues – route entry, capacity and pricing, but there was also specific focus on the right of establishment and route licensing. These last two issues were symptomatic of the fundamental problem of getting all Member States to act according to common criteria. Britain's liberal airline and route licensing policy sought to enable competition, including from foreign owned airlines set up in Britain; but other Member States used their licensing policy as a means of excluding foreign owned airlines and protecting their national flag carriers' routes. This was a major issue for the British and for competition in Europe in general.

External relations presented important, pressing and very difficult problems. They were important because without Member States sharing equal commercial rights for operations outside the EC, the idea of a level competitive playing field for them was an illusion. They were a pressing issue, first, because of the anomalous position of fifth freedom rights noted above; second, because SAS was jointly owned and operated by Denmark, Norway and Sweden, among which the latter two were at the time outside the EC; and, third, because of pressure for Community ASAs from Austria, Switzerland and other members of the European free trade area (EFTA).[31] External relations were difficult because the Commission did not have the resources to take over negotiating ASAs on behalf of the Member States, and the Member States were unanimous in not wanting it to do so for practical reasons and as a matter of principle concerning sovereignty. Despite all these challenging problems, and the fact that reaction among the Member States had forced the Commission to withdraw previous proposals it had made about external relations, it still began to make moves on this issue as soon as Package 1 had been approved.

In letters despatched in January and November 1988, 'the Commission requested all Member States to provide full and detailed information on the relevant national legislation and administrative practice which cover bilateral air service agreements with other Member States and third countries and also shareholdings in the control of national air carriers by non-nationals'.[32] The Commission's mission garnered strength on external relations in April 1989 from the European Court of Justice's ruling in the Ahmed Saeed case, which established external competence for the application of the Community's competition rules. Nicholas Argyris, Head of Division for Transport and Tourist Industries, in DG IV, now pressed ahead even more vigorously, and in September the Commission sent a letter to the Member States 'requesting them to amend all their bilateral air service agreements according to Community law without delay'.[33] By the autumn, the Commission had drawn up proposals to send to the Council. It had been working on competition block exemptions for routes to and from the Community, but it was unclear what conditions might apply, and in any case this was a hugely controversial issue and one that the Council would prove exceedingly reluctant to act on.[34] According to a British official involved at the time, he and his colleagues were dismayed in October 1989 at what they saw as 'the Commission's incomplete grasp of the practical as distinct from the legal issues' concerning external relations. They thought that the attention of DG IV 'needed to be refocused on more immediate practical issues affecting competition much nearer home'.[35]

In actual fact, the Commission had good grounds for believing that this was a practical problem that affected competition and the integrity of the developing SEAM. For them it was a 'domestic' issue and officials in DG IV continued to work on what they thought was a compelling argument for action. And it was compelling, at least until it ran up against political interests of the Member States. Furthermore, if the Commission had not made proposals to the Council for acquiring competence over external commercial airline operations, it could well have been deemed to be in dereliction of its duty after the Ahmed Saeed case.

Speaking at a conference in Montreal in 1989, Argyris said some had thought both the domestic and international civil aviation of the Community lay outside the scope of Regulation 3975/87 and enjoyed a degree of *de facto* anti-trust immunity, but the 'Ahmed Saeed Flugreisen judgement has changed all that'.[36] The Court made it clear that the Community's competition rules applied extraterritorially.[37] It acknowledged that 'Article 85 ... cannot be directly applied by a national court to deal with anti-competitive agreements prior to a decision taken by a national authority or by the European economic community (EEC) Commission under Articles 88 and 89 of the EEC Treaty,[38] but with regard to Article 86 the 'abuse of a dominant position is not susceptible of any exemption whatsoever'. And that it 'must be concluded that the prohibition laid down in Article 86 of the Treaty is fully applicable *to the whole of the transport sector*' [emphasis added].[39] These arguments demonstrated that the competition rules applied to agreements with countries outside the EC, which therefore came under the notional competence of the Community. Argyris explained it was partly because Ahmed Saeed had created some uncertainty about the legality of agreements, made by Member States with third parties that the Commission sent the Council of Ministers proposals for block exemptions from the competition rules of the Treaty of Rome for the entire air transport sector, including its extraterritorial operations.[40]

There was a strong logic to the Commission's claim, namely, 'The Community must be considered as one market both internally and externally.'[41] On 24 January 1990, the Commission adopted proposals that called for competence for itself for negotiating ASAs on behalf of the Community with outsiders.[42] When the Commission sent these proposals to the Council in February, it reminded the Council that the Ahmed Saeed case had indicated that there was no need for implementing legislation and that Article 86 could be applied directly to 'the behaviour of carriers concerning routes between the Community and third countries'.[43] It then proceeded to catalogue the reasons why competence over external relations was necessary and pressing. The limitation on fifth freedom rights that applied to Member States, but not to countries outside the Community, was an anomaly that had already received considerable attention, but the Commission now added a range of other reasons why fifths along with other external relations needed to be brought under the aegis of Community competence. Its view on fifths was inextricably entwined with its determination to assert Community cabotage as a logical consequence of establishing a single market. This would not result in countries outside the Community losing their existing fifths. Those would be grandfathered, but any applications for new fifths would have to be submitted to the Commission and existing fifths would have to be brought into line with Community law. Among other things, this would strengthen the hand of the Community in negotiating air rights from other countries, which would no longer be able to exploit lack of Community unity.

> Individual Member States have faced the refusal of some very large partners [i.e. the US] in aviation to grant comparable traffic rights to European carriers. This has created an imbalance in market opportunities. By declaring a Community cabotage area, a level playing field is created and thereby a basis for more balanced negotiations.

The Commission was doing nothing less than following the logic of existing Community law and the requirements of a single market. There would have to be community, not national, airlines. A single market entailed cabotage and that required unified control over fifth freedom rights. If there were to be a level playing field, another way of saying a single common market for community airlines, then they would all need to have the same rights, not just within the EC, but also regarding their operations outside, particularly as that is where most of them made their profits. However, the Commission was realistic in recognizing that it currently lacked the resources to deal with these issues. The Member States literally had hundreds of bilateral ASAs: the UK had 72, France and the Netherlands 85 each, and so it went on to an accumulated total of about 600. So, the Commission recognized there would be:

> a serious risk that efficiency and speed would be impaired if the Community were to take on an exhaustive negotiating role for all bilateral agreements immediately. By taking up its responsibilities gradually the Community can better prepare itself for its task both in expertise and in resources.[44]

Thus, Member States would be authorized to continue to negotiate ASAs, but they would have to coordinate with the Commission, keep it informed and proceed in accordance with 'a common framework for the negotiations'.[45]

The arguments were forcefully and cogently put, but the Commission underestimated the political opposition this proposal would provoke and it made a serious error in the way that it tried to ground legal competence for the new powers it had sought. The Commission argued for competence on the basis of Article 113, concerning common commercial policy and over non-commercial matters on the basis of the AETR case, which provided for the extension of competence into areas external to the Community, if they would affect the operation of common rules that had been adopted for application within the Community. 'It is a basic rule of Community law that as the Community develops common internal rules it acquires the authority over external negotiations which might affect those common rules.'[46] However, the idea of trying to separate the commercial from non-commercial matters in external air service relations was hardly practical and for all intents and purposes the Commission's case really stood or fell on the basis of its claim for competence under Article 113. Its arguments were seen by many to be inadequate, but whether they argued that sincerely or in a sophistic manner in order to discredit the Commission's case and keep bilateral ASAs securely in the hands of national governments is difficult to say.

The British Department of Transport was strongly against the Commission's proposals and explained a sound financial reason why.

> The financial implications are uncertain but could be substantially disadvantageous to the UK industry. The UK's leading position in international air transport means that UK air carriers enjoy very significant worldwide traffic rights, contrasting conspicuously with the UK's comparatively small domestic market. Were worldwide traffic rights in future to be negotiated by the Community on behalf of all Member States as a bloc and then divided between them, UK air carriers could well see a decline in their share.[47]

In addition to the ideological opposition to the growth of power in Brussels that was widespread in London, and throughout the Community, here was a sound pragmatic reason why the British opposed the Commission's play for competence over external relations. Two years later, in its report on the Commission's proposals, the House of Lords Select Committee on the European Communities also opposed granting competence to the Commission, but restricted itself to legal considerations.

> We are not convinced by the Commission's arguments that the draft Decision can properly be founded on Article 113 as proposed. The arguments indeed appeared to lack conviction as well as substance. The powers given by the EEC Treaty have certainly shown a tendency to evolve and to expand, but not in such a way as to alter structural divisions clearly laid down in the Treaty itself. ... The case law of the European Court, as well as the previous practice of the Council and the Commission, point to Article 84(2) as the appropriate legal base.[48]

Weight of opinion in the European Parliament and most importantly, but not surprisingly, in the Council, was also against Article 113 and in favour of

Article 84(2). As the House of Lord's Committee observed, actually anticipating findings by the European Court of Justice, it was unusual for European law to cross the structural divisions laid down by the Treaty of Rome and, therefore, as there was an article (i.e. Article 84(2)) that applied to sea and air transport and which was clearly separate from that dealing with commercial relations generally (i.e. Article 113), then that was the appropriate place to ground the legal basis for the Commission's claim for competence in external aviation relations. The only problem with that for the Commission was that Article 84(2) would require Council action, and as all Member States were opposed to granting competence over their external civil aviation relations to the Commission, it was highly unlikely that it would ever get a result. Not surprisingly, the Commission clung to Article 113 with determination. But it was all to no avail. A senior official from DG IV explained in May 1991: 'it's quite clear that ... Members are not keen on this kind of development'.[49] That was putting it mildly. The Council had still not discussed the Commission's proposals even after Package 3 had been agreed in June 1992.[50] When the Council did finally consider the Commission's claims for competence over external aviation relations in March 1993, it followed the argument that Article 84(2) should apply and not Article 113. There then ensued a standoff between the Council and the Commission until a few months later when the European Court of Justice also lent its authority and concurred with the Council's reasoning about Articles 113 and 84(2).[51]

This did not entirely curb the Commission's ambitions. It was granted authority to conclude some external agreements, for example, with Norway and Sweden because external relations had direct impact on community rules as SAS was jointly owned and operated by Denmark, Sweden and Norway. Agreement was reached in April 1991. The Commission was also granted a mandate for negotiations with EFTA members Austria, Switzerland, Finland and Iceland in the framework of negotiations for the European Economic Area.[52] In October 1996 the Commission was granted authority by the Council of Ministers to negotiate with east and central European countries who were candidates for entry into the European Union. But, there was no denying the fact that thwarting the Commission's main ambitions created uncertainty and ambiguity for third parties outside the Community. The House of Lord's Select Committee noted this so perceptively in 1992 that its observations are worth quoting at length.

> The Community must decide how its aviation relations with the rest of the world should be conducted. There are both legal and policy reasons to resolve at least the guiding principles which should apply. If the Council does nothing, there is a risk that the Commission may bring legal proceedings before the European Court – either against the Council or against the Member States. Third States will be uncertain with whom they should be negotiating. In the absence of a Council Decision, the principles of Community law ... give the Community exclusive competence in areas where common rules have been adopted. The Community alone will therefore conclude the Agreement which is now being negotiated with Norway

and Sweden – a clear case, since it amounts in effect to the geographical extension of the Community rules. Agreements with other States will not be so clear-cut. If, for example, a Member State revised its air service agreement with the United States allowing it to designate additional airlines on a route to New York and lifting capacity restrictions on all routes to the United States, while allowing United States carriers new fifth freedom rights from its capital to further points in the Member States, would the conclusion of such a bilateral agreement by a Member State individually, or its content, violate Community law?[53]

The fact was, however, that the Member States simply refused to move on external relations in any meaningful way: by September 1992, for example, no state had taken any steps to comply with the September 1989 request from the Commission that they should bring their ASAs, and in particular their national ownership clauses, in line with Community legislation.[54]

While the Commission's attempt to gain control of external relations ran into fierce opposition, it had more success with problems arising from CRSs. CRSs were vital components of the post-US deregulation airline system. They made the massively expanded operations of airlines with their hub-and-spoke operations possible. They were essential for any large airline to be successful, and they were important commercial ventures in their own right. When Robert Crandall, Chief Executive Officer of AA, was asked whether he would prefer to be president of Sabre or AA, he said without hesitation that from an earnings point of view he would prefer to be president of Sabre.[55] CRSs were an industry marvel, but they could be used in ways detrimental to competition. Somewhere in the region of 80 per cent of all airline bookings in the EC were made by travel agents in 1987 and of those 80 per cent were made through airline-owned CRSs, and of those 80 per cent were taken from the first display screen. As the Commission put it these figures:

> give an indication of the temptation for airlines which control CRSs to build into their systems a bias in their own favour, either in terms of presentation, comprehensiveness or reliability of information, or to deny access to the system to other airlines or to charge prohibitive or unreasonable fees for participation in the system.[56]

In the aftermath of US deregulation, the European airlines had had to play catch-up with their American counterparts in order to be effective in the global market place. However, the main strategy that they chose compounded difficulties with CRSs, which were already becoming evident for the Community's competition rules. In Europe, consortia of airlines came together to create Galileo and Amadeus, that were clearly falling foul of Article 85's prohibition of cooperation between enterprises and threatened also to clash with the provisions of Article 86, concerning dominant positions. The Commission had two distinct competition problems to deal with. The first was posed by the danger of dominant positions and cooperation between airlines in creating Amadeus and Galileo. The second was a whole range of other practices that could undermine competition, but which were not captured in the scope of either Article 85 or 86. The first problem was dealt with by DG IV under the block exemption provisions of Regulation 2672/88, which exempted joint ventures, such as Amadeus and Galileo, from the competition rules, but still provided that competition there must be. Access had to be open to all carriers who wanted to participate. They were to have the right to switch easily between competing CRSs. Displays had to be neutral and information, data up-loading and fees had to be handled in a non-discriminatory way. The underlying rationale was to enable:

> European carriers to get together in order to resist the challenge which is coming from CRSs in third countries and, in particular, from the other side of the Atlantic, by producing competitive computer reservation systems so that they can resist the challenge.[57]

Regulation 2672/88 effectively addressed the issue of jointly-owned systems, but it was left to DG VII to deal with the broader problems. After some initial faltering, DG VII worked closely with ECAC, drawing on its expertise in this area, to draft a comprehensive binding code of conduct.[58] ECAC drew up principles for a code of conduct in June 1988, and the Commission approved them and then developed them further to meet the legislative needs of the Community. DG VII was concerned to bring non-discriminatory practices and neutral displays to all CRSs that operated within the Community, including those that were foreign- owned. In October 1988 it sent proposals to the Council of Ministers

> for a general and detailed mandatory code of conduct to apply to all CRSs offered for use and/or used in the Community for the distribution and sale of transport products irrespective of the states or nationality of the system vendor, the source of information used or the location of the relevant central processing unit.[59]

The Commission's proposals provided criteria for ranking orders of displays, required neutrality of treatment, and insisted that foreign-owned CRSs operating in Europe played by the Commission's code of conduct or else they would be excluded. Interestingly, CRSs in the US soon began to adopt guidelines which were the same as, or similar to, those promulgated by ECAC and the EC, though, as we have already noted, this was largely driven by the agreement struck between AA and BA. If the code of conduct were breached, then the Commission had the power to levy a fine of up to 10 per cent of the delinquent's annual turn-over. In June 1989 the Commission's proposals were approved.[60] The Commission had a major success story. The problem of CRSs was not fully solved, and the governing Regulation would be updated periodically, and eventually ICAO also entered the field to encourage uniformity on a global scale, but this had been a major step forward for the Commission and a real achievement in helping to deal with a significant problem for competition, which did not just have impact in the Community's airline industry, but internationally.[61]

Airport slot allocation and all-cargo services were two other issues taken up by the Commission, but they were still undecided, when Package 2 was approved; nevertheless, they warrant a brief mention here. Commission proposals that would have involved prising slots out of the hands of the national flag carriers ran into a veritable storm of protest. The Commission sought to 'improve access to slots for new entrant carriers and to provide for more transparent slot allocation procedures'.[62] The major airlines argued that losing slots would undermine their vast investments at their hub airports, and for BA it would have also diminished its value for shareholders. In December 1990 Leon Brittan, Commissioner for Competition, was forced to back down, and DG IV began to craft less forceful measures, which they put forward the following year.[63] There was some slight change in IATA's international scheduling conferences, which gave a little more room to manoeuvre for new-entrants, but it came no where near solving the problem.[64] It would still be down to the Commission to try to make things more amenable for new entrants and established independent competitors.

There were far more promising developments on airline all-cargo services. The Member States were moved here by global competition – the encroachment into Europe of the large US cargo carriers, Federal Express (Fedex) and United Parcel Service (UPS). The message was clear: failing reform, European airlines would continue to lose business and fail to compete effectively with their US counterparts. The Commission's proposals included third, fourth and fifth freedom rights between any Community airport involved in cargo services, liberal pricing and even cabotage. In the process of negotiation and review in the Council and the Parliament, some of the more radical edges were knocked off, which brought it closer to the general principles that eventually prevailed in what was to become Package 2, but even so when it was finally approved by Council on 17 December 1990, it still provided unlimited third, fourth and fifth freedom rights and free setting of cargo rates. All-cargo air services represented the most liberal achievement so far in the Community's developing civil aviation regime.[65]

The Commission's fortunes in championing the reform of issues that were seen to obstruct competition and the creation of a single market were varied. It did not have much success with external relations and slot allocations. The story with CRSs and all-cargo services was more favourable. But more important for the reform agenda during the period from early 1988 to June 1990 was the change of atmosphere. Setbacks with slot allocations and external relations were simply that. They did not apply the brakes on reform elsewhere, and successes with CRSs and all cargo services encouraged and emboldened the reformers. The vulnerability of European cargo services and the problems with CRSs had both emphasized the need for Community-wide action to deal with challenges from the global marketplace. They could not be ignored, and they could not effectively be dealt with by individual Member States. At the same time, even the most conservative regulatory states began to realize that there were opportunities to be seized as well as challenges to be met. There was also an increasing sense that a do-nothing default position was not tenable and that substantial liberalization of the airline market was both inevitable and necessary, if it were to survive in Europe. Although not a disinterested observer, nevertheless, Nicholas Argyris's words in 1989 are significant: 'I detect among the airlines a growing recognition that the old cartel days are over.'[66] Such thoughts and feelings made up part of the backdrop to the Commission's work in drafting proposals for Package 2.

Drafting and Negotiating Package 2

At the end of July 1989 the *Independent* newspaper announced:

> Sir Leon Brittan, European Community commissioner for competition policy, has just unveiled proposals which if accepted by EC transport ministers would dismantle the maze of restrictions currently preventing competition in the air.[67]

That was not to happen immediately, but there was substantial delivery with Package 2 and the promise, with firm deadlines, of significantly more to come.

The proposals were largely crafted through an inter-play between British ministers and officials on the one hand and officials from DG IV and DG VII on the other. In the wake of Margaret Thatcher's historic third General Election victory in a row, John Moore made way for Paul Channon as Secretary of State for Transport. Channon vigorously lobbied Commission officials, including, Karel van Miert, the new Transport Commissioner, on the need to push ahead with the liberalization of air transport. Van Miert proved to be a strong proponent of liberalization. He was energetic in his attempts to make the Member States and the airlines comply with Community rules, and he was a liberalizer, but one who was politically astute and who realized the need for pragmatic accommodation. At times, that pragmatism stretched too far for his colleague, Sir Leon Brittan, at DG IV, particularly on the issue of subsidies for state airlines.[68] By the summer of 1989, the agenda, purveyed by Channon and supported by the Commission, was in the public domain, and was clearly reflected in the proposals that the Commission was developing for the Council of Ministers. In addition to predictable proposals on fares, capacity and route entry, the British had particularly pushed the need for the right of establishment to become a reality in the Community. They wanted a liberal licensing policy for Community airlines and routes. Member States used licensing as a means to protect their domestic airlines, and this was seen by both the British and the Commission as a major obstacle both to market entry and to effective competition. Van Miert lent his support to the proposals. Among other things, like the British, he had a strong belief that 'existing restrictions to foreign shareholding at an intra-Community level and the right of establishment have to be considered as one of the most important problems to overcome'.[69] It took resolute determination on the part of Van Miert and Brittan to push their full range of proposals through to acceptance by the Commission in a series of meetings in July 1989.[70] Notably, for the future fortunes of these proposals, both French Commissioners Christiane Scrivener and Jacques Delors voted against their acceptance. The French were to lead the opposition to the more liberal aspects of Package 2. They tried hard to bury them, but only succeeded in effecting modest delay.

The Commission's proposals were radical. They called for double disapproval pricing and application of competition rules to fares on routes to third parties outside the Community. They aimed at phasing out capacity restrictions and called for a move to a 25 per cent safety net on 1 April 1992. They proposed a liberal licensing regime, and a series of measures that would have run in parallel with those to ease market access. The measures included opening up cabotage, lifting restrictions on fifth freedoms, lowering the threshold on multiple designation, and opening up major airports to regional traffic. The Commission also sought specific authority to negotiate with third parties, namely Norway and Sweden and EFTA. When taken together with the Commission's demands for general competence over external civil aviation relations of the Community, and its proposals on all cargo services, CRSs, and airport slot allocations, one can get a real feel for the truly ambitious liberal agenda that was being championed. However, as we have already seen, parts of that agenda soon fell by the wayside, and some of the proposals for Package 2 were to suffer a similar fate over the following six months.

The net result of the Council of Ministers rejecting some of the Commission's proposals and delaying the introduction of others was assessed differently by different constituencies. Nicholas Argyris of DG IV thought that the 'Council postponed the adoption of the most dynamic aspects of the Commission's proposals.'[71] Loder feared that it would be 'a repeat of the 1987 sell-out'.[72] British officials, however, were more than pleased with the outcome of Package 2. The Department of Transport thought the result of the December Council, which more or less determined the form of the package, was better than could have been expected. Cecil Parkinson, with whom Margaret Thatcher had replaced Channon as soon as transport issues became really important, and many of his officials had been deeply concerned that the French and their allies would sidetrack further liberalization, by insisting on harmonization measures and reforms of specific problems such as air traffic control and airport congestion.[73] Those matters would have taken a very long time indeed to sort out; but, in fact, all that the regulatory conservatives managed to do was to cause a very limited delay. Transport Minister of State, Michael Portillo, announced after the December Council meeting that the proposals that emerged 'will mean more opportunities for British airlines' and James Moorhouse, conservative member of the European parliament (MEP) for London South and Surrey East, and someone who had specialized in air transport for over a decade, declared 'I am personally delighted with the outcome.'[74]

Those different views about what Package 2 delivered raise questions not only as to the substance of the provisions but about the role of the French Presidency, which oversaw the consideration of the Commission's proposals between July and the end of December 1989. The French Presidency determined how Package 2 would eventually emerge into Community law, and some see the French as moving sharply away from their regulatory conservatism, and allowing what still amounted to liberal content going forward in Package 2. Others see the French role as emasculating the Commission's proposals, which would suggest less of a Damascene conversion than is sometimes suggested. The truth lies tantalizingly in between.

As soon as the Commission's proposals were published, the French convened an informal meeting of the Transport Council 'rushing to set a corset of Council decisions around the Commission's proposals in order to restrict the action and policies' that its successor presidency, that of the Irish, would be able to pursue in the final months before the deadline for Package 2 in June 1990.[75] Supported by the AEA and trade union representations, the French urged caution and the need for harmonization, adequate social provisions, the continuation of exemptions from the competition rules and the continuation of bilateral relations rather than a move to multilateral competence for the Commission. The French Presidency set up a High Level Group, composed of Directors' General of Civil Aviation, to hammer out detailed policies. Some saw this as a tactic to minimize opposition to French conservative regulatory views. However, President Mitterand issued instructions to French officials in October that they should be prepared to make concessions in order to make the French overall presidency, including in the Transport Council, a success. A senior British official Handley Stevens discerned some impact from that in meetings of the High Level Group on 15/16 November, which tabled a draft set of decisions agreed upon by majority vote. However, John Loder noted of the outcome of those same meetings: 'In two major respects it overturns the Commission's proposals: it rejects Double Disapproval of air fares and substitutes a new zone', which was remarkably similar to one advocated by AEA, ECAC and the European Parliament. And second, 'it rejects moves to a 75/25% country pair capacity balance'.[76] When these decisions were referred to the COREPER a few days later, they were approved. The report sent up to the Council thus rejected double disapproval pricing, the liberalization of capacity to a 25 per cent safety-net and insisted that harmonization was 'essential'. Furthermore the market access provisions seemed to:

> reject the Commission's proposals on right of establishment and removal of States' rights to maintain national airline monopolies. To date, no State has replied to the Commission's letter ... demanding withdrawal of the airline and aircraft ownership nationality rules and amendment of the bilateral agreements with 3rd countries to cover ownership of airlines by Community nationals. Similarly cabotage is to remain subject of 'deep study'.[77]

With regard to external relations, the only progress to be made was on authority for specific negotiations with Denmark's SAS partners and with EFTA: there was no action to be taken on any other aspect of the Commission's agenda for exercising competence over external relations. Much of the substance of the Commission's proposals had either been struck out or else had no clear timetable for further action. So far there was little indication that the French had in fact conceded much at all to the liberalization camp.

It was in the final Council session 4–5 December and in two further meetings of the High Level Group that the situation was retrieved, at least in so far as establishing a future timetable for implementing what the Commission had wanted to achieve immediately through Package 2. It was at this point that the French really shifted their position. If they had wanted to do so, they could have led the regulatory conservative majority and outvoted the reform states led by Britain and the Netherlands. Even under the new rules for qualified majority voting, the 'liberalizers' could not muster enough votes to push things through. Why the French shifted ground will be examined shortly, but first the outcome, the actual content of Package 2, will be considered.

After the December Council there were still heated exchanges about Package 2 during the Irish Presidency, but there was little actual change to the content between December 1989 and June 1990 when the Package was formally adopted. On fares, there were new zones of flexibility with prices based on a reference fare (the normal economy fare, or arithmetic average if more than one applied, or if there were no economy fare, then the lowest fully flexible fare). Fares that met the conditions of the zonal provisions and fell within the following parameters would automatically be approved: 95–105; 94–80; and 79–30 per cent of the reference fare. Air fares generally had to be accepted if they were reasonably related to costs, and that provision was supported by a robust consultation and arbitration procedure. Finally, anything above 105 per cent of a reference fare was subject to double disapproval within 30 days of it being filed. Any fare that was not captured by these provisions was still subject to double approval until 31 December 1992.[78]

On capacity, any state had the right to increase capacity automatically up to 60 per cent. Thereafter, subject to the possibility of invoking a freezing clause in the event of difficulties arising, a state would have the further right to increase capacity by 7.5 per cent a year.[79]

On market access, Package 2 permitted third, fourth and fifth freedom rights between any Community airports, but with fifths restricted to 50 per cent of the seasonal capacity. Thresholds for multiple designation were lowered; in Sorensen's view, they were 'reasonably low',[80] and the possibility of designating a route as a public service was also introduced.[81]

In fact these provisions did not move liberalization much further forward. As Argyris explained: 'The second liberalisation package agreed by the Council on 18 June 1990 ... provides for a regulatory regime for the next two and a half years which will be much more restrictive than the Commission had proposed.'[82] The Council had postponed action on operating and route licensing and on the introduction of double disapproval pricing (with one exception), both of which, if introduced, would have strengthened 'opportunities for new carriers to enter the market and compete effectively'.[83] Other proposals from the Commission on entry into the market-place had been diluted, capacity restrictions continued for the time being, and the idea of extending the competition rules to pricing on routes to third parties outside the Community had been set aside. All this was bad news for the reformers, but the good news, which was somewhat overlooked by the more radical liberalizers, was that most of these issues had only been postponed: they had not been buried by the forces of regulatory conservatism. In the meetings of the High Level Group on 4–5 December various timetables were accepted. There would have to be uniform licensing criteria by July 1992. Double disapproval pricing and capacity freedom would be introduced by January 1993. And, though hedged with more uncertainty about delivery, cabotage would have to be part of the SEAM. When one adds to this the successes with all-cargo services, the mandatory code of conduct for CRSs, developments on noise controls, airport consultations, the development of positions on slot allocations, the concept of community airlines and the success the Commission experienced in gaining authority to negotiate first with Norway and Sweden and then with EFTA, it becomes clear that things were now firmly moving in favour of liberalization. This is not to say that there was uniform movement across the range of issues that needed attention – on external relations and slot allocations, for example, the Commission's ambitions were frustrated for years to come – but it now seemed further change was inevitable. That fact partly explains why the forces of regulatory conservatism began to give ground more quickly, and why the French Presidency between July and December 1989 substantially shifted its stance.

One British official who observed the deterioration of the French position of opposition to liberalization, rather illuminatingly expressed things as follows:

> The French were like fish out of water. They thought that they could control this process. It was fascinating to watch them lose it.... They were getting desperate about the whole thing. They tried to link it to harmonisation and other things. None of them worked. You know, it was just fascinating.[84]

The French, from this account, made errors of judgement and were coerced into further change by the market and policy-preference dynamics released by the original modest steps of liberalization as much as by the proponents of liberalization in the Commission, Britain and the Netherlands. More specifically there appear to be three reasons why the French moved to accept gradual liberalization: the need to be seen as good Europeans and to achieve something during their presidency; the need to accept the reality of the legal situation; and the opportunity to benefit Air France. Stevens, who was a British official involved in the negotiations, records that President Mitterand and the leadership of the French bureaucracy instructed their officials that they should make concessions if that were necessary for the French presidency to have achievements to its credit. A senior official in DG VII, looking back, thought that the French changed their stance because of 'political consideration [about] Europe. I think that was the main thing, at least, that was my impression'.[85] In addition, the French Transport Minister Michel Delebarre may have had personal political ambitions, which could have been facilitated by a success story from the Transport Council, and second he may have thought that Air France could benefit from liberalization.[86] Hard evidence is difficult to come by here, but Stevens is not the only one who believed that there was a growing sense of the inevitability of liberalization, in French government circles, and if that were the case they had to manoeuvre to diminish the damage to their position that change threatened and to maximize the benefit for French airlines.

The second element of persuasion was the legal reality facing the French, which had helped to push the liberalization programme forward and which showed no signs of relenting. 'Legally speaking there was no possibility for the French to resist ... they would have to accommodate us [i.e. the Commission].'[87] Argyris explained the hold that the Commission had over those Member States reluctant to accept liberalization: 'The Commission's willingness to renew the block exemptions up to the end of 1992 depends on the Council adopting proposals of the kind which have been tabled.'[88]

The third factor to affect the French position was a combination of the realization that liberalization was going to happen whatever they might do and that with it could come some advantages for Air France. Less than a year after the French Presidency agreed to what became the substance of Package 2 and its timetabled promises for further liberalization, Air France received a decision from the Commission that would strengthen its position in a more liberal dispensation.

The main problem that eventually struck down both TWA and Pan Am. was their lack of an adequate domestic feeder system for their long-haul operations. That, Air France determined, was not going to happen to it. In November 1990 the 'Commission ... cleared Air France's takeover of French carriers Air Inter and *Union de Transport Aérien* (UTA) giving the state-owned flag carrier its own domestic service network and access to all French international routes.'[89] In return, Air France had had to agree to open up eight domestic and fifty international routes to domestic French and overseas airlines. Leon Brittan commented that the French had opened up their market in 'a way that would have been unthinkable a few months ago'.[90] That might have been true, but what we see here is not so much an opening up of the French market as a re-positioning, through collusion between Air France and the French Government, to sustain the national flag carrier's dominant position and to reap what rewards it might from liberalization. Lord King, Chairman of BA, certainly saw things in that light when he spoke at the Royal Aeronautical Society in May 1991.

> It is instructive to note how France is preparing for these [competitive] challenges. Air France, Air Inter and UTA have been consolidated in a single airline which now carries many more passengers than British Airways. The

number of European destinations served by Air France has been rapidly increased. The authorities are investing heavily in Charles De Gaulle and in the surface transport systems which serve that airport. The aim is to displace Heathrow as Europe's premier gateway and make Paris Western Europe's premier hub.[91]

In a way, once liberalization of the marketplace began, it became contagious. The forces of globalization were stripping the wings off the conservative regulatory project's flying machine. If European airlines wanted to continue to operate, they would have to change their system, become more competitive, and seize the opportunities presented by a more open marketplace. That did not mean deregulation. In Europe it meant getting rid of the old cartel-style system of airline-government collusion and adopting new measures of regulation that would encourage competition to thrive. When one adds all these factors together: bad judgement, the need to be seen as good Europeans, legal realities, and the effects of and opportunities offered by what seemed an inevitable opening up of the European airline system, it becomes evident why the French position changed.

Package 2 was warmly welcomed by those Member States in the vanguard of reform, but they also recognized that many difficult issues still demanded attention. In the UK, the CAA feared that inappropriately regulated market forces might diminish rather than increase competition. On the one hand, in theory, opportunities for competition had been increased by Package 2, but on the other hand, the de facto reality in the industry indicated that there was 'little prospect that this will actually occur'.[92] The national flag carriers dominated their domestic markets, the major airports and the key take-off and landing slots and the most important routes. Congestion would severely limit the opportunities for new entrants; and opening up the framework for competition without supplementary measures to deal with predatory behaviour, the power of alliances, consolidations and takeovers might very well reduce rather than increase competition. Such views were widespread in the industry among the smaller airlines. Andrew Gray, Managing Director of Air UK, expressed strongly-held doubts in March 1991 that competition would flourish because he did not believe that it would be possible to get airport slots, for example, in countries like France and at airports like Charles De Gaulle.[93] This catalogue of problems and difficulties was intimidating, but the Commission was engaging with them. It had taken action, albeit not always successfully as yet, on pricing, capacity, market entry, establishment and licensing issues, CRSs, all-cargo services, slot allocation procedures, compensation for denied boarding, consultation procedures for airline users and airports,[94] noise regulations, harmonization of technical and legal matters, and external relations. Perhaps of equal importance, Package 2 delegated policy powers to DG VII.

> It is significant that the Commission has been given powers of decision concerning too high or too low fares, traffic restrictions at airports, protection of

new services, public service obligations and the freezing or reduction in capacity growth ... These powers have so far in the EEC been reserved for the enforcement of the competition rules.[95]

Not only did Package 2 achieve more liberalization, and produce concrete promises for more to follow, but the Commission had also grown in the process, deepened its expertise and strengthened its bureaucratic powers. The most important strategic battle in the development of the SEAM had been fought and won by those states in favour of a liberal regulatory system and the Commission with strong support from legal decisions from the European Court of Justice. Achieving Package 3 would come with much more ease, but it did not answer all the problems that needed to be addressed for the SEAM to flourish in the way the reformers intended. Problems that the UK CAA so clearly identified, and others, would have to be solved or at least ameliorated before that could happen.

7 Package 3
Delivery in 1992

> It's a process [liberalisation]. First of all we need to put in place all the rules which are necessary for this to occur. Airlines have to adapt themselves to a new situation and make use of opportunities and then we have to see actual evidence of competition between airlines. So it will take a number of years, but I am quite sure that is the way things are developing.[1]

Commission officials had always seen the development of the SEAM as a process, even though, at the outset, they were unsure precisely what would be its outcome. They knew it would take time to change embedded positions that underpinned the old system and had few illusions about the strength of the regulatory conservatives or the vigour with which they would defend their enormous vested interests against the threat posed by liberalization. Furthermore, they also knew that the process would not be straightforward. It would not simply be a matter of formulaic changes. The modest liberalization achievements of the first two packages quickly brought a series of issues into sharp focus that would have important bearings on whether or not competition would actually flourish even after the old regulatory constraints were dismantled. These issues needed creative tending to devise suitable policies for dealing with them. Deregulation, tantamount to a laissez-faire system, had never been the intention of European reformers. Instead, they wanted to remove regulations that inhibited competition and replace them with others that would nurture competition, but not to the extent of excluding consideration of public service obligations, or of ignoring either the interests of organized labour or environmental, social and welfare issues.

In July 1990 Argyris acknowledged that many complexities would trouble the Commission's ambition to create a liberal competitive aviation market. He conceded that there would probably still be some restrictions on pricing and market entry after the SEAM came into being in 1993, and that there would be even more significant 'non-regulatory barriers to entry.' These would encompass both infrastructure problems and operating practices of the flag carriers. Chief among the infrastructure problems were insufficient capacity at key airports and air traffic control (ATC) inadequacies. Europe was plagued by a mosaic of exclusion zones reserved for military aviation, and for its civilian traffic it had '52 ATC centres serving 31 national systems, with equipment from 18 suppliers and running 70 different programming languages. By contrast, the USA ... [had] one system, a single area and only 20 centres'.[2] And that was for a much larger area.

Reformers in Europe could learn from US experience and not only in the field of ATC. The likely behaviour of the major carriers, if US experience were anything to go by, would involve anti-competitive practices 'designed to discourage new market entry' through the use of CRSs, FFPs, incentives for travel agents, takeovers and mergers. Between 1978 and 1987 market share of the eight leading US airlines rose from 81 per cent to 92 per cent. Argyris was disturbed by such prospects and did not want them to materialize in Europe, but at the same time he noted that it was unlikely that the EC would be able to sustain its twelve existing flag carriers.[3] There would probably be some consolidation of the European market, but acceptance of that likelihood lent even more force to his argument that there must be strong benign regulation to nurture competition.

The British Government shared most of these concerns. In December 1990 a memorandum by the Department of Transport reiterated commitment to liberalization:[4]

> The Government's objective in the forthcoming Community discussions will be to limit the extent of remaining regulation to that necessary to ensure safety and the fitness of operators combined with the introduction of safeguards designed to prevent exploitative practices or unfair competition. The Government believes that this approach, together with initiatives to promote access where airport or airspace capacity is scarce, offers the best guarantee of a single market, operating in the interests of the consumer.[5]

Thus after Package 2 had been delivered, while the focus for Package 3 continued to be on market entry, capacity, pricing and common airline and route licensing criteria, the reformers placed increasing emphasis on problems with ATC systems, allocation of take-off and landing slots at congested airports, subsidies, external relations, and a raft of difficulties with the dominant flag carriers and their ability to manipulate the market in order to disadvantage their competitors and repel potential new entrants from boarding the system. In addition to the use of CRSs and FFPs, mergers and alliances, this raft included the power and influence that came with dominant positions in relationship to government, airport management and consumer perceptions.

The national flag carriers all sought ways to maintain their positions and exploit the marketplace and its changing regulatory regime. As time passed, it became clear that their priority was to adjust strategies in order to compete globally, and that had some negative consequences for nurturing competition in Europe, particularly in terms of making space for new entrants at their international hub airports. Ironically, in some ways, it was developments with BA that really began the re-positioning that this priority prompted. Privatization resulted in a leaner, more efficient and competitive BA that then proceeded to gobble up B.Cal., and later the scheduled routes of Dan Air, and to craft a joint venture agreement in 1987 with the world's largest airline, UA. This involved integrating their networks, coordinating ticketing, schedules and baggage handling and sharing of terminals at Chicago, Washington, Seattle and New York JFK. Entry of UA into Heathrow four years later compromised that agreement, but meanwhile, in the face of those developments, as one analysis put it at the time: 'the rest of the European industry is scrambling for strategic alliances, or positions of defence and survival, in the looming of a new era which is menacing but ill-defined.'[6] Lord King of BA might have rather woefully observed Air France consolidating its position in the French market, but BA had in fact shown the way.

Those were problems enough for liberalizing the European airline system, but Saddam Hussein's invasion of Kuwait on 2 August 1990 added a further dimension, which was to trouble the industry profoundly over the next two years. The Middle East crisis and the war that followed in 1991 pushed the world's airline market into a crisis not matched until 9/11 and its aftermath. Achieving Package 3 actually turned out to be relatively easy compared with the passage of its predecessors; however, trying to ensure competition would really happen in the face of infrastructure problems, the shenanigans of Europe's flag carriers, with their main attention on global challengers rather than on European competition, and the need to ward off the threat to liberalization from the effects of recession were much more difficult objectives to achieve. How successful the reformers and the European airlines were at adjusting to the new framework and in riding out the effects of the recession became clear in assessments of the industry towards the end of the decade: those will be examined at the end of the next chapter. In the meantime, the focus is on Package 3.

The immediate context for Package 3

Three general factors helped the passage of Package 3. First, commitments had been approved in Package 2 for further liberalization with specific deadlines, namely uniform licensing rules by 1 July 1992; and the abolition of bilateral capacity agreements and the introduction of double disapproval pricing, both by 1 January 1993. There was also a vaguer commitment to the introduction of cabotage.

Second, there were developments in the marketplace. Modest progress with Europe-wide liberalization and the impact of Britain's liberal bilateral agreements demonstrated the benefits of increased competition. At the same time competitive challenges from the global marketplace demanded responses. The most immediate and pressing manifestation of this was the market share being taken in Europe by US cargo companies such as Fedex and UPS. The European response was a liberal all-cargo regime that more or less offered everything short of cabotage to airlines of the Member States. Thus both the attraction of benefit and the need to rise to global competitive challenges encouraged the Europeans to move further along the liberalization pathway.

And third, movement for liberalization was also now less inhibited by fears aroused by the spectre of deregulation, which was being rapidly exorcized from the debate about the SEAM project. During the mid 1980s, the forces of regulatory conservatism repeatedly invoked the mantra of deregulation to provoke resistance to the programme of reform of the airline system. Even though the Commission had always been careful to disavow any intention of promoting US-style deregulation, opponents continued to allege that this was its agenda. As time passed, and the Commission's version of the SEAM gradually began to take shape, charges that deregulation was the objective became more and more difficult to sustain. In particular, during the passage of Package 2, the development of parallel proposals for regulations needed to nurture competition made it abundantly clear that the Commission favoured liberalization, but under a controlled environment. Just abolishing old regulations and allowing a laissez-faire approach to take the industry wherever it may was not the agenda and never had been. Time and again, even the most vociferous in calling for reform made it clear that liberalization, not deregulation, was their intent. Bethell, Richard Branson of Virgin Atlantic, Sorensen, Van Miert, Brittan and even the father of US deregulation, Alfred Kahn, cautioned against US-style deregulation in Europe and talked instead of liberalization and the need for new regulations that would nurture real competition. In early 1993 Kahn warned Europeans about the 'troubling surprises' that US deregulation had produced: 'Reduction in quality of service, the disappearance of airlines and price discrimination ...'[7] He also advised that infrastructure bottlenecks would need attention, such as air traffic control and airport congestion. It was the profile that these kinds of issues had attained, which required a new regulatory system if competition were to flourish, which in turn made the allegations that Europe was heading for US-style deregulation implausible. Not only was the Commission gaining ground in terms of introducing substantial reform, but it was also undermining the opposition's propaganda to the point where there now seemed to be only one argument left about the way the European airline system must go.

In addition to these three general factors there was a more specific and rather unexpected development on fares, which eased the way for further liberalization in Package 3. As early as 1988, changes in the European airline system were beginning to pose the major airlines with a dilemma, and that dilemma intensified as liberalization gained momentum. Once it became clear that there would be some reform, there arose the danger of being disadvantaged if they did not join the bandwagon. They became torn between their commitment to the cosy system they had enjoyed for so long and the need to adjust to what increasingly seemed like inevitable change.

> ... uncertainties surrounding the ... single aviation market is causing concern to airline executives who would just as soon see the Commission handle aviation matters on behalf of all EC states to avoid what one of them calls 'another agricultural disaster' [i.e. similar to the trouble caused by the Common Agricultural Policy]. He shudders at the prospect of a 'continuous

flow of regulations and directives valid only for a part of the Community irrespective of what is happening in other member states.'[8]

This was the other side of the coin to the danger of being disadvantaged by liberalizing ahead of other states: there were also dangers that national carriers would be left behind in the global competition if they did not follow the lead of those states like the Netherlands and Britain, which were rapidly liberalizing the market environment for their carriers. The major airlines realized that it would be better for them to prepare for and to influence the course of change, rather than simply be subject to it in a form determined by others. Some had already been seduced by the chances for opportunistic gains, like Aer Lingus with fifth freedom rights out of London, and others were soon to succumb to similar temptations. Air France and BA acted robustly to strengthen their positions not only for more Europe-wide competition and opportunities, but primarily for global challenges. The old flag carriers were not only gradually realising that reform would come, but also that it offered them some opportunities as well. According to a senior Commission official from DG IV, by the time of Package 3 in 1992, the airlines had 'gone overboard.' They 'wanted to go beyond what the Commission was proposing. For instance ... the Commission proposals on tariffs in the Third Package – the airlines said, hey, that is not good enough....'[9] They wanted something more liberal than the Commission initially proposed. But there is need for caution here. This did not necessarily mean that the traditional flag carriers had been converted to the cause of competition as envisaged by the Commission.

When Air France and BA consolidated their domestic dominant positions further, most perceived of this as diminishing, rather than enhancing, the potential for competition. So what exactly was going on when these same airlines agreed to what seemed to be a pro-competition fares agreement, and one more liberal than the Commission originally proposed, in Package 3? It should be clear by now that the national flag carriers were not threatened so much by the removal of regulations – pricing freedom for example – as they were by new regulations designed to help new entrants and existing independent airlines to compete on a level playing field – for example, by getting access to take-off and landing slots at major airports at prime times. In fact, free pricing, in conjunction with advantages that the flag carriers had inherited from the traditional system such as brand recognition, possession of the best slots and superior infrastructures, could allow them to take on their challengers and drive them from the marketplace. This is precisely what had happened in the US, with increasing consolidation of the market in fewer hands. Competition through the eyes of the national flag carriers looked rather different from the idea of competition seen through the eyes of those in the Commission and the UK's CAA. The latter's chairman, Christopher Chataway, in February 1991 put his finger on the difference when he emphasized that the 'primary objective of liberalisation must be to increase competition and to enable a multiplicity of airlines to survive.'[10] He rejected the 'doctrine of contestability', popularized in the US, that the *threat* of a possible competitor entering the market would be sufficient to discipline airlines in monopoly route positions. He insisted that there had to be a multiplicity of competing airlines for competition to work, but the response to this by the likes of Air France and BA was that only majors could compete with majors, and US experience indicated that when airlines reached that kind of size, like People's Express and America West had done, they went bust. BA and Air France were looking to expand in order to compete, not so much in Europe, but globally, and they did not want the requirements of the vision of competition often shared by the UK CAA and the Commission to get in the way of their strategic plans. Those strategic plans continued to pose problems for years to come so far as the Commission was concerned, but in the short term, the net impact of all this for Package 3 was that changes in pricing were much easier to achieve than in either of the first two packages.

That specific factor along with the three more general ones, considered above, all helped facilitate the emergence of Package 3. Its coming was a lot easier than either Package 1 or 2. Nevertheless, there were still difficulties. Britain was not willing to support some of the Commission's proposals, one of which, on external relations, subsequently languished in limbo for a long time after January 1993. The regulatory conservative states also continued to try to slow liberalization down, partly by insisting that it should not forge ahead of harmonization. Their hands were strengthened by the onset of severe recession in the airline industry as a result of the Gulf War, but the effects of the recession were not uniformly favourable to the regulatory conservatives. On the one hand, the recession gave them arguments for delaying the implementation of reforms, and on the other, it gave the airlines the excuse to shed staff and become leaner and fitter for competition. And, for many, the issue soon became a choice between moving ahead with liberalization and creating a more efficient and competitive European airline system, or else continuously handing out state aids to rescue ailing airlines, some of which were clearly unviable commercially and seemed destined to remain so even after large cash injections. Between 1991 and 1995, over £6.5 billion of state aid was given to European airlines.[11] Package 3, therefore, came not without difficulties nor without a growing sense that it would not be the end. There would still be things to do to ensure a fully working competitive airline system, but it was a vital further step forward on the liberalization pathway.

There's a difference between having a mission and being on mission. Officials in DG VII had believed that they had had a mission for over a decade; now they were truly on mission. There was progress, and the prospect of further dramatic developments beckoned. The small group of people in DG VII and DG IV, who had driven the SEAM forward over the previous six years, had grown in stature and experience and were now impatient to consummate the project. On some issues they were overambitious, and the result was frustration, disappointment and visible signs of irritation. On others they underestimated what was immediately achievable. On most things they took sound negotiating positions and largely got what they wanted. The Dutch and British governments continued to throw their weight and influence behind the liberalization programme, and relations between them and Commission officials continued to be close. However, it is significant that the British Government was ambivalent on some issues, for which the Commission hoped for substantial progress in Package 3. On these issues national interest overrode Britain's commitment to liberalization.

On slot allocations, the British professed to want 'a system that can generate fair and vigorous competition, and reward efficiency': this sounded promising for reform. Unfortunately these changes were only to be rung providing they did not sacrifice 'the flexibility and practicability of the existing system'.[12] The idea that there was flexibility in the system of slot allocations must have been some official's idea of a joke. Inflexibility was the nature of the problem. In fact, there were divided loyalties in the British Government between those who did not wish to weaken BA's competitive ability in the global marketplace by taking valuable slots away from it, and those who thought that that was a necessary price to pay for generally increasing competition in Europe. In March 1991 the Secretary of State for Transport, Malcolm Rifkind, took what many saw as the first major political step to remove British Government support from BA. Following a recommendation from the UK CAA, he abolished the traffic distribution rules, notionally opening up Heathrow (though not to more than two US carriers as per the agreement of 1980 and not to other airlines if they could not get slots). He then moved to approve an agreement reached with the US to replace TWA and Pan Am at Heathrow with AA and UA, after the former two had gone bankrupt. Even though the new arrivals took over their predecessors' slots and were far more effective competitors, overall the deal was highly favourable to the British. Nevertheless, BA's fortress Heathrow had been weakened, and Lord King was furious and withdrew BA's financial support to the Conservative Party in retaliation.[13] So far as slot allocations were concerned, it highlighted just how important, valuable and controversial they were. For the time being, none of the Member States, including Britain, had a clear solution to this most intractable of problems, though there was a strong preference in Britain for some kind of market solution, whereas the Commission's position favoured redistribution where possible on the basis of need. In the event European action on slots was excluded from Package 3, not solely because of what had happened in Britain, with the problems at Heathrow, and its difference of opinion with the Commission on how to proceed on this issue, but it is noteworthy that the Member State most associated with liberalization did not energetically pursue changing the slot allocation system at this time. The major area, however, where Britain withheld its support from the Commission was regarding its ambition to take over external aviation relations. The British Government's view was

> that such an assertion is at best premature while the single market in aviation remains incomplete, and furthermore that EC air transport matters fall within the scope of Article 84(2) [and thus not under the commerce clause as asserted by the Commission].[14]

The main lesson to be drawn from looking at the British Government's position here is that it would be unlikely that the Commission could ever get its way if there were no support even from the most enthusiastic Member State for liberalization. The Commission at this point was the most powerful and effective driver of reform, but that does not mean that it could get its own way on everything, even when logic and law seemed to support it.

Commission officials were fully aware of both the reservation of their closest and strongest ally in the campaign for liberalization about Community competence over external relations and the opposition from other Member States on issues such as cabotage, but it was important for DG VII to lay out a robust negotiating position for Package 3. The main responsibility for drafting the proposals to go to the Council of Ministers lay with Frederik Sorensen. Debate and consideration of the contents of Package 3 began in June 1990 and continued for some twelve months. It was noticeable that the debate had widened in scope and now engaged more vigorously with infrastructure and non-regulatory obstructions to competition that would need regulating. Parliaments, industry, interest and lobby groups, NGOs and the Member States, all made their views known to the Commission, but such views were largely to do with timing and tactics. With the caveat of certain specific areas that the Member States effectively vetoed, the agenda in fact was dictated by what had gone before, the legal requirements of the Community, and Commission officials. The key issues were to do with how quickly regulations restricting competition could be phased out; how quickly harmonization could be ushered in; and how infrastructure problems and anti-competitive behaviour of the national flag carriers could best be dealt with. That was clearly the position in the summer of 1990, but as the Gulf crisis broke and developed into war, there arose a serious challenge to the reform agenda. In the end there was to be no, or at least little, turning back even in the face of a deep industry-wide recession, but that outcome was by no means clearly foreseen or necessarily expected at the time.

There might have been little turning back, but there was no denying that European airlines teetered on the verge of disaster as a result of the onset of the Gulf War in January 1991. In February 1991 the AEA predicted that operations in 1990 would yield the first combined loss for its members for over a decade as a result of spiralling costs, a depressed US market and the initial impact of the Gulf crisis. Such losses paled to insignificance compared to what was to happen in 1991. When hostilities began, traffic dropped by 10 per cent during the first week. By the second week it had dropped by 25 per cent. Load factors slumped to around 35 per cent, which was over 15 per cent down in the same period a year before.[15] By January 1993 estimates of accumulated losses for scheduled world airlines between 1990 and 1993 stood at $10 billion. By April that had risen to $11.5 billion with European airlines accounting for nearly a half of those losses.[16] In just over a month after the onset of war, the European airlines had announced over 20,000 job losses in the airline industry alone, besides reductions in aerospace manufacturing and support industries. BA was set to lose 9 per cent of its workforce, after already implementing reductions in previous years. KLM's reduction was 12 per cent, Sabena's 18 per cent, Iberia's 10 per cent, Alitalia's 8 per cent, and SAS's 16 per cent. In contrast both Air France and Lufthansa strove to avoid job losses, even though Air France, according to its Chairman Bernard Attali, fell into massive deficit representing 5 per cent, 12.5 per cent and almost 50 per cent of IATA airlines' total deficits respectively in 1990, 1992 and 1993.[17] These grim figures provided France and other regulatory conservative states with ammunition to argue for slowing down and, in some cases, for reversing liberalization. They also provided the rationale for demanding state aid. The issue of state subsidies was thus thrust very visibly into the limelight, and it proceeded to cause serious worry to Commission officials, BA and other private sector airlines and to the leaders of the liberalization movement among the Member States for some time to come. What success the reactionary forces had we shall assess shortly. In the meantime, it is important to note that not everyone saw the crisis as inimical to liberalization's prospects: *Flight International* observed that the 'Gulf War provides many with an excuse to slim down ready to compete when growth returns'.[18]

The crisis that was rapidly unfolding in early 1991 prompted Van Miert to try to head off what he knew was coming: attempts by the regulatory conservative states to revert to protectionism and the provision of state aid. He called a meeting of airline and Commission officials and tried to be as accommodating as he could, without abandoning the liberalization agenda. BA, as the only privately owned airline and thus not eligible for state aid, predictably was in the forefront of opposition to the idea of financial bailouts. Van Miert noted that direct Community subsidies were not possible and that the Commission could only offer financial help with infrastructure improvements, but added, rather ominously for the liberal camp, that the Treaty of Rome could be flexible where state action was concerned. Over the following five years, that flexibility stretched the credulity of many as billions of pounds of state aid poured into inefficient and some clearly unviable airlines. No firm decisions were made at the meeting, but DG VII continued to consider 'the airlines' demands for temporary relaxation of competition rules; allowing capacity sharing between carriers on low-traffic routes; freedom to raise fares more quickly; and liberalisation programme delay'.[19] Worryingly, in May, the outgoing chairman of the UK CAA, Christopher Tugendhat, predicted 'no competition yet' for Europe because government ownership and interest in airlines still remained too strong and congested airports would also stymie competition.[20] He dismissed the notion that BA still needed to be cosseted in order to strengthen it for global competition and pointed out that on routes where more than one British carrier operated, the British share of the market was greater than where there was only one. It was against this backdrop of economic crisis in the industry and gloomy prognostications by reformers that Sorensen had to craft the Commission's proposals for Package 3.

Drafting and negotiating Package 3

By June 1991, Sorensen was in a position to circulate an important paper that laid out much of what was later incorporated into proposals agreed by the Commission on 17 July and sent to the Council of Ministers in September as COM(91)275.[21] In words virtually identical to those in COM(91)275, Sorensen argued in June:

> Experience has shown that competition is desirable. However, a completely unregulated market may lead to abuse, and indeed to anticompetitive behaviour and a certain regulation is therefore necessary to guard against such practices ... and to protect consumers.
> However, there should be no need to intervene unless things go wrong.[22]

Emerging from these considerations came four main thrusts of policy for liberalization; harmonization; the infrastructure; and external relations. There is no need to go through Sorensen's paper item by item, but it is instructive to note some significant changes between his paper and what eventually emerged in COM(91)275. These changes came about in the final stages of intra-Commission negotiations in the summer of 1991, and they provide insight into what Commission officials thought might be possible of achievement given the then existing power relations within the Council of Ministers. With the notable exception of external relations, Sorensen's paper was much less detailed than COM(91)275. On licensing, the situation between June and July 1991 moved from simply acknowledging that provisions were needed for specifying common safety and technical standards and financial probity requirements for carrier licensing to be applied across the Community. Under the section on market access, provisions also appeared for non-discriminatory national route licensing policies. Protection was only allowed for public service routes and for new routes for two years when operated by aircraft of no more than eighty-seat capacity.[23] The former, among other things, eased the situation for the introduction of cabotage by diluting the fears of the regulatory conservatives about disruptions to national markets. The Commission clearly did not intend that access to cabotage should result in the closure of routes deemed to be of public service value.[24] The two year protection for new regional routes was an attempt to avoid the damaging cycle of start-up and disappearance, through takeover, merger or collapse, of airlines as witnessed so often under deregulation in the US with the net result of yet further consolidation and domination of the market by a small number of carriers. On market access, the lifting of restrictions on fifth freedom rights, already flagged in Package 2, remained in place, but the Commission was now also calling for the introduction of full cabotage. On capacity, the Package 2 commitment to abolish bilateral capacity restrictions by January 1993 was simply carried forward for Package 3.

On fares, there was considerably more movement in evidence. Sorensen's paper simply noted Package 2's commitment to double disapproval, but there had been some misgivings that such a pricing regime might act in a retrograde way in areas where free pricing had already been introduced and the national flag carriers were now generally in favour of a liberal pricing regime.[25] The result of Commission consultations, particularly with the airlines, thus resulted in a more liberal regime than had been envisaged in Package 2 and one more liberal than Sorensen himself originally thought likely to succeed. By July the Commission had amended its position and proposed that on routes, where normal competition conditions existed, free pricing should be introduced in 1996 after a three-year transition period. An example of 'abnormal conditions' would, for example, be where a lack of available slots restricted competition. In addition, the Commission took steps strictly to limit the possibility of any fare disapprovals in the meantime under the vestiges of the double disapproval system:

> It is proposed to restrict the possibility of submitting an air fare for examination by the Commission to fully flexible fares being charged on routes on which, for one reason or another, competition is limited. This will restrict the use of safeguards to be added to a double-disapproval system to situations where this system would not work well because of insufficient competition.[26]

The proposals that went to the Council of Ministers also elaborated on the harmonization issue. For the first time, there was real emphasis on the need for harmonization. Previously the emphasis given to this had always come from the forces of regulatory conservatism as a tactic to delay progress. Now, while aware that such a danger still existed, the reformers saw it as a necessary complement to liberalization to ensure that it worked in favour of competition:

> The very fact that the liberalisation really will create one air transport market within the Community has created the need to ensure that norms and standards in a number of areas are harmonised in order to ensure a level playing field for competition among EEC air carriers irrespective of where in the EEC they are established.[27]

The list of areas requiring action was long: safety and accident investigation, airworthiness; licenses; flight-time limitations; CRSs; slots; consultation between airports and users; denied boarding compensation; liability; noise and emission controls. On infrastructure the two key areas were ATC and airport congestion.

The main difference, however, between Sorensen's paper and COM(91)275 was the space devoted to external relations. In Sorensen's paper it ran to several pages; but in the proposals sent to the Council it was a scant couple of paragraphs. It is clear from his own paper that Sorensen was agitated by the lack of progress in gaining Commission competence in external relations and the ill-disguised irritation was one thing that was carried forward from his paper into the proposals sent to the Council of Ministers.

> ... *it must be said that this is not only an intellectually amusing question* the fact is that an agreement between a Member State and a third country in nearly all instances will affect the commercial situation inside the Community for air carriers from other Member States (emphasis added).[28]

Sorensen offered five reasons why the Commission needed to take competence over external aviation relations. Three were to do with the logic of the single market and tactical bargaining with countries outside the Community; the heart of his case, however, lay in what he took to be compelling legal arguments. They had continuing resonance over the following years and eventually became so important over a decade later that they need to be quoted in full.

> a) A large majority of the nationality clauses which form part of the standard clauses in bilateral agreements between Member States and third countries are illegal since they limit the carriers which can be designated to operate on the routes which are contained in the agreements to those carriers which are substantially owned and effectively controlled by nationals of the signatory States. This should be considered as discrimination on the basis of nationality and consequently these clauses will have to be replaced by Community clauses.
> b) In bilateral negotiations, rights are being exchanged, which form part of existing Community legislation, without inter-Community consultations, e.g. traffic rights between Member States, access to computer reservation systems, without inter-Community consultations. According to the jurisprudence of the Court of Justice this is not acceptable.[29]

All of this was lost from the proposals that went to the Council of Ministers. Sorensen's irritation at non-action was still there, but otherwise the Commission restricted itself to emphasising 'important reasons' for acting with 'urgency': 'The procedural problems are dealt with in a specific proposal COM(90) [about which Sorensen correctly observed in June that they had not been discussed in Council in any detail] but action must soon be taken in order to avoid squandering Community assets.'[30] The reality was that external relations were so controversial and the strength of opposition was so overwhelming that in fact '[i]t was not on the Commission's agenda.' All that even the determination and commitment of Sorensen could achieve was effectively to flag the issue for future action.[31]

The proposals for Package 3 contained far-reaching measures, but once they were made public it soon became clear from comments made by Van Miert that the Commission did not expect to get all that it was bidding for. While he hinted that even more liberal pricing might be proposed, namely free pricing in 1993 with double disapproval solely for those routes which still did not enjoy free competition, on a range of other issues he clearly expected difficulties and some temporary retreats. He dubbed the licensing proposals 'a political "hot potato"', because it would enable any airline meeting the licensing criteria to have access

146 Package 3: delivery in 1992

to any market within the EC. 'If a government turns them down, they would have the right of appeal to the Commission, which would probably find in the airline's favour.'[32] And on cabotage, he thought that the Commission would have to accept a transition period: 'total adoption of cabotage is "doubtful."'[33] He recognized that it was a touchy issue and said that he could live with some kind of gradual phasing in, but '[w]e'd like to get it moving so that the people who think it is so revolutionary can get used to it'.[34]

Van Miert's position was a rather curious mixture of low-key radicalism with a pragmatic willingness to compromise. He declared that '[w]e must have a proper balance between liberalisation and putting on limits. We want to keep the notion that it is possible to serve our communities – even if they are non-profitable routes.'[35] And new regional routes operated by low capacity aircraft would be protected for two years until they had had time to become commercially viable. The rough and tumble of a US-style free-market would not happen in Europe. At the same time Van Miert was not insensitive to what could be learnt from the US and in particular that it still did not make sense to charge such high prices in Europe. 'There is something wrong if airlines can charge less for a trip to the USA than between Brussels and Milan.' He went on to add with rhetorical flourish: 'Do you really think you can maintain such a system?'[36] And finally, Van Miert, like many of the officials in DG IV and VII, emphasized the need for infrastructure reforms. So far as he was concerned, the most pressing was in ATC, where EUROCONTROL needed to move from being an international to becoming a supranational organization in order to deal with what was rapidly approaching chaos. Van Miert knew that the package would provoke lively debate in the Council of Ministers, particularly as the world airline system was then currently experiencing what was often referred to as apocalyptic damage because of the recession precipitated by the Gulf War. In fact, although the regulatory conservatives protested and tried to amend things in such a way as substantially to delay further liberalization, it is a clear testimony to the strength and impetus that had developed in the Commission's reform agenda and in the marketplace that they only had modest success.

COM(91)275 was the starting point for discussion in the Council's Transport Working Group, chaired by Ruy Veres. Notwithstanding that the Council presidency was in the hands of the regulatory conservative Portuguese, attacks on COM(91)275 were largely repulsed. Furthermore, pressure from the airlines moved the position on fares to an even more liberal position. The Council of Transport Ministers meeting in Brussels on 26 March decided that there should be free pricing with safeguards only for fares being raised too high or pitched too low. The double disapproval regime was thrown out as too timid.[37] At the same meeting it was agreed that Norway and Sweden would be admitted into the Package 3 regime, but on two other important issues – cabotage and common licensing rules – matters remained undecided. Concerns about the recession in the industry had prompted caution about cabotage. There were fears that opening up cabotage in 1993 could be damaging to Member State domestic airlines that were already suffering badly. Although the European Council had spoken up the previous year in favour of opening up cabotage the European Parliament and the Economic and Social Committee both asked 'that a transitional period lasting until 1 January 1995 should be allowed during which cabotage could only be exercised subject to certain conditions'.[38] As it turned out such calls would later seem quite moderate. The effects of the recession were also clearly evident in the thinking of the Council of Ministers and in the Commission, but in the latter in a rather different way.

> The Commission has ... received a confidential report on the level and nature of subsidies used by most European countries to bolster the positions of their national flag carriers. With liberalisation, subsidies are becoming an issue. The Commission is to investigate further items such as tax breaks, route subsidy, waiving of landing charges and duty-free trade concessions to state owned carriers.[39]

The Commission was already engaged with a whole series of issues that would need attention after Package 3 was accepted.

Final delivery

The final stage of bargaining took place in June and July 1992. In Council on 22 June, attempts by France, Germany and Italy to put the brakes on liberalization by linking further forward movement to progress on external relations and slot allocation rules, both of which were heavily bogged down, failed. Just how bogged down the issue of slots was became clear when proposals were completely set aside: ' "We'll negotiate that later," [said] an EC official. "It is very sensitive." '[40] The situation was similar on external relations. On market access, there were also some disappointments for the liberalisers. Full introduction of cabotage was delayed on the insistence of France, Germany, Greece and Italy for four and a half years, until 1997. The British and Dutch had favoured its immediate introduction, or at worst a year's delay. Until 1997 carriers could only engage in consecutive cabotage up to 50 per cent of the seats on the first leg of the journey. Consecutive cabotage was rather like a fifth freedom right except passengers could be picked up and set down between two points *within* another state. Market access was eased with unrestricted fifths made available between most Community airports and with the introduction of 7th freedom rights, which allowed the airline of one country to originate a flight in another and fly to a third party Member State. Access could still be denied on environmental or congestion grounds, but such denials had to be non-discriminatory and were subject to adjudication by the Commission. National ownership criteria were abolished as of January 1993 and were replaced by the concept of Community carriers. The most radical aspect of Package 3 was on licensing. '[I]t requires member states to grant a licence to any airline which meets the (not exacting) standards.'[41] Such licensing was general, not specific to a particular route, but combined with other liberal market access policies this was a formidable step forward in encouraging a multi-airline competitive regime. There were still restrictions for public service routes and there were dangers here. The Commission had tried to limit a Member State's ability to designate public service routes by restricting them to routes with less than 30,000 seats a year, but this had been lost in Council negotiations.[42] The ability to protect new entrants using aircraft with no more than eighty-seat capacity on routes with less than 30,000 seats per year against anything other than a like competitor for two years was also a restriction on competition that some feared would be abused. The fare regime was unchanged from the decisions in March and Van Miert declared: 'This package should now lead to lower fares.'[43] The three Regulations on licensing, market access and capacity, and on fares that made up Package 3 were all adopted and set to come into force in January 1993.[44]

'Seen in the light of the intended aim of the completion of the internal market by the end of 1992, there is no doubt that the package falls short of this aim.'[45] So wrote one of the airline journals in July 1992. And it was correct. On the other hand, liberalization had travelled a long way in a decade. Comparing the architecture of the European airline system in 1982 with what was achieved by 1992 was simply staggering. Even though the *Financial Times* entered the caveat 'in theory', nevertheless its summary of what Package 3 achieved was still very impressive:

> European airlines will be free to set their own fares from the beginning of next year. They will also be free to fly between any EC country. They will operate under a single EC air licence and from April 1997 they will be free to run domestic services in other member state[s].[46]

These achievements were especially impressive, considering the strength of the embedded position of the flag carriers in 1982, when only two out of the ten Member States favoured reform and the Commission was weak and had little expertise and few resources dedicated to air transport. Nevertheless, it is true that the SEAM had not yet become a reality. Much would depend on how continuing problems with both infrastructure and practices of the flag carriers, which could exclude or overwhelm would-be competitors, were addressed. Much would depend on how the relationship between governments and flag carriers were controlled, especially in the fraught area of subsidies. Much would depend on how and whether the Commission could solve the problem of external relations. And finally much would depend on whether the new system would be exploited by the airlines. Would they actually compete?

8 Impact and developments after Package 3

> There would be no low-cost airlines were it not for deregulation. It would have meant perpetuating flag carriers if deregulation hadn't come about. It is difficult to understate its importance.
>
> Tim Jeans, sometime marketing director Ryanair[1]

Reaction to Package 3 raised a whole series of observations, which were an interesting mixture of cautious optimism and what seemed at the time to be well-warranted pessimism about the chances for improvement in the European airline system. 'Not Liberal Enough?' was the way *Flight International* greeted Package 3 and 'Clouds over open skies' and 'Softly, softly on EC fares' were story lines in the *Financial Times*.[2] The recession was biting deep and creating financial problems for the airlines that inhibited expansion onto new routes. In 1991, the combined losses of European airlines exceeded $1.3 billion. More specific things that inhibited change were the high costs of launching new routes because of airport and rising navigational charges, lack of available slots and the negative impact on airline finances of the costs of denied boarding compensation, the threat of adding VAT to the cost of airline tickets, the removal of revenue through the phasing out of duty-free shopping and the idea of a 3 per cent carbon tax. There were also fears that flag carriers would use the transition period to consolidate their positions even further and that individual Member States would not apply the licensing provisions of Package 3 in the spirit that they were intended, that they would continue to provide state aids, that they would use the public service provisions imaginatively, that they would object to competitive fares and that they would generally foot-drag on liberalization. Sir Michael Bishop of BM cautioned: 'There is still a long way to go before European carriers can enjoy the practical benefits of highly competitive low-cost air travel and we should not underestimate the difficulties of implementing the package'.[3]

These cautions were well founded. The recession did have a negative impact on the chances for liberalization, but it did not last for ever. Costs did remain high, burdens were added to the industry and revenue-gaining possibilities were removed with the phasing out of duty-free shopping. There was further consolidation such as the financial stake taken in Sabena by Air France, and airline cooperative practices through alliances, code sharing and FFPs posed competitive challenges for the smaller airlines and for the regulators. Licensing and establishment rights caused problems periodically, for example, with regard to access for BA to Orly airport in 1995, even after the European Court of Justice had ruled in 1994 that France must open up its domestic routes to competition.[4] However, there is a danger of losing perspective here. As we shall see later in this chapter, the European airline system did develop and move forward between 1993 and 2000, and the Commission tried to keep the momentum going with its White Paper on Transport in 2001, which set out further ambitions and targets for transport in general.[5] The SEAM was generally a success story, and actors such as Ryanair and EasyJet, which were later to drive competition forward aggressively by exploiting to the hilt the new industry structure created by the Commission, had already arrived on the scene.[6] Success of liberalization was tangible and real by 2000, but there had been, and continued to be in some cases, substantial problems that needed to be addressed. These were subsidies, slot availability, ATC provisions, strategies of the major airlines which still challenged the ability of others to compete effectively and external relations.[7] It is important to look at the first four here in order to grasp the magnitude of the problems that remained before examining the analyses of what the SEAM had achieved by 2000. In Chapter 9, we shall turn to examine the last major remaining and most persistent problem – external relations.

Subsidies

Subsidies was the most troubling and controversial issue of the early years of the SEAM.[8] They were politically highly sensitive on both sides of the divide, and many thought that the Community's provisions for dealing with them were far too flexible. However, even Leon Brittan recognized that some help would have to be given to the airlines because of the extraordinary circumstances brought on by the Gulf War. He acknowledged that capacity would have to be reduced and was prepared to look at fare changes and joint ventures. Even state subsidies would be considered, though not at the expense of unduly distorted competition 'to the detriment of consumers and airlines whose governments do not think that giving subsidies is an appropriate response to the current problems'.[9] As the flow of demands for state aid became a torrent, Brittan's position hardened, but Van Miert felt that some accommodation had to be made. Political pressures were too great to resist, and if the Commission had tried to do so, it could have politically endangered the whole liberalization programme.

There was no specific legislation on state aid for airlines. The matter was dealt with under the authority of Articles 92 and 93 of the Treaty of Rome and guidelines laid down in both the Commission's 1984 Memorandum 2 on aviation and further elaboration on those during 1992 and 1993.[10] Prior to liberalization, state subsidies had not been a major issue, but as John Steele now pointed

Table 8.1 State aid 1991–95 (£ million)

1991	Sabena	584
1992	Air France	665
1992	Iberia	670
1993	Aer Lingus	170
1994	Tap-Air Portugal	710
1994	Olympic Airways	995
1994	Air France	2,400
1995	Iberia	445[1]

Note
1 H. Stevens, *Liberalization of Air Transport in Europe: a Case Study in European Integration*, London, European Institute, LSE, 1997, pp. 5, 10–11, citing 'Aviation State Aid' briefing by UK Department of Transport, 5 October 1995, similar figures except expressed in ecus may be found in K. Button et al., *Flying Into the Future: Air Transport Policy in the European Union*, Cheltenham, Edward Elgar, 1998.

out 'as the single market takes shape, hidden subsidies are coming to count for more'.[11] He was right, but the situation of the airlines in the early 1990s was such that open calls for subsidies became commonplace. Air France, Sabena and Iberia led the way in demanding large subsidies and provoked outrage among private airlines and those most robustly in favour of liberalization. In July 1992, Van Miert asked his fellow commissioners to approve a £670 million subsidy for Iberia. Brittan opposed, but he was the only one to do so. This in fact was just one of many huge hand-outs approved between 1991 and 1995 (Table 8.1).

By September 1993, the movement for subsidies had not only increased in momentum, but it was also beginning to carry a more general intent to put the breaks on, or even reverse, liberalization. In the *Daily Telegraph* on 25 September 1993, there was an article headed 'Sabena leads move against open skies'.[12] There was also concern among reformers about the committee of twelve wise men – *Le Comité des Sages* – set up by the Commission in July 1993 to examine the present and future of European airlines. Chaired by Herman de Croo of Belgium, the committee in addition to the liberal inclinations of its chairman had only two self-evidently pro-competition members, Geoffrey Lipman, President of the World Travel and Tourism Council, and Pieter Bouw, Chairman of KLM. Many of the representations made before the committee were critical of liberalization. Bernard Attali of Air France went so far as to baldly claim 'deregulation [sic] has not worked'.[13]

In the end, the apprehensions of liberals about the *Comité* proved unfounded. Its report, issued in January 1994, was unambiguous in its general support of liberalization.[14] 'The *Comité* firmly advises against any rollback of liberalisation. This would be inappropriate and self-defeating. It would render the global competitiveness impossible.'[15] The general tenor of the report was clear, even though there were still two ideologically opposed camps for and against liberalization led respectively by Britain and France. A heading in the *Financial Times* read '"Wise men" favour open skies policy'.[16] The report called for the full implementation of the three packages, with reliance on the safeguards therein agreed and the termination of any special treatment for flag carriers. There was, however, a little more of the devil inserted into the detail by the conservative camp, particularly on state aids.

> For a brief transitional period, however, the *Comité* reluctantly recognises the need for some states to act on a genuine 'one time, last time' opportunity to put airlines on a normal commercial footing. The reasons for granting exceptions are essentially political.[17]

At least one could not fault the committee for its honesty. State hand-outs were justified as one-off financial events that were supposed to restructure the ailing airline in question, make it competitively fit and suitable for privatization, though this latter possibility was not a compulsory requirement for receiving state aid. The subsidy packages were supposed to accord with normal commercial practices and market investor principles. The reality however was difficult to assess. From one perspective, financial bail-outs instead of preparing airlines for competition simply seemed to featherbed them in their uncompetitive ruts, reward their inefficiency and grant them unfair advantages vis-à-vis other European airlines. The Commission did strive to link approval of capital injections into state airlines to obligations of the host Member State to move forward on liberalization, for example with France in 1995 when there were major problems in trying to prise open the dominant domestic position of Air France.[18] Most galling of all for the liberalizers was that some airlines and governments seemed incapable of understanding what 'one' and 'last time' actually meant. For those who favoured the development of a competitive market, the string of state aids and what appeared to be the weakness of the Commission were deeply troubling and disillusioning. And indeed difficulties with state ownership and state aids continued well beyond the spate of capital injections between 1991 and 1995. For example, Christian Blanc, in rather stark contrast to his predecessor Bernard Attali as head of Air France, resigned in September 1997 when the incoming socialist government reneged on previously given pledges on privatization that had been made in the wake of financial help for the airline. The new French Government refused to proceed down the path of privatization.[19] And, in 2003, the Commission took Olympic Airways to the European Court of Justice because it refused to comply with the Commission's decision in 2002 on state aid.[20]

But, in fact, all that extravagant expenditure on inefficient state airlines in the 1990s sensitized many to the benefits of liberalization. Gaining state support for airlines proved in the end to be a Pyrrhic victory in more ways than one: some just did not get any better and continued to distort competition and supply excess capacity and that provided further ammunition to those who wanted to stop subsidies altogether. As time passed, the Commission displayed, to the surprise of some, growing resolution. This shift was not entirely voluntary. The British Government helped with its fulminations against subsidies as did a legal case brought by BM, BA, KLM and SAS to the European Court of Justice in

1994 against the Commission's approval of state aid for Air France. As one Brussels official put it at the time: 'If nothing else, this legal challenge is likely to stiffen the Commission's spine and toughen its attitude over future applications for state aid'.[21] In the summer of 1998, the Court declared the Commission's approval illegal, and both Commissioners Van Miert and Kinnock seemed rather pleased.[22] Attitudes to the whole issue of state aid gradually hardened. Parallel to the development of this hardening were gradual moves towards privatizing European airlines. That momentum stalled in France, but by the end of the 1990s, BA as a privately owned airline had been joined by KLM and Luxair, and state holdings in SAS, Lufthansa and Austrian Airlines had been reduced respectively to 50, 52 and 52 per cent. By March 1997, even someone as generally sceptical about European liberalization as Michael Bishop felt able to say: 'We're seeing much greater scrutiny of state aid. It's not being squeezed out, but it will be over the next two or three years'.[23] His prediction turned out to be pretty accurate.

When the post-9/11 recession hit the airlines, the Commission was less generous than that bastion of deregulation the US in what it was prepared to do to help the airlines financially. In the twelve months following 9/11, the US government in response to nearly $10 billion of losses and the shedding of 90,000 jobs in the US airline industry provided $5 billion of cash aid and guarantees for $10 billion of loans, and in 2002 the Congress passed the Terrorism Risk Insurance Act by which the US Government provided insurance cover to US airlines for terrorist attacks.[24] In contrast, the Commission was tired of its ailing airlines and, though the words would never be publicly spoken, the post-9/11 recession was not altogether unwelcome because it would now force some European airlines to the wall or into mergers and takeovers. This was a process of consolidation that many in DG TREN (DG 7) and the DG for Competition (DG 4) believed was necessary if European airlines were to become more effective and competitive and were to survive not just in Europe but in the global marketplace.[25]

Soon after 9/11, the *Observer* reported that the European Transport Commissioner, Loyola de Palacio, was strident in insisting that there would be no 'government rescues for stricken airlines. There must be a shake-out of the industry, with weaklings going bust or being bought out and the stronger becoming bigger and taking on the world'. 'A market such as air transport is a global one, competing with the great US and Asian carriers. We need in Europe, also, world-size carriers which can compete'.[26] Some relief was provided in Europe by governments, for example, the Commission allowed Member States to compensate their airlines for their losses during the four days immediately following 9/11, and there was also help with insurance and security costs, airlines were allowed to hold on to valuable slots even though they were not being used because of capacity reductions and the imposition of VAT on aviation fuel was delayed.[27] All this was much less than aid provided to US airlines and did not prevent Sabena becoming the first Community flag carrier to disappear: it did so within three months of 9/11.[28] Later, there were also mergers, the most important

154   Impact and developments after Package 3

of which was KLM with Air France. The process of the demise or merger/takeover of state-owned national flag carriers in Europe had begun. This process had been deemed to be a political impossibility a bare twenty years before when liberalization began: both the ECAC COMPAS and the European Parliament Klinkenborg report had declared the political impossibility of a national flag carrier being allowed to fail or to be taken over by a rival.[29] They were wrong: state aids, and the status and protection of national flag carriers were gradually becoming phenomena of a bygone age.

Take-off and landing slots

Slots proved to be a more enduring problem than state subsidies and for many a more serious one for obstructing competition. In Richard Branson's opinion: 'The clearest demonstration of the nature of barriers to new entrants is to be found in the rules governing the allocation between airlines of airport take-off and landing slots in Europe.'[30]

Until the Commission entered this fraught area of airline operations, the world's slot allocation regime was coordinated through IATA and its Scheduling Guidelines, which essentially worked in favour of the major scheduled airlines and helped to consolidate their dominance over the years through the grandfather principle: use of a slot in the past established the right to use it in the future. At congested airports, this created a major entry obstacle for both new competitors and for established privately owned airlines that wanted to expand. Under pressure from liberalizers, IATA modified its guidelines marginally in 1991 in order to give more priority to new entrants, but this was really only a placatory nod in the direction of trying to deal with the problem. The Commission had struggled to introduce a more liberal version of the IATA regime in Package 3 but, when confronted with implacable opposition, had been forced to abandon it. It was not easy to recommend even modest reform when that would put Europe under a different regime to IATA's and when interoperability between the two regimes was essential.[31] The opposition often couched its objections in mild and accommodating language, but insistence on keeping the grandfather principle provided them with an impenetrable defence.[32] Nevertheless, negotiations continued, and by the end of 1992, the Commission succeeded in getting the Council of Ministers to approve Regulation 95/93 promulgating common rules for the allocation of slots at Community airports, and in July 1993, bloc exemption from the competition rules was granted for the collusion necessary for implementing them.[33]

The Regulation required congested airports to have a scheduling committee and an independent coordinator whose job would be to apply the rules transparently and impartially. It required the Member States to take action at congested airports, provided a legally binding set of rules for slot allocations and went some way beyond IATA guidelines for prioritizing slots for new entrants. But this regime, while a step forward, was not radical. The Commission had had to recognize the grandfather principle, which lay at the heart of the old conservative regulatory slot system. After conceding that, only tweaking at the margins of the problem was possible. Once an airport was designated as 'fully coordinated' because of congestion and allocation problems, then any slot not utilized 80 per cent of the time would be tossed into a pool for reallocation by the coordinator. Up to 50 per cent of that pool would then have to be reallocated to new entrants if there were demand from them. Unfortunately, the pools remained small and populated by unwanted off-peak slots. A new entrant was defined as an airline with less than 2 or 3 per cent respectively of an airport or airport system's daily slots. The *Comité des Sages* claimed that the rules set 'out common rules aimed at ensuring neutral, transparent and non-discriminatory decisions on the allocation of slots at congested airports'.[34] And one could agree with that with certain *caveats*, but the essential point was that the new regime only released a modest amount of unattractive slots for reallocation. The system might now be fairer, but with limited and low-quality raw material to work on little could be achieved. And at times, even the fairness of the operation of the new system came under question. Many major European airports found reasons to deny slots to would-be competitors for their flag carriers. In 1997, Virgin Express executive Jonathan Ornstein complained of the difficulties in getting slots at Brussels airport even though it was 'an airport where you can fire a canon down the runway most of the time without hitting anything'.[35]

The only occasions when the Commission had any really significant impact on the distribution of slots were in cases of cooperation and merger agreements where it stepped in to prevent increasing market dominance through concentration of slots in limited hands. Cases where it acted thus include BA and both B.Cal. and TAT; Air France and both UTA and Sabena; and KLM and Transavia.[36] Also notable was the demand for the release of slots at Gatwick and Heathrow as a condition for the BA alliance with AA in 1996: the price of giving up 267 slots, as demanded by the Commission, was considered too high and was one of the two deciding factors in the failure of the proposed alliance.[37] Attempts like this by the Commission to open up congested airports caused widespread anger and resentment among the old flag carriers. Jürgen Weber, Chairman of Lufthansa, argued: 'We cannot be expected to be weak in our home markets and at the same time act as world-class players in global competition'.[38] Once again, the requirements for competition in Europe, as seen by the Commission, and competition in the global marketplace, as seen by the major airlines, collided.

Slot reallocation remained a fraught issue. Disagreements abounded on a whole range of issues, but the two fundamental problems were the extent to which the grandfather principle should be modified and which underlying principle should inform any procedure for the redistribution of slots: should it be along market lines or according to some concept of the public good and operating needs? The Commission took exception to those who wanted to introduce a purely commercial market for slots. Van Miert in a speech in early 1998 observed: 'Some people say that trading is the best solution because the slots will be bought by the most efficient companies. Is this necessarily so? What about smaller carriers which do not have deep pockets?'[39] BA did have deep pockets, and four years later, it busied itself paying small airlines like Lithuanian Airlines to move from Heathrow to Gatwick so that it could take over their slots.[40] The Commission thought that 'the slot allocation system should be considered as a system whereby the slots are allocated as public goods, based on certain rules, to the most deserving air carrier'.[41] This highlighted a serious problem that not only divided the Commission from the major airlines, but also from those states that generally favoured liberalization: they favoured a market style solution to the slot allocation problem whereas the Commission feared that that would simply allow the dominant carriers to wield their financial strength, dip into deep pockets and become even more dominant, as BA was busy doing in 2002 at Heathrow.

In fact, although Weber and other major airline executives were troubled by what the Commission was trying to do with slot allocation, the changes wrought by Regulation 95/93 had only had minor impact. However, the Regulation required that there should be further monitoring of slot allocation policy, and as a result, Coopers and Lybrand was commissioned to carry out an analysis. It reported in 1995, and its findings were largely supported by a later report by Price-Waterhouse-Cooper in May 2000.[42] Both saw the need for further reform and clarification. In the debates that followed, there were dire warnings from the flag carriers and the AEA about the threat to the major carriers that slot redistribution posed. Karl-Heinz Neumeister of the AEA emphasized the extent of potential damage if there were a 'gradual withdrawal of grandfather rights, exclusion of alliance partners from new entrant status and confiscation of slots held by incumbent carriers'.[43]

By the time the Commission made proposals to the Council of Ministers to amend Regulation 95/93 in 2001, it was clear that radical change was not possible. A number of issues were dealt with, for example, there were ongoing problems with the legal status of slots. Were they something that airlines could own? And there were several other questions about how effectively some Member States implemented the Regulation, the designation status of major European airports, the independence of coordinators, and the way coordinating committees operated. But the fundamental problem was still recognized to be that grandfather rights were too inflexible and that they prevented striking the right balance between 'incumbent air carriers and new entrants at congested airports'.[44] The rule of use it 80 per cent of the time or lose it was proving to be decreasingly effective as slots were traded between alliance members to avoid them falling into the redistribution pot. Start-up and independent airlines thus continued to have a hard time. Unfortunately, the Commission could find little that was politically acceptable for solving any of the substantial problems that afflicted the distribution of slots.

On 21 April 2004, the Council finally promulgated Regulation 793/2004 to replace 95/93. It did little to improve the situation and did marginally less than the Commission had asked for.[45] Differences among the Member States and between them and the Commission and the essentially intractable nature of the problem of slots severely limited what could be done to improve the situation. Generally, the new Regulation sought to ensure the independence of coordinators, clarify the legal status of slots – they could not be owned or bought and sold by airlines – and link the problem of slots with the possibility of further improving ATC. More specifically, the Commission had thought that there might be a profitable trade-off between quantity and quality of slots in the redistribution pool that would help new entrants and the smaller airlines. In the aftermath of the Coopers and Lybrand Report, it had considered reducing the percentage of slots in the pool earmarked for new entrants from 50 to 30 per cent, but only if that 30 per cent were of improved quality: they would not be for off-peak times of marginal commercial value.[46] In the event, the percentage remained at 50. The Commission had also proposed that a 7 per cent slot holding would be a more realistic cut-off point for defining new entrants. The new Regulation did move the percentages below which airlines would be considered to be a new entrant, but only from 2 to 4 per cent and from 3 to 5 per cent respectively for airports and airport systems.[47] There remained so many contentious and conflicting views among the Member States that in fact no really substantial improvement to the system was possible. Officials at DG TREN in September 2006 observed that the number of slots coming under the auspices of the reallocation rules was still only a small percentage of the slots needed by airlines seeking better competitive positions and that the Commission continued to struggle to find a better solution to the problem. Slot policy was again in the autumn of 2006 under Commission review and among other issues that of selling and buying slots was revisited, partly because the major airlines have drastically shallower pockets than they used to have and 'newcomers' have substantially deeper pockets than they used to have.[48] Nevertheless, the slot redistribution problem currently abides as a serious obstacle to greater competition. As a report for DG TREN put it in 2005, since 2001 'no groundbreaking reform of the slot allocation [system has] been achieved', and little looked likely to happen until 2007 or 2008.[49]

Controlling the traffic

In July 1992, Pieter Bouw of KLM claimed that ATC in Europe was 'the greatest source of concern for the European air transport industry'.[50] Delays in European airline operations in 1991 were 21 per cent up on the previous year with an accumulated 106,000 hours of delays.[51] In 1961, EUROCONTROL had been set up to try to develop a single sky in Europe for commercial aviation that would operate according to the needs of scheduled international routes and not national boundaries, but even after expanding from its initial membership of 6 to embrace most European states, it still had little power of enforcement and was worryingly ineffective. A year before Bouw spoke out, Van Miert had bemoaned the lack of power in EUROCONTROL, the lack of political will among its members to do something effective about ATC and lack of effective participation by the EC. The Director General of EUROCONTROL, Keith

Mack, responded with characteristic institutional jealousy and with emphasis on the international as opposed to any sense of supranationalism in EUROCONTROL. He did not favour EC membership because that would produce double representation for its member states and also he asserted that the EC did not have the expertise required for effective action in this sphere.[52] EUROCONTROL had launched a major new initiative in 1990, the European Air Traffic Control Harmonisation and Integration Programme (EATCHIP), and, working closely through ECAC, $3.6 billion were approved in March 1992 for the implementation stages of the programme.[53] But many in Europe were still profoundly dissatisfied with ATC arrangements.

The *Comité des Sages* was particularly outspoken in 1993. 'The anachronistic fragmentation of the European ATC system is a serious problem indeed'. 'The *Comité* deplores the lack of political willingness by the EU Council of Transport Ministers to tackle this ATC problem with the urgency needed'.[54] Delays cost European airlines dearly, and those costs came on top of European navigational and airport user charges that were higher than in the US and amounted to 13.5 per cent of total airline operating costs. National sovereignty in Europe posed problems not encountered in the US, and air space reserved for military flights was also more complex and intrusive. Something better than EATCHIP was needed, so far as the *Comité des Sages* was concerned, because while it represented 'an essential step towards improving Europe's ATC system in a pragmatic way ... there is no alternative to a truly Single European Air Traffic Management System'.[55]

The calls from the *Comité des Sages* went largely unheeded, and only incremental reform and improvement took place for most of the 1990s. Closer cooperation between the EU and EUROCONTROL did develop, and Directive 93/65 enabled the Commission to adopt standards laid down by EUROCONTROL, and in 1995 the inception of further cooperation through the introduction of the Central Flow Management Unit (CFMU) was to lay an important platform for future performance improvements. However, for that to be effective, there would have to be more robust implementation powers. In 1997, with that aim in mind, EUROCONTROL embarked on self-reform, but with only limited success. As the AEA pointed out, observers would be disappointed because the member states of the organization failed to 'agree to pool sovereignty, or allow it to be exercised collectively on their behalf by EUROCONTROL'.[56] The only significant change was a move from unanimity to weighted majorities in decision-making.[57] Notwithstanding disappointment with these reforms, the EU decided the following year to press forward with negotiations for membership. The pace of development picked up in 1999, partly due to the ATC problems that the crisis in Kosovo produced, and partly because of the vigour of the new Transport Commissioner Loyola de Palacio and the Commission's publication of COM(1999)614 Final, calling for 'The Creation of the Single European Sky'.[58]

Action was still desperately needed. Michael Ayral noted in a speech in Maastricht in February 2000 that in ECAC 'Ministers have noted that the current delay situation is most unsatisfactory and that further measures will be necessary to respond to [the] demand'.[69] About 350,000 hours of flying time were now being wasted in Europe each year because of delays and non-optimal routing, though not all of the delays were by any means solely generated by ATC difficulties. Between 1991 and 1999, delays in Europe had risen from 12.7 per cent of movements in 1991 to 30.3 per cent in 1999.[60] Thereafter, delays in commercial flight operations continued to fluctuate. They declined from 21.6 to 18.2 per cent respectively in August 1999 and August 2000.[61] They rose again in 2001 and then dropped back. In the face of these costs and inefficiencies and EUROCONTROL's seeming inability to cope with them effectively in its then present form, political views finally began to coalesce in favour of reform. The Commission's Single European Sky initiative garnered support in the Parliament and in the Council of Ministers, and in November 2000, the High Level Group appointed by the Council issued its report.[62] In its forward, Commissioner Loyola de Palacio wrote of two overriding priorities:

> ... we face the challenge of organising the involvement of the military air traffic control service in the single sky. We will need the continued interest and support of the highest political authorities to build adequate structures that enable military air traffic authorities to gain confidence and to work closer together with their civilian counterparts. Second we must develop synergies with Eurocontrol as well as the Community's own capabilities to establish an agenda for reform and to implement changes.[63]

On 8 October 2002, the EU joined EUROCONTROL, and this eased the way for closer cooperation and for more effective action. By 2003, EUROCONTROL was claiming that 'delays attributable to air traffic management have been virtually eliminated'.[64] And indeed progress was now evident, although there had also been a significant reduction in flights because of the accumulated impact of 9/11, the SARS virus and the war in Afghanistan and from March 2003 in Iraq as well. On 22 December 2003, a Memorandum of Cooperation covering implementation of the Single European Sky, research and development, data collection and analysis, satellite navigation and international cooperation was signed. These developments, culminating in a new legal framework for the 'single sky' in 2004, have greatly eased Europe's ATC problems in terms of delays, but costs are still high, and there is still fragmentation and need for more effective technology and computer software.[65] In 2004, with the fastest annual growth rate in traffic since 1999, delays were at an all-time low.[66] Since then, ATC delays have increased again, but not dramatically so, and the EU continues to make advances to improve the coherence and effectiveness of the system, harmonize technology through the Single European Sky Implementation Programme (SESAME), create a single framework and 'provide integrated seamless air traffic management'.[67] Between June and August 2006, over 13 per cent of all flights suffered some delay, and the average air traffic flow management delay (ATFM, the time between the aircraft's last request for a take-off time and the time finally allocated) was 2.6 minutes up from 2.3 minutes the previous year.[68] There is no doubt that concerted efforts by EUROCONTROL and the EU to improve traffic flows have met with substantial success, but as EUROCONTROL, itself, acknowledges:

> In spite of much effort to modernise and streamline it, Europe's air traffic management system remains safe but fairly costly. It is also hampered by heterogeneous working practices and constrained air route networks, which in the main, are based on national borders and not traffic air flows.[69]

Clearly some problems remain, and there is still only an ineffective framework for dealing with the problem of air space for military use. Nevertheless, a report commissioned for DG TREN reported in 2005 that ATC development and reform were 'on track' to achieve the goals laid down in the Commission's 2001 White Paper on transport.[70]

Dangers from anti-competitive airline strategies

Of the strategies of the major airlines which posed challenges for the Commission's vision of a competitive SEAM, the story of alliances, mergers, takeovers, code sharing and FFPs is the most important. It is also deeply complicated and spills over as an issue into the realm of external relations. The flurry of activity for repositioning by the major airlines began well before the delivery of Package 3 and was largely driven by global strategy as even the largest airline in the world, UA, realized that it alone was incapable of dealing on its own with the vast potential of the global market. What followed was a series of relationships that varied in their intensity, often dependent upon tactical considerations, but more often on what regulators would permit. For example, over the years AA and BA were never granted anti-trust immunity, which prevented the kind of code-sharing partnership that would have produced great efficiencies in marketing, coordination and mutual feeder services: UA and Lufthansa on the other hand were granted immunity, and they went on to form the heart of the Star Alliance in May 1997. In Europe, immediately before and in the wake of Package 3, parallel strategies to those first seen in the US developed with increasing momentum. BA set up Deutsche BA and took over the French airline TAT in order to operate more effectively in Germany and France respectively. It also at various times courted different partners in Europe, notably Sabena and KLM, but without success. Lufthansa and Air France acted in a similar manner, but none of the consolidation that happened really substantially changed the architecture of aviation in Europe, and certainly the impact was negligible compared with that of the no-frills airlines which were soon to revolutionize the European airline system. Of more impact than takeovers and mergers in Europe were alliances of global scope.

Alliances are generally seen as a second-best alternative to mergers and takeovers, but with national pride in European airlines still strong and with insuperable legal difficulties preventing transatlantic mergers, alliances with coordinated schedules, code sharing, joint marketing, common FFPs and other cooperative arrangements became of great significance and were attractive to European and US airlines alike as well as to the travelling public. Prima facie, however, alliances would appear to epitomize old cartel-type operations and hence anti-competitive practices. One of the reasons that the regulators insisted on a price for their alliance, which BA and AA considered unacceptable, was fear about its impact on competition. BA and AA in a close knit alliance would have dominated 70 per cent of the transatlantic market. But from another perspective, alliances helped to overcome artificial barriers erected in the marketplace by nation states with their sovereign air space. In particular, they help to overcome the problem of the exclusion of foreign airlines from domestic feeder services for international flights. This was why there was a widespread view that the BA-US Air Alliance formed in 1992 'could become a watershed in overcoming protectionism' because US Air would provide BA with US domestic feed for its transatlantic flights.[71] The later alliance between UA and Lufthansa was also designed to overcome each others' feeder problems for transatlantic flights and it diminished the attractiveness of setting up 5th freedom operations because each partner in their home base was in a much better and more efficient position for providing onward connections to third-party destinations. Thus, alliances made operations more seamless, efficient and cheaper and opened up new markets and, according to many, contributed to competition rather than detracting from it. Certainly, a report authored largely by Randy Bennett of the US Department of Transportation favoured that view, but for the agnostic some doubts might abide.[72] A more rounded account of the impact of alliances might indeed register that they overcome artificial barriers erected in the marketplace by nation states and as such diminish protectionism, but they also pose the problem of cartel dominance and create potential for abuse. How those dangers are handled largely determines whether or not alliances actually increase competition. Alliances in and of themselves are not necessarily a good thing for competition.

The US was quick off the mark to seek better access to the European market before the SEAM came into effect. The US Department of Transportation embarked on a series of open-skies negotiations with the individual Member States, partly to advance its international policy established in the Carter days of deregulation, but also to ensure that the position of US airlines in the EU was not weakened by the SEAM and the assertion of European cabotage. The deal on offer was straightforward: in return for open-skies access, the US would allow alliances with US carriers and grant them anti-trust immunity. This general strategy did not go unnoticed by the Commission, but it was not aware of specific negotiations, particularly those with the Netherlands that dramatically delivered the first US–European open-skies agreement. The first that Van Miert heard about it was 'from the Americans'.[73] On 4 September 1992, Jan Weck and Carl Cundiff, respectively for the Netherlands and the US, signed the first of what was to be many open-skies agreements between the US and the Member

States of the European Union. These agreements offered free fare setting, capacity and access (except for cabotage) and encouraged commercial cooperation between airlines to the extent that both sides committed themselves to 'provide fair and expeditious consideration to any such agreements or arrangements filed for approval and anti-trust immunity'.[74] By October 2000, even France came to agreement with the US, which then had twenty open-skies agreements in Europe.[75] The only significant Member State to resist open-skies courtship was Britain. These open-skies agreements enabled the emergence of powerful alliances in the 1990s between KLM and Northwest Airlines, Lufthansa and UA and between Delta, Austrian Airlines, Sabena and Swissair, though the latter's wings came off at the end of the decade to be replaced with ties between Delta, Continental and Air France. AA also developed its alliance, though, as we have noted, its ability to get close to BA was restricted by the regulators and compromised by the failure of Britain and the US to consummate an open-skies agreement. Nevertheless, the formation of the Star Alliance with UA and Lufthansa at its heart and Oneworld headed by AA and BA were formidable formations. The US Department of Transportation credited them with bringing fares down on transatlantic routes, increasing passenger numbers faster than non-alliance operators, creating greater efficiencies and delivering more seamless travel.[76]

> Alliance-based networks are the principal driving force behind transatlantic price reductions and traffic gains. The 'Alliance Network Effect' will therefore play a key role in the evolving international aviation economic and competitive environment.[77]

But from the perspective of the Commission, all was not quite so rosy. There had always been concerns about the market being allowed to have its way, especially if that led to dominant positions. In 1990, Argyris urged the need for 'effective safeguards against anti-competitive behaviour' in the same breath that he noted that since 1978, the US authorities have not opposed 'a single merger'.[78] By September 2001, alliances were causing real concern in the Commission. The Star Alliance 'is virtually squeezing out other US carriers' and 'was reducing or eliminating competition in a large part of the European market'. At the time, Austrian Airlines was looking for a new alliance partner and was eventually drawn into the Star Alliance. The Commission would have much preferred it to have gone into the Oneworld Alliance: 'But we cannot say it'.[79] And while a senior BA official termed the Star Alliance a 'basket case' in February 2002 because he thought it was volatile, the figures for alliances tell an undeniable tale: the Star Alliance with nineteen members and the largest geographical embrace with airlines from Africa, Latin America, North America, Europe, Asia and New Zealand reaps 25 per cent, Sky Team 19 per cent and Oneworld 14 per cent of total global airline revenue, i.e. collectively not far short of 60 per cent of the world's total.[80]

Alliances posed a growing problem in Europe, and opinion was and is divided. In February 2002, Sorensen observed that 'the old Articles 88 and 89

... are rather cumbersome to apply' in this area and that there 'has also been a certain hesitation of uncertainty as to what to do about these alliances because they are much bigger than what we've seen so far in aviation'.[81] This is not to say that the Commission has not acted when it has seen dangers of dominant positions compromising competition, and the requirements laid down for the BA–AA alliance is good evidence of that, and also in 2006 the SkyTeam alliance was under scrutiny by the Commission.[82] The Commission's general policy of promoting transparency also helped to clarify things such as code-sharing agreements so that passengers knew beforehand exactly what was involved in terms of change of aircraft and carrier. Nevertheless, Commission, like US, officials see alliances generally as a positive thing and one that will gradually give way to takeovers and mergers, and indeed within Europe, there is now evidence of that. For similar developments involving the major transatlantic alliances, the law, particularly in the US, will have to be changed, but if it were that also could lead to further transnational consolidations in the airline industry. The Commission appears confident that it could police such developments. Its reasoning is that dominant carriers are not a problem, provided the regulators can prevent them from abusing their positions and that under such guidance they deliver a more competitive, efficient and seamless service. Even if an OAA were consummated between the EU and the US, which lifted restriction on mergers and takeovers, the attitude is: 'they [the Commission] can redress the situation if abuses arise or prevent moves that would be anti-competitive'. They also believe that in an OAA, there would be vastly 'improved contestability'.[83] Others are more sceptical. But this is about as far as the discussion can be taken at this stage without trespassing into the area of external relations and that is the focus of Chapter 9.

The SEAM as a success story

ATC issues, subsidies, scarcity of slots at congested airports, alliances, mergers, takeovers, code sharing and FFPs all posed problems for the Commission's vision of a competitive SEAM. Those were all ongoing operational problems, but there was also a major incompleteness in the SEAM, namely, its external relations. So, clearly, in a very real sense, the SEAM was not completed in 1992. There was still an ongoing task to nurture it and develop it into a fully functioning system. Nevertheless, 1992 was recognized as a turning point, and assessment of what was achieved between 1992 and 2000 indicates just how much of a turning was taken.[84]

Early reports were sanguine about intent and Commission action, but thin on the substance of changes. The Commission noted in June 1994 that European carriers continued to lag behind their US counterparts' productivity levels by a margin of 20 per cent, that fifth freedoms and cabotage rights were little used in the EC and that there was little evidence of increasing multiple designation on European routes. It added rather wistfully that the more competitive structure that had been created might be more vigorously exploited as the airline market recovered from recession.[85] In 1995, a UK CAA report was more up-beat, at least about the decisiveness of the Commission in implementing Package 3: 'overall, liberalisation has been implemented with impressive success'.[86] The *Financial Times* pointed out that the CAA's optimism however was hard to justify 'by results in the market'.[87] It was correct. There had been some improvements among those previously heavily restricted domestic markets such as Germany's and Spain's, BM had sparked some price competition on routes that it operated on and there was a small decline in the dominance of the national carriers, but: 'Most damningly, Europe's notoriously high air fares have been slow to fall'.[88]

The first three years had not been very auspicious, but things were about to change. First of all, the industry was finally emerging from recession and secondly it was on the cusp of a dramatic change that was to be injected into the system by no-frills, low-cost airlines. There had always been the worry among Commission officials that no matter how the system might be changed to be more competition friendly, if the airlines refused to compete it would all be to little avail. A month after the CAA report on the SEAM, Stelios Haji-Ioannou's EasyJet took its first booking. EasyJet along with Ryanair became the no-frills market leaders. In addition to spawning a host of imitators such as Debonair, they also prompted BA to launch Go, KLM to launch Buzz, BM to launch BMI Baby, Virgin to launch Virgin Express and airlines such as Braathens and Maersk Air to develop copycat strategies. By 1998, Ryanair was offering a return fare of £99 for the London-Stockholm route, which compared favourably with BA's return fare of £500. Not surprisingly reports on the success of the SEAM after 1995 became increasingly fulsome in praise of the results of Package 3 and of the way liberalization was delivering results to the industry and to the consumer.

By 1996, routes had increased from 490 in 1993 to 520. Those using promotional fares rose from 60.5 to 70.9 per cent of total passengers over the decade from 1985. Over 30 per cent of routes were now served by two operators and 6 per cent by three or more and 90–95 per cent of passengers were travelling at significantly lower prices than those in 1993. The Commission recognized that more still needed to be done. The price of fully flexible fares, favoured by business people, continued to rise significantly, and there was lack of transparency about how they were set. Infrastructure costs were high at 25 per cent of total airline operating costs and were 40 per cent higher than in the US. Even so, the general feeling was that the internal market was 'flourishing'.[89]

Ironically, even Karl-Heinz Neumeister, Secretary General of AEA, had to concede that progress had indeed been made by the Commission's reforms.

> It is good to remember that in Europe until a decade ago the governments ... controlled the rights of entry, frequency and capacity, allocating only as much to the carrier of the other side as their own national carrier thought it could exploit. The airlines themselves sat in smoke filled conference rooms negotiating everything from tariffs to meal contents and to seat pitch so that

no airline would have a competitive edge. Compared to those days we are now light years away and all the elements required to achieve competition are in place. There are no restrictions on entry, capacity, frequency, tariffs and service conditions.[90]

Further evidence from reports by the UK CAA in 1998 and COM(1999)614 from the Commission in 1999 confirmed that progress had been achieved. The dominance of national carriers in terms of output on all scheduled routes within the EC had declined from 80 to 70 per cent. The number of private scheduled carriers had increased by 24 per cent. Domestic route monopolies had declined from 50 to 25 per cent. Multiple designation throughout the EC had only risen from 4 to 9 per cent by 1999, but on the densest routes the rise was more dramatic from 12 to 26 per cent. The number of routes had increased by 30 per cent. Where there were new entrants prices dropped, elsewhere they tended not to do so, but 'the range of tariffs proposed has widened and most passengers now fly at discount fares'.[91] By 1999, EasyJet was carrying 3.5 million passengers a year and Ryanair six million.[92]

If dramatic changes in prices were the measure of the SEAM's success, then by 2000, it was a success. In February 2000, Michael Ayral, Director for Air Transport in the Commission, expressed this anecdotally at a conference in Maastricht:

> The benefits of liberalisation in the air sector have been remarkable – new low-cost airlines, new routes and schedules etc. In 1992 a return flight from London to Madrid cost 205 euros but only last week one travel agent was selling a similar return flight for 15 euros and to his surprise a prospective customer indicated that he needed time to think about it![93]

The SEAM had indeed progressed well. The changes crafted by Package 3 had created an environment more conducive to competition, and the no-frills airlines were busy exploiting that to the hilt by the turn of the millennium and more was to come. But the SEAM is a dynamic system, and strategies of the major carriers continued to cause concern and many of those strategies connected with the last major incompleteness of the system – external relations. The Commission was well aware of this major defect.

> The Commission's role in regulating ... alliances and developments is becoming ever-more important. While ... Europe's internal market is flourishing the full potential of the changes [created by the SEAM so far] will not be felt so long as their [sic] is no single external market.[94]

9 External relations and the SEAM

> ... even those who dispute the Commission's claim that aspects of aviation negotiations are part of the common commercial policy agree that greater Community involvement in external affairs is inevitable.[1]
>
> One of the lessons we have learnt in Europe is that it is not enough to deregulate only internally. If this industry is going to operate as any other normal business, it requires some major changes to the way it is regulated internationally.[2]

From the mid-1970s, it had been clear that the Commission had ambitions to take over competence in external relations: it had also been clear from that point that the Member States, including those who were later in the vanguard of liberalizations, were opposed to the loss of important foreign policy sovereignty over the negotiation of bilateral ASAs. By 1990, the Commission's formal achievements in this sphere were meagre, amounting to Regulations 69/494 on progressive standardization and 80/50 on consultation procedures.[3] There were a host of reasons for the opposition which had restricted the Commission to such paltry gains. Not all states subscribed to all of them, and the importance they attributed to each varied and changed over time, but collectively they amounted to a formidable obstacle to the progress of the Commission's agenda.

From a practical point of view, was it feasible that the Member States argued for the Commission to negotiate as if the SEAM were a single entity before it was actually completed? And furthermore, what would be the practical consequences of the Commission declaring a SEAM cabotage? Would this be compatible with the existing international aviation system and what impact might those developments have on relations with other countries, particularly the US? Even if the Commission did assume competence over external relations and addressed the issue of an OAA with the US, would a majority of Member States want their airlines to compete in a more open market with the US mega-carriers? There was such apprehension about this in Europe that any EC–US liberalization progress seemed highly unlikely in the 1990s. In the light of that, countries such as Germany, Belgium, Luxemburg and Britain, which were attracted by the lure of open-skies, or at least wanted to change their ASAs with the US, preferred to continue with bilateral negotiations.[4] Certain Member States, including

Britain, were not eager to see Brussels accumulate more power and were sceptical of the prospect of the Commission representing the Member States in international organizations. There were fears, certainly well founded in 1984 and for some time after, that the Commission did not have either the expertise or the person-power to assume responsibilities in external affairs. And finally, possibly the most difficult practical problem for the Commission would be:

> how benefits from any agreement will be shared out and the principles [determined] which would guide regulators when trading rights where benefits and losses fall on different airlines and states. This share of pain and gain is one of the most difficult issues which governments with more than one airline face today.[5]

This kind of gain and pain issue was complicated enough even for single states with a multiple airline industry: for the Commission, with multiple states and multiple airlines to deal with, a nightmare loomed. Those states that were the major players in the airline industry tended to wield the most influence in the sector, and they were fearful about how traffic rights would be distributed by the Commission. As we have seen, the British felt that there were dangers that some of their operations would be redistributed to the carriers of other Member States. Those with the most stood to lose most through any regulatory interference in the distribution of traffic rights. Would the Commission, as negotiator, add value or simply redistribute fixed benefits? Furthermore, there was not only the prospective danger of individual airlines losing out in a Commission distribution regime, there was also the danger that aggregate Community benefits might be eroded in negotiations between the Commission and powerful competitor states, such as the US, if they were not handled skilfully. 'Fixed benefits' might turn out to be diminished benefits. Would the Commission be able to manage and consummate negotiations successfully? Here were very real and substantial problems, which provided ammunition for those resisting the Commission's bid to take control of external relations.[6]

From the Commission's point of view, on the other hand, there was a whole series of compelling arguments why it needed to assume competence over external relations. All the flag carriers made their main profits, not within, but outside the Community. Unlike their main competitors from the US, European airlines had a division of 30 per cent domestic operations to 70 per cent overseas operations: the figures for US airlines were neatly and exactly the reverse.[7] The commercial health of Europe's airlines was largely determined on overseas routes, and that had major implications concerning how they could operate within Europe. Thus, if one carrier was in a privileged position on important external routes vis-à-vis other Community airlines, then prospering on those routes would strengthen its ability to compete within Europe even if its operations there were less efficient and its service standards lower. It could lose money in Europe and still continue to offer capacity there to the detriment of other more efficient carriers because of profits made outside Europe, which would keep it afloat as a company. Tilts in the playing field could not be levelled simply by creating common rules of operation within Europe because the external playing field was tightly hinged to it and was capable of moving the competitive terrain.

In addition to the need for a level playing field, the Commission had arguments derived from the changes that it had introduced both prior to and with the coming of the three packages. The Commission reminded the Member States periodically, for example in September 1989, and in March and July 1990, of their legal obligations under existing Community regulations to consult and coordinate with the Commission concerning external relations and to adjust their ASAs, but it did so without effect.[8] In particular, the replacement of nationality clauses with a community clause that enabled any Member State airline to operate from anywhere to anywhere both within and outside the EU – providing the foreign state in question agreed – opened up some interesting issues. Lufthansa was no longer a German, but a Community airline, just as Sabena, Air France, BA and the others were. Unfortunately, their ASAs with non-Member States all restricted the exchange of commercial rights to airlines substantially owned and controlled by the national citizens of each side. But, Community law now made such agreements discriminatory as between the Member States and therefore illegal. At least that appeared to be the logic of the legal situation, but it was not actually enforced in law for some time. Nevertheless, here was another strong argument to promote the Commission's ambition for control of external relations: it needed to bring all Member States' ASAs into line with Community law.

Finally, the Commission argued that if it were empowered to wield a common negotiating position on behalf of the Community, the position of all would be strengthened. By the autumn of 1992, it could point to the successful conclusion of negotiations with Norway and Sweden for entry into the SEAM, and negotiations with EFTA were well in hand.[9] Here was at least some evidence of Commission negotiating ability. At the same time, the US–Netherlands open-skies agreement exacerbated the fear of the Commission that Member States might be picked off one by one, that individual states would be disadvantaged in such negotiations, that Europe would suffer relatively as a whole and that further discrepancies would arise between the positions of Member States in relation to external commercial relations. In September 1992, the 'Transport Directorate [was] adamant that open-skies negotiations should be carried out at EC level'.[10] As we saw in Chapter 6, at the time of the acceptance of Package 3, all these arguments were to no avail. Nevertheless, even before the Netherlands–US open-skies agreement became public knowledge, the Commission was busy striving yet again to seize the initiative on external relations.

Further commission failures and the rising threat from open-skies agreements

The lack of success of its proposals sent to Council in 1990 as COM(90)17 disappointed the Commission but did not dissuade them from taking further and rather similar action again in the autumn of 1992. It will be recalled that neither the Council nor the European Parliament was convinced by the grounding of the Commission's legal argument on Article 113 for competence over external aviation relations. The Council also wanted a longer transition period than that suggested by the Commission and the establishment of an aviation committee to discuss and advise on issues. Ludolf van Hasselt was largely responsible in the Commission for re-shaping the proposals made in 1990, and he asserted that in their new incarnation, they were 'very pragmatic, setting out procedures to be followed in negotiations rather than grand policy outlines'.[11] The Commission stressed the need for action especially as the development of the internal market had prompted a flurry of negotiating activity with third parties. 'The fact that some fundamental Community principles are endangered by the present situation forces the Community to consider relations with third countries without delay'.[12] The Commission sought to address the existing situation, develop Community policy and devise a transition period. 'A cautious and gradual approach should ensure that the restructuring of the market can take place in a balanced way'.[13] Be that as it may, the proposals actually did not fundamentally differ from those put forward in 1990.

Crucially, the Commission stubbornly insisted on its general competence in virtue of Article 113. More specifically, it also asserted that ASAs fell within the scope of Decision 69/494, derived from the authority of Article 113, and its requirement for notification to and authorization from the Commission for any commercial agreements to be made or extended between Member States and third parties. It proposed a transitional period until 1999, but no longer could ASAs be negotiated without notification and involvement of the Commission. Member States would now have to negotiate according to the following guidelines: they could not negotiate in areas already taken up by the Commission; they would have to be explicitly authorized to conduct negotiations; and any such negotiations would have to be within the parameters of both Community policy and law. A new aviation committee was proposed, which would have input into procedures for bringing existing ASAs into line with Community rules. The Commission repeatedly tried to strike a compromising and accommodating tone, for example acknowledging that even after the Ahmed Saeed case it had not implemented the Community's competition rules to airline routes to third parties, but then went on to argue that this was a major legal concern to it along with nationality clauses in ASAs and future non-discriminatory allocation of traffic rights. It also specifically raised Member State non-compliance with Decision 69/494. It explained that it had refrained from mounting legal infringement procedures for their failure to consult and coordinate with the Commission because it wanted an open debate on external relations, but then went on to wield the threat of legal action. Reminiscent of tactical legal leverage it had introduced at the time of Package 1, the Commission warned that 'in the case that no progress can be made in this area by the end of 1992 the Commission will be obliged to take up its responsibilities without further delay'.[14] Unfortunately for the Commission, none of the Member States accepted the legal arguments about Article 113 and Decision 69/494, and therefore not surprisingly it soon transpired that both the COREPER and the Council remained unmoved by the Commission's legal arguments. The Commission was heading for a massive tactical defeat.

After a preliminary consideration of the Commission's proposals on 7 and 8 December 1992, the Council referred matters to COREPER for detailed consideration. On 4 and 10 March 1993, the COREPER duly examined the proposals in the light of findings by the High Level Group on aviation. At the second meeting, the representatives of the Member States unanimously agreed on draft conclusions to be submitted back to the Council. The findings of the committee were devastating for the Commission's position. Article 84(2) not Article 113 was deemed to be the 'proper basis for an operational development of an external aviation policy'.[15] They agreed with the Commission that pragmatism and cautious and gradual movement were needed in the light of the changes in law that had culminated in Package 3, but then insisted that the legality of existing ASAs must not be challenged, that member States 'shall remain fully responsible for their relations with third countries in the field of aviation unless and until action has been taken by the Council'. Any negotiations authorized by the Council would have to be of a kind where a common interest existed among the Member States and where it was judged that the Commission could conduct things better for such collective good than individual states.[16] The message that went out to the Commission was clear: Member States would not relinquish their prerogatives in the field of external aviation relations. The Commission was told it could continue to work on proposals for procedures on relations with third countries, but only within the constraints of the findings of the COREPER. In effect, there would be further study and talk within the new Aviation Committee that was to be established. As the EC Bulletin put it, the remit of the new committee was to:

- exchange information on a mandatory basis and consult on relations with third countries, provided that business confidentiality is respected;
- investigate areas where Community law might come into conflict with bilateral agreements, or where Member States' respective interests might clash, and any appropriate methods of resolving the conflict;
- define areas of interest common to all Member States prior to undertaking any Community negotiations authorized by the Council.[17]

A few months later, the European Court of Justice, which had been so helpful for the Commission's aviation agenda in the past, also seemed to desert it when it lent its authority and support to the Council by concurring with its reasoning about Articles 113 and 84(2).[18]

The *Comité des Sages* did its best to promote the Commission's case and urged the Council to declare an external relations policy under Article 84(2) of the Rome Treaty.

> The question is ... not whether there should be a common external policy, but what its component elements should be, where and when it should be applied, and how, in particular, to handle the transition from national policies effectively, equitably, without competitive distortion and major disruptions.[19]

Unfortunately, as the *Comité* also observed 'Member States – for a variety of reasons – have so far been reluctant to move forward on this issue'. And current urgings by the *Comité* had little effect in dissipating that reluctance. All the Commission's energy and repeated efforts to move along the track of assuming external competence had barely lifted it off the starting blocks.

The Commission now had to endure a long period of frustration and anger. Transport Commissioner Neil Kinnock became truculent about the lack of progress. He was highly exercised by what he saw as the disadvantages for the Community as the US picked off Member State by Member State in its pursuit of open-skies agreements. In the summer of 1995, he went so far as to declare that those open-skies agreements 'could put in peril the whole of European deregulation'.[20] Throughout the 1980s, the global market share of US airlines had risen steadily, and in the 1990s, they made significant inroads in Europe. By 1995, US percentage of passengers carried between France and the US and Germany and the US had risen respectively since 1978 from 42.5 and 38.3 per cent to 71 and 61 per cent. Apart from the carefully regulated US–UK market, the story was similar throughout much of the EC.[21] Worried by such US encroachments into Europe through their open-skies programme of negotiations, the Council responded to Kinnock's urgings and granted authority to the Commission to explore the possibility of a TCAA. Desultory conversations followed, but the US soon withdrew in April 1997 because of its conviction that it could achieve more through continuing with bilateral negotiations with individual Member States. By the end of 2001, it had twenty open-skies agreements in Europe, including one with France, and only Britain of the major European players had continued to refuse US overtures.[22] At first glance, the fact that Britain refused to enter an open-skies agreement appears rather odd given its vigorous pursuit of liberalization and its constructive role in the creation of the SEAM. And in some ways it was, but the British position was one that was soon to be taken up by the Commission and it thus deserves some attention.

Ever since the negotiation of Bermuda 2 in 1976–77 and the follow-on agreement in 1980, which among other things restricted US carriers at Heathrow to Pan Am and TWA or their corporate successors, the British had held important cards for future negotiations with the US. As Jeffrey Shane of the US Department of Transport commented in the spring of 1991:

> Every city pair market is restricted in terms of entry. Every city pair market is restricted in terms of capacity. Every city pair market is restricted in terms of the fares the airlines may charge the passengers. There is no aspect of the market that is not being regulated pursuant to UK insistence.[23]

There was a note of bitterness in Shane's tone and that was understandable because he spoke shortly after the British had extracted further concessions from the US in the succession rights talks to allow AA and UA to take over from Pan Am. and TWA at Heathrow. The British managed to cap the capacity of the new airlines to that enjoyed by their predecessors for three years, but most significantly they were granted what they assumed at the time to be unrestricted code-sharing rights with US carriers.[24]

Although BA was furious, as we have seen, because the agreement brought strong carriers into Heathrow and UA into direct competition with BA, which among other things undermined their cooperation agreement, BA was in fact in a good position to exploit the new situation. At the time, it was the only major airline making a profit in the recession precipitated by the Gulf crisis and at the time it had almost unbounded ambitions. The corporate strategy was to construct a hub-and-spoke operation throughout the world through its subsidiaries and alliance partners. At various times during the 1990s, BA tried to establish a network of spokes reaching out from Heathrow to KLM/Amsterdam or Sabena/Brussels on the western tip of continental Europe to its subsidiary Deutsche BA's operations in Germany and on to a prospective partner in Moscow. Far East connections would be enhanced through a tie up with Qantas, and to the west there would have to be an alliance with a major US airline. In 1992, US airlines were sinking into deep debt with Delta, US Air, AA and UA together losing somewhere in the region of $2 billion between them in 1992. They were all eager for some cash injection, and after several suitors BA opted for a deal with US Air, from which in return for $750 million it would receive 25 per cent of the company's voting shares, a veto over company policy and the opportunity to code share extensively in order to improve US domestic feed into BA's transatlantic flights. Over the next four years, opposition from the other US airlines, US Air's undistinguished performance and attempts by the US to try to push Britain into an open-skies agreement by only granting code-sharing rights with US Air for one year soured the whole arrangement. The US argued, somewhat disingenuously, that the code-sharing rights agreed to in the Heathrow succession rights talks did not apply to all situations, and BA's 25 per cent equity in US Air was not one of the conditions envisaged. In the end in 1996, the US Air alliance gave way to the attraction of one with AA. However, that also ran into problems with the regulators on both sides of the Atlantic over slots and with the US government's refusal to grant anti-trust immunity to any close alliance involving code sharing and the like, unless it were within the framework of an open-skies regime. This may appear to be something of a diversion from both the external relations of the SEAM and the discussion of Britain's apparently uncharacteristically protectionist position vis-à-vis the US, but in fact it brings us to a position where we can profitably return specifically to both issues and cast light on what were to be major problems in the SEAM's developing relationship with the US.

The British Government's position in Bermuda 2 and thereafter and BA's quest for a close partnership with a US airline arose from the same considerations: access to the vast US market. The Americans always argued that the British were protectionist and the clearest, and for them the most damaging example of this was the refusal to allow free competition into Heathrow. The British response was that they were in favour of competition and if that were also truly the case in the US then why should competition cease at the water's edge? The US had about 40 per cent of the entire world's airline market within its cabotage. The British argued that restricting access to that market was protectionist. This was the issue that had exercised the British Government and BA since 1991 and before. It would soon emerge as a problem for the SEAM as well.

The British had long contended that cabotage allowed US airlines to compete unfairly against foreign airlines because they could draw on their domestic feeder services to supply passengers to their international hubs for on-ward flights across the Atlantic. The US could hub-and-spoke from the US into the international marketplace: no other airline could. BA had tried to overcome these problems by buying into US Air, but US law limited foreign ownership to 25 per cent and had even more stringent rules concerning foreign control. The British thought that they had extracted code-sharing possibilities from the US, and they had, but in the event the US interpretation was more restrictive than the British thought that they had a right to expect. The US insisted on wedding open-skies agreements and anti-trust immunity for close knit alliances. The British and BA in the end, in the context of their proposed alliance with AA, were sceptical of the price that would have to be paid for open-skies in the long-run. They felt that the advantages that abided for the US in its vast protected market were too great and feared that foreign partners of US airlines would never be in charge of their own destiny: US airlines could always pull out of alliances if results were turning out to be overly favourable to their foreign partners. The British were also irritated by what they saw as hubris in the US position with their Fly America Program, the operation of the Civil Reserve Air Fleet (CRAF) for military purposes, which was worth $2 billion a year to US carriers, their prohibitions on wet-leasing and their stringent ownership and control regulations.

Such concerns were shared by the Commission. In 1997, it decided it must begin to address them and once again asked for empowerment in applying competition rules externally.[25] The Council in its turn again refused to act, but it could not quell the Commission's ambitions. If anything they became even more expansive. The Commission began to think increasingly in terms of symmetrical bargaining with the US on the basis of a European cabotage position, and as more and more open-skies agreements were struck by Member States it became ever more concerned that aspects of the new agreements both weakened the European hand and were contrary to Community law. In April 1998, Karel Van Miert, who was then the Commissioner for Competition, explained the Commission's concerns.

> Companies are now adopting global strategies to market their products and services. For antitrust enforcement, this presents the challenge of having to

> deal with competition problems on a geographically much wider, global scale. I am thinking in particular of 'global alliances' between EU and US carriers. These are often presented as code-sharing arrangements. In fact, the airlines decide to co-operate on fares, frequencies, schedules, relationships with travel agencies, etc. Actually these alliances are often very similar to mergers. The companies in fact operate on the market like one entity and eliminate all competition between them. These alliances raise new, important and difficult competition issues.[26]

Of course, these transatlantic alliances came on the back of open-skies agreements between the Member States and the US, but the Commission rightly viewed them as 'contrary to the basic principle of the single market and [that] they should be replaced by an EU–US open skies agreement'.[27] While Van Miert recognized that benefits for passengers could be delivered by alliances through their extended networks and cheaper fares, there was also a danger of anti-competitive behaviour, and it was not 'self-evident' that this danger was avoided by competition between alliances.[28] At the time, the US applied its competition law to alliances and that imposed conditions, not only on US, but also on European airlines without taking the latter's legal position within the SEAM into consideration. Thus the German–US open-skies agreement gave all kinds of benefits to Lufthansa, but they were denied to Deutsche BA because it was owned and controlled by nationals other than Germans.

> These provisions which limit competition and discriminate between airlines should disappear and we consider that they should be amended prior to the granting of any exemption [from competition rules]. These difficulties could of course be solved in a global open skies agreement with the US negotiated by the EU Commission.[29]

In the light of these views, it hardly came as a surprise when the Commission took eight Member States to the European Court of Justice in 1998, alleging that their recent bilateral ASAs with the US were contrary to Community law. The following year, the Commission strove to keep the focus on the global challenge that confronted the SEAM with its paper 'The European Airlines Industry: From Single Market to Global Challenge'.[30] In September that same year, the AEA lent its support to the Commission's agenda by coming forward with a proposal for a TCAA and just over twelve months later it claimed:

> It appeared that support was growing among EU Member States, which could lead to the Commission receiving a mandate to negotiate with the United States.[31]

Unlike in the early 1990s, US airlines did not look quite such formidable competitors as they had, European airlines looked fitter for competition, and they were all already embedded in alliances with their US counterparts. Removing national regulations that constrained transatlantic cooperation and mergers thus appeared more attractive than it had, but not so attractive that the Council of Ministers was moved to grant full authority to the Commission to negotiate a TCAA with the US. The Commission re-echoed once again its intention to achieve a higher degree of competence in external aviation relations in the White Paper 'European Transport Policy for 2010'.[32] To some, this sounded like a tired and repetitive refrain, but in fact things were now on the cusp of a radical change.

Rather appropriately on the British fireworks, or Guy Fawkes, night, 5 November 2002, the European Court of Justice delivered its opinion on the cases brought by the Commission in 1998 against eight of the Member States. It was to explode most of the long-held reluctance of the Council of Ministers to grant competence over external aviation affairs to the Commission. The Court held that nationality clauses were illegal because they prevented any European airline, not owned and controlled by the European state party to a bilateral ASA, from fully benefiting from the Community's establishment rules. Consequently, Austria, Belgium, Denmark, Finland, Germany, Luxembourg, Sweden and the UK had acted illegally in signing ASAs containing nationality clauses with the US in recent years.[33] Furthermore, following the principle established in the AETR case, ASAs that dealt with CRSs, fares and slots were also illegal as the Community had assumed competence over those areas by already introducing governance over them. However, in full awareness of just how politically explosive these issues were, the Court stopped short of granting the Commission exclusive competence over external civil aviation relations. Instead, it argued that there was shared competence between the Commission and the Member States and that therefore Council action would be required under (the now old, because of Treaty reform) Article 84(2). In effect, the Court had denied the Commission its wish for full competence, but it had also made it virtually impossible for the Member States to continue as they were: they would now have to work constructively with the Commission and take appropriate decisions within the Council of Ministers in order both to advance things and to reconfigure ASAs so that they were no longer illegal.

'The Commission's aim to receive an exclusive mandate to negotiate air service agreements ... has failed':[34] to have and to have not

Two weeks after the Court's pronouncement, the Commission despatched a Communication to the Council of Ministers concerning its consequences. At the heart of the paper were three key issues, first: 'neither the Community nor the Member States have a free rein to conclude air transport agreements'.[35] The Community had certain powers and authority and the Member States had certain powers and authority, but only by working together could progress now be made. Second, the illegalities that now clearly existed and had been declared so by the Court – nationality clauses, and bilateral policies in the fields of slots,

CRSs and fares that ran contrary to Community legislation – would have to be addressed. Third, and the issue that most urgently needed attention, was the relationship with the US.

> The relationship with the United States is central to the European Union's air transport relations. It is of the utmost importance to open Community negotiations that will offer the opportunity of correcting problems in the bilaterals that were the subject of the Court's judgements and creating a better balance within the Transatlantic relationship. The two sides must take steps towards an open environment for the provision of services and investment, complemented by a framework of high standards. The Commission considers that the Council should approve a mandate for negotiations as soon as possible on the basis of the preparations already undertaken addressing not only market access conditions but also the regulatory environment.[36]

For the time being, the Commission instructed the eight defendants in the Court case to take steps to denounce the offending parts of their ASAs with the US and advised seven other states with US open-skies agreements similarly.[37] All Member States were asked not to make any agreements out of line with Community policy.

Two other important considerations under-girded the Commission's position: the recession precipitated by 9/11 and the size of European carriers. In the previous chapter when dealing with the issue of subsidies, it was noted that the Commission sought a shake-out of the European airline industry rather than hand-outs. Loyola de Palacio made it clear that for global competition, there had to be strong European airlines. As job and financial losses piled up in the worldwide industry, over 200,000 jobs went within two months and 2001's estimated annual financial losses jumped from $2.5 billion to $7 billion in the same time frame according to IATA estimates; it was obvious, at least to de Palacio, that European airlines needed rationalization.[38] More specifically, the traditional majors needed rationalization. No-frills airlines such as EasyJet not only rode out the depression: they thrived on it. Instead of putting fares up as the majors did they cut fares, and by December EasyJet passenger numbers were back where they were before 9/11 and still rising. From the end of January 2002 to end of January 2003, it carried 17.7 million passengers 'which made it Europe's largest low-cost airline and the UK's second biggest'.[39] The performance of these no-frills, low-cost airlines simply made the situation of the traditional flag carriers more untenable and their need for strategically beneficial mergers, takeovers and cash injections more urgent. The Commission noted that comparative passenger figures for the largest US and European airlines in 2002 were 110 million for AA and forty million for Lufthansa. BA with the largest European fleet had 280 aircraft AA over 800.[40] Size matters and the Commission wanted to open up more opportunities for mergers and takeovers, not so much in Europe, but on a transatlantic basis. After being dragged along on the coattails of US deregulation and liberalization policies for nearly thirty years, the unthinkable was about to happen: Europe was preparing itself to make radical proposals for liberalization for an OAA, which, if accepted, would take things beyond the US's most ambitious agenda.

Three months later, the Commission returned to the Council with more detailed requests. By then, it was clear that there were growing concerns about the legal uncertainties and over what the future policies of the Community might entail among both the Member States and their airlines and third party states and their airlines. While the Commission acknowledged these problems, it firmly declared that 'the *status quo* is not an option'.[41] The Commission reiterated many of the legal arguments expressed in November, but also added emphasis for action because of the need for restructuring as a result of the recession in the wake of 9/11.

> It will not be possible to carry out the necessary reorganisation of the sector if the competent authorities at national and Community level do not display the response and dynamism needed with regard to international relations in civil aviation.
>
> It is therefore essential for the Community to take the measures necessary to ensure in the short term that a new regulatory framework is put in place which is in conformity with Community law and meets the needs of economic operators.
>
> The overriding objective must be to develop a balanced and effective way of working at Community level that makes full use of the weight of the Community to further the interests of our industry and consumers.[42]

The Commission reiterated its demand for a full mandate for negotiating with the US as the first among its concerns. It also requested what became known as the 'horizontal mandate' to deal with the illegalities of all the other ASAs of the Member States, for transparency that would allow all the Member States and the Community's institutions to be aware of how negotiations were progressing and for appropriate procedures to ensure effective implementation. The negotiating mandate was granted by the Council in June, and in April 2004 Regulation 847/2004 was promulgated on the negotiation and implementation of ASAs with third countries.[43] Before moving to the EU–US negotiations, we need to dwell for awhile with the problems with existing ASAs.

Regulation 847/2004 established a legal framework within which the Member States could continue to negotiate bilateral agreements and adjust existing ones. They were required to seek standard clauses in order to keep new or bring old agreements into line with Community law and keep the Commission fully informed of what was going on.[44] However, there was still uncertainty about what the consequences would be if the Member States ignored the Commission's urgings. Caught between a rock and a hard place, when France was confronted by Chinese demands to retain a nationality clause for their new ASA, it acquiesced, clearly in breech of Community law.[45] Finland, Italy, Germany and Portugal were all warned by the Commission to cancel bilaterals signed since 2002, which included illegal nationality clauses.[46] As the Director of Air Transport, Daniel Calleja, put it in November 2004:

> Member States are no longer free to negotiate with third countries alone. They may only do so within a Community framework. [but] today, these judgements have still not been executed. The legal situation is fragile. The Commission, as guardian of the Treaties has taken steps to ensure respect of the Treaty.[47]

More importantly, the political situation was fragile. Europe was once again enduring a period of reflection and self-doubt. The strains of enlargement and reform were ubiquitous and corrosive of the Commission's status and authority. The rejection of the European Constitution by France and the Netherlands was a clear demonstration of the limitations of the political power of the Community, and progress on the external relations of the SEAM had to be pursued with diplomatic delicacy. The prospective talks with the US and their outcome thus became of great significance for the EU and the Commission's ambitions in external relations. If the Commission could acquit itself effectively and deliver on the negotiations, then it would gain in stature and respect and authority in a way that would ensure the success of its ambition to take control of the full range of external civil aviation relations of the EU.

European radicalism and American conservatism

Four moths after the Council granted a mandate to the Commission, full-scale talks with the US began with the Commission delegation led by Michael Ayral and the US side by Richard Byerly, Deputy Assistant Secretary of State for Transportation Affairs. The US had its standard open-skies agenda, including unlimited 5th freedom rights within and beyond the EU. The European agenda was more radical. The Europeans wanted to create an OAA that would merge European and US cabotage, that would permit 100 per cent ownership and control of US airlines by Europeans and vice versa and a harmonization of competition and safety regulations. Having largely achieved this in Europe, the Commission sought to reproduce its success with an OAA for Europe and the US. In 2002, it had received an analysis from the Brattle Group, and the findings had been very encouraging. The report suggested that an OAA would generate upwards of seventeen million extra passengers a year, deliver $5 billion of benefits to consumers and boost employment in both Europe and the US. In addition to those benefits was the possibility that a EU–US agreement might become a model or template for global reform with further benefits following for European and US airlines.[48]

The stakes were enormously attractive. The Commission recognized that this was an ambitious agenda and that it would have to be achieved in stages, but a prerequisite for moving forward had to be better access to the US market for

European airlines. Better access would come either through opening up cabotage or through changes of ownership and control, or ideally through both. The changes mooted for cabotage and ownership and control were deeply radical, and there was a major question mark over whether the US Congress would ever accept such changes even if they were recommended and strongly supported by the US Administration.

The talks were not easy, and after only a few weeks the Americans were protesting that they could not deal with some of the highly charged political issues that the Commission had raised because a presidential election campaigning was just round the turn of the year. However, they held out the prospect of some progress on ownership and control if the Europeans would only be patient. Since 1991, there had been talks on and off in the US about raising the allowance for foreign ownership from 25 to 49 per cent, and it was on the understanding that the US side would strive to implement progress on this that it was agreed that talks would continue during this first stage.[49] Talks proceeded, and there were six sessions in all between October 2003 and June 2004, but, disappointingly for the Europeans, delays in the 'interagency clearance process' in Washington prevented the proposal to change the percentage of foreign ownership in US airlines from seeing the light of day in the US Congress.[50] Nevertheless, by June, considerable agreement had been reached. Unlimited 5ths for the US had still not been fully sorted out, but there was a commitment to open-skies, which for the US crucially meant lifting restrictions on US access to Heathrow, all restrictions were to be lifted on 3rd and 4th freedom flights and the US recognized the concept of community airlines, which would allow Lufthansa, for example, to operate from anywhere in the EU to the US.

Unfortunately, this was not good enough for the Council of Ministers, which rather brutally 'bloodied the Commission's nose'.[51] Of the Member States, only Ireland and Spain seem disposed to accepting what had been agreed in the negotiations, but the opposition, with Britain in the lead, was so strong that there was a united Council rejection of the draft agreement. The Council declared that there was not enough balance of benefit, and in particular even if the US raised the ownership and control allowance for foreigners to 49 per cent that would not be significant because it would not alter the inability of foreigners to control US airlines. This was particularly troublesome for the Council because it was well aware that ever since the 1930s, the US had applied an extremely strict interpretation of control. 'If there were any semblance of foreign control [the US regulators] would disallow proposed ownership'.[52] So, there was little progress with access to the US market through changes of ownership and control. Similarly, there was no progress on the cabotage issue. In fact, if anything matters went into reverse here as the Americans defined cabotage very broadly to encompass consecutive cabotage, code sharing and wet-leasing. The only 'concession' that the US offered was to allow indirect air carrier services. In other words, EU carriers would be allowed to buy space on US carriers and sell seats as a charter service. The Europeans rejected this as a concession, arguing that subject to US regulatory approval, this kind of operation was already available to them and that they did not want acceptance of this to prejudice their attempts to get more substantial and meaningful concessions. As far as the Council was concerned, insubstantial progress had been made on access to the US market, and there were also remaining problems with wet-leasing, separate from cabotage, with the Fly America Programme and the CRAF. The Europeans wanted the Fly America Program to be abandoned and for European airlines to be eligible for the CRAF programme. Things had arrived at an impasse and one that could not be addressed until after the US presidential election had run its course.

Within days of the re-election of George W. Bush, Daniel Calleja, the Commission's Director of Air Transport entered the lion's den. On 16 November 2004, in a speech at the International Aviation Club in Washington DC, he had the temerity to quote the US's own 1995 air transport policy statement and part of a speech from President Bush's re-election campaign in order to urge the Americans to embrace proposals from Europe:

> Simply put, we cannot let old labor/management paradigms or protectionism hold hostage the enormous benefits to consumers from removing price, capacity, frequency, destination and ownership restrictions between the United States and 25 European Union countries.[53]

This was almost impertinent. Calleja pulled no punches. He simply laid out the three key aims of the EU's objective. There had to be regulatory co-operation and convergence. EU and US carriers must have the 'freedom to operate as they choose between any two points within the combined territories of the EU and the US'.[54] And without ceremony, he dismissed the US proposal to raise foreign ownership limits from 25 to 49 per cent as 'of little or no value to the EU or its airlines'. Instead, he reiterated that: 'We wish to remove the restrictions on the foreign ownership and control of EU and US airlines in respect of EU and US nationals. In other words, to allow US nationals to own or control EU airlines and vice versa'.[55] He acknowledged that there were important security issues involved in the CRAF programme but professed himself convinced that special arrangements could be made to open this up to EU-owned carriers. And finally before expressing optimism that a deal could be cut, he took it upon himself to 'express our concern at the level of financial assistance given to US airlines and its negative effect on competition'.[56] Europe had indeed come a long way since the uproar and dismay at the disruption caused there by US pressures to liberalize transatlantic air fares and the rather modest changes wrought by the 1982 US–ECAC memorandum of understanding. It was now Europe's turn to beckon to a way forward.

The EU spent most of 2005 trying to get the US negotiators back to the table. In March, the new Commissioner for Transport, Jacques Barrot, spoke passionately of the need for an EU–US agreement. Depending upon one's perspective, it was either poetic justice or poetic irony that a Frenchman should be the one to urge the US to enter the most radically liberal agreement covering airline services that had ever been tabled.

External relations and the SEAM 181

Il y a, à mes yeux, essentiellement trios thèmes au cœur de ses négociations. Le premier est celui de la coopération entre Européens et Américains sur le plan réglementaire.... Le second thème est celui de l'accès au marché.... Le troisième est de réussir ensemble à assouplir les règles qui empêchent la création de marchés ouverts de l'aviation et entravent le développement du secteur économique et du monde des affaires. Il faut normaliser le secteur de l'aviation et supprimer les règles qui handicapent sa croissance.[57]

For some time, the US Secretary of Transportation Norman Mineta remained unmoved. He argued that the US would only return to the negotiating table if the EU would guarantee to the US from the outset that they would be granted 5th freedom rights throughout and beyond the EU. The European response was that they would talk about that issue but would not concede it ahead of talks and that the US must agree to negotiate on cabotage, or, if they would not on that, then on ownership and control. Eventually, the US came forward with a proposal to break this impasse, which they believed would deliver to the Europeans what they wanted, but without having to go to the Congress and ask for changes to the law on ownership. The proposal was that the US Department of Transportation would issue a notice of proposed rule making (NPRM) which would aim to change the longstanding strict interpretation that the US had applied to the concept of foreign control. It would modify the situation. Strict control over security, safety, decisions relating to the CRAF programme and organizational documentation would remain in American hands, but over all other matters of control, namely commercial policies, a minority foreign investment could wield a decisive say.[58] The Transportation Department tried to justify this shift of approach to its domestic constituency by arguing that it was time 'to increase the availability of off-shore capital to the US airline industry' and that larger scope for international investments would strengthen alliances and allow US airlines more freedom for investing in foreign airlines.[59]

On the basis that the NPRM would extend real control opportunities to European airlines, talks were resumed and moved rapidly forward. By November, they had an agreed text. There would be open-skies agreement with no restrictions on 3rd and 4th freedoms and unlimited 5ths for the US within and beyond the EU. The US accepted that Community carriers could operate from anywhere in the EU to the US. There would be gradual harmonization on competition and safety rules. And there would be 7th freedom all-cargo rights for European carriers to the US, but without any concessions to the US on all-cargo services. This latter provision was really politically motivated so that the Commission could say that it had held something back. But it was understood that all this hinged on the success of the NPRM. The Council of European Ministers made it clear and iterated and reiterated the point in Council on 5 December 2005, 27 March 2006 and on 9 June 2006 that its approval of the agreement depended on the outcome of the NPRM.

> The Council reaffirmed its unanimous satisfaction with the draft EU/US air transport agreement resulting from the negotiations in November 2005,

while noting that it will await the outcome of the US rulemaking process in relation to the control of US air carriers by foreign nationals before deciding whether to proceed with the agreement. It stressed the crucial importance of clear, meaningful and robust policy changes in this area.[60]

Unfortunately for the fate of the OAA, opposition was growing in the US to the draft agreement. Under Secretary for Policy at the US Department of Transportation, Jeffrey Shane, later acknowledged that while they had all expected some opposition to the NPRM 'none of us guessed how *much* controversy there would be'.[61] Labour and the pilots association generally opposed and Continental was 'one very angry company'.[62] Alone of the major US airlines, Continental looked unable to exploit the agreement to get access to Heathrow: UA and AA were already there, and Delta and Northwest Airlines looked all set to gain entry through their alliance partners Air France/KLM. In early 2006, opposition was fuelled by a controversy over the proposed takeover of several major US ports by a Dubai company. The controversy became so politically charged that the deal fell through, but not before the opponents to the proposed OAA had made comparable points about the control of US airlines and the strategic dangers that would pose. The situation was hardly helped by provocative remarks by the chief US negotiator John Byerly that the future of the OAA 'really rests in Europe's hands', and that restrictions at Heathrow Airport were 'despicable' and a 'thirty-year abomination'.[63] Similarly intemperate language and controversy were widespread in the Congress and with mid-term elections looming in November 2006 and the Bush Administration's popularity in free-fall because of the tragedy in Iraq, the Department of Transportation issued a supplemental NPRM to explain 'somewhat more clearly what we had intended'.[64] It argued that it was simply making something explicit, which had always been implicit, namely, that any control powers delegated to a foreign minority ownership could always be revoked. The Europeans however saw this for what it was: a major retreat by the US Department of Transportation, which placed in question the value of the whole deal.[65] However, while the Europeans saw the change as pandering to those who vehemently opposed changing US ownership and control, 'the clarification did little to mollify the opposition'.[66] As a result, in the summer, the US Administration took further steps to slow things down and to reassure the Congress that their legislative prerogatives would not be usurped by executive fiat.

> That decision reflected the Administration's view that a change of this importance, even if wholly within the purview of the Executive Branch – as we maintain that it is – should not and cannot be implemented over significant opposition from members of Congress.[67]

Immediate further consideration was ended in July when the US Department of Transportation said that it would have a full formal proposal issued by August/September of 2006, but then in August Mineta resigned and Maria Cino the acting Secretary contacted President Barroso of the Commission to say that the US would not be able to keep to that timetable. At the time of writing in November 2006, the situation remained unresolved, but with the Democrats gaining control of both the House of Representatives and the US Senate, the prospects for the OAA look a little forlorn. Commission officials, however, with vestiges of optimism still in evidence were 'awaiting to see how the US Administration intends to proceed with the rulemaking on control ...'[68]

Gradually, but with the most difficulty experienced in any aspect of developing the SEAM, the Commission is gaining competence over external aviation relations. It is taking an inordinate length of time because this aspect of civil aviation intrudes most directly into political and strategically important matters, and the Commission finds itself in the realm of sovereign foreign policy making. Over the years, the Commission has incrementally encroached with procedural and then substantive powers of negotiation with states that either stand in a privileged position vis-à-vis the Community or were prospective candidates for membership. And now it has taken on the US in negotiations that could produce governance for two-thirds of the global airline industry. However, the basis on which it is conducting this most ambitious of negotiations is still not entirely clear. The Commission's claim for exclusive legal competence over external relations on the basis of the commerce clause Article 113 (original Treaty of Rome) has never been regarded as valid, but in 2002 the European Court of Justice made existing ASAs impossible to sustain and the negotiation of future ASAs impossible to consummate without cooperation between the Member States and the Commission because of the illegality of nationality clauses and the competence over pricing, slot allocations and CRSs already ceded to the Commission. But all this, of course, is still clouded by political difficulties, and in time-honoured fashion, the EC has tended to obfuscate things regarding what the consequences for Member States might be if they do not fall in line with the legal requirements, which now in theory, govern European civil aviation. Thus, the nature of the cooperation that the Court has effectively called for is still a matter for debate, and the outcomes are still unsure. Having acknowledged that, it still seems likely that there will be further developments in the Commission's external competence. It would now require a massive retreat in the powers of the Commission and a serious unravelling of the SEAM if developments were to go into reverse. Even putting developments on hold now holds the danger of serious complications and disruptions to the international airline system. Jeffrey Shane's ruminations on the prospects of the possible failure of the OAA illustrate clearly what the dangers of inaction now are not only for the EU, the US and all other states in relationships with the European Member States, but also for the global airline system as a whole because of the threat to global alliances.

Without an open-skies or similar kind of agreement between the EU and the US, which addresses the issue of community as opposed to nationality clauses in ASAs, the transatlantic civil aviation system could unravel. Existing open-skies agreements and changes to the UK–US ASA had all been declared illegal by the European Court of Justice. As Shane pointed out:

> If we lose the current open-skies agreements, we face the very real prospect of dismantling the US–EU airline alliance structure that provides so much international aviation competition today, as well as the emerging cross-border airline mergers.
>
> Antitrust immunity, which has helped to facilitate the efficient operation of many of the current alliances, is necessarily predicated on underlying open-skies agreements. Without legally secure open-skies agreements with their guarantee of open market entry, it is very difficult to see how we could continue to justify immunity from antitrust enforcement for airlines that are potential competitors.[69]

The world's aviation system is now a deeply and inextricably interdependent and inter-penetrated system. The Europeans had devised a Community-wide policy as a means of responding to those emerging facts in the 1980s and 1990s and now found themselves being propelled further. A regional level playing field was not enough. Their airlines had to operate in a global marketplace and according to rules that would not discriminate between their players. Gradually that had pushed them into moving more and more competence over external aviation affairs to the Commission in order to ensure that a uniform policy would be developed and applied to all Community airlines. There were still important political and legal difficulties involved in consummating this wide-ranging agenda, but opportunities beckoned and difficulties threatened if progress were not made. There is still uncertainty about the way things will develop in this most fraught area of the SEAM, but few would question the importance of the fact that the Commission has conducted negotiations with the US, the most important actor in global civil aviation, and that the agreement that they have reached, but which lies unapproved at the moment, is iconic in its actual and symbolic importance.

> In the (OAA's) potential for transforming the transatlantic market, the agreement represents the next important step in deregulation and globalization – the removal of regulatory barriers to the emergence of the European airline, the establishment of an EU-wide open-skies regime with the United States, and trans-Atlantic cooperation in areas such as security, competition policy, and consumer protection that goes well beyond what is contemplated in our more traditional open-skies agreements. Moreover, the EU and the U.S. agreed to begin a second stage of negotiations within 60 days of the effective date of the agreement.[70]

Europe has still not fully consummated the SEAM, but it has travelled a long way indeed since the French Seamen's Case and the First Memorandum on civil aviation and is now engaged with the last remaining area in order to complete a coherent aviation system.

10 Concluding thoughts
The dervish shall whirl again

> The European liberalisation packages of the 1990s and their impact on fares, service quality ... and employment have shown that policy measures have a dominant effect on the development of the transport sector.[1]

With the major exception of competence over external relations, by 2006 the Commission had largely achieved what it had urged the Council of Ministers to do in its First Memorandum on Civil Aviation in the summer of 1979. The amazing achievement of the architectural build of the SEAM emerged in 1997, as a result of the three packages of reform. Against all odds, the Commission, Britain and the Netherlands had managed to push an agenda forward that eventually triumphed after being opposed first by the other eight and then after the admission of Spain and Portugal into the EC, the other ten Member States. Following the wake of the creation of the SEAM came the work of existing independent airlines like BM and Maersk Air and new no-frills low-cost airlines such as EasyJet and Ryanair. These airlines drove the market to its present dynamic and competitive condition. But, without the architectural changes wrought in the European airline system, there would have been no dramatic impact from the likes of Ryanair and EasyJet.

The route to where we are now has been difficult to negotiate. Help came initially from both new economic theory and the impact of US deregulation in the global marketplace. Then, following the French Seamen's Case, there developed a changing coalition of forces that encompassed DG VII and DG IV, regulatory liberal Member States, and a varied group of mouthpieces voicing support for change in the European airline industry. That coalition was helped by continuing pressure from market forces, the Single Market project and other judgements from the European Court of Justice. The latter two provided targets and legal drivers to push things forward and enabled the Commission to develop tactics that brought pressures to bear for change on the recalcitrant regulatory conservative states. At the same time a key alliance formed between Britain and its officials within the institutions of the EC and the Commission and key individuals there like Frederik Sorensen. This alliance did more than anything else to promote reform. From time to time, there were useful inputs from other sources and even from conservative quarters at times, such as the European Parliament and ECAC, but for much of the reform agenda things were driven by Britain and the Commission. A notable exception to that was competence for the Commission over external affairs. Here the Commission had to rely on the European Court of Justice and Community law for the kind of support that eventually moved this part of the agenda forward in 2002.

Creating the SEAM was one thing, making it work was another. Officials in the Commission always worried about whether the airlines would actually compete, once they had made it possible for them to do so. EasyJet provided perhaps the best relief possible for those worries. Its online ticket purchasing, its development of less glamorous airports such as Luton, and its willingness to compete with drastically lower prices than those offered by the established major airlines have been a recipe for success. Ryanair's strategy is similar except it has been even more dependent upon the SEAM's reforms, which have enabled it to open up various regional airports with low-cost charges (sometimes including what are now deemed to be illegal local authority subsidies) and thrive commercially. Both airlines have exploited the opportunities for competition provided by the packages of reform, sold tickets cheaply and maximized capacity levels: each airline has passenger capacity loads averaging around 84–87 per cent. In the old days of regulatory conservatism the kind of pricing that is sensitive enough to the market to achieve such load factors was just not available. The rules were too inflexible. It was on the back of these aggressive pricing and marketing strategies that the new airlines grew. By 2002 EasyJet, after buying up Go, had annual passenger numbers exceeding a staggering twelve million: Ryanair was not far behind with eleven million. And EasyJet and Ryanair were by no means alone. There was a whole new generation of airlines in Europe. They were now the norm. It was not like being a lone maverick as Freddie Laker had been in the 1980s.

The SEAM is a reality. For most intents and purposes airlines within the EU operate within a single market. The airlines are free to operate on the basis of commercial strategies and pricing, capacity, frequency, route selection and scheduling that they freely decide to be in their business interests. Nothing, however, is perfection, and slot restrictions at key airports and the looming dominance of alliances such as at Frankfurt and Paris, where the Star and SkyTeam alliances, respectively, control 60 per cent of capacity, continue to raise competition issues. Some states are not as cooperative as others and much depends on how the Commission polices the system. And that is no easy task. As the Commission's brief has widened and shifted somewhat from a focus on reform in Europe to the wider global marketplace, it has become more sensitive to some of the needs of the traditional flag carriers and their concerns about positioning for global competition. This has been one of the factors driving the Commission's desire for an OAA with the US. Global competition is also behind the Commission's support for alliances and intra-European mergers and takeovers. 'The Commission takes a positive stance towards airline mergers in Europe'.[2] It thus swiftly approved the Air France-KLM merger and that of

Concluding thoughts 187

Lufthansa and Swiss International Airlines (SWISS). Respectively they created the world's third and fifth largest airlines. The Commission believes that this is necessary for European airlines to be effective competitors with their US and Asian counterparts. While these developments raise the spectre of dominant positions and possible abuse, not just by these mega-carriers, but also through their alliance connections, the Competition DG remains confident that it can deal with problems if they arise.[3]

The main focus of this study has been on the overtly commercial aspects of civil aviation that the Commission has reached out to and reformed, but it is also important to note that it has entered virtually every aspect of the civil aviation industry with Regulations and Directives on everything from noise pollution to insurance and compensation for denied boarding and delays.[4] Just how broad the remit of the Commission now is becomes clear from an evaluation of the implementation of policies promulgated in the Commission's 2001 transport White Paper (Table 10.1).

The SEAM has been a great success story for the Commission, market liberalization, for at least some European airlines, and for the European consumer. For the time being some problems still remain and there continues to be the incompleteness because of the Commission's failure to seize full competence in external relations. This continues to be a great worry and as Chapter 9 noted, if the EU–US fail to consummate the agreement achieved in November 2005, then there could be serious complications for alliances and anti-trust immunity, which could lead to an unravelling of the existing global system. This continues

Table 10.1 Evaluation of policy implementation, its impacts and effectiveness[1]

Measure	Policy implementation	Potential impact on air transport sector development
Creation Single European Sky	High	High
Technical harmonisation and safety	Very high	Medium
Insurance requirements	Very high	Low
Airport charges	Medium	Medium
Slot allocation policy	Low	High
Noise management	Medium	Very low
Unfair competition from third countries	High	Very low
Safety of third country aircraft	High	Medium
ASAs with third countries	Medium	Very high
Airport capacity expansion	Low	High
Introduction of fuel tax	Very low	High
Introduction of differential air navigation charges	Very low	Medium
Compensation of air passengers	High	Medium

Note
1 ASSESS: *Assessment of the contribution of the TEN and other transport policy measures to the mid-term implementation of the White Paper on the European Transport Policy for 2010*. Transport and Mobility Leuven, 28 October 2005. Annex XIV, Qualitative Analysis of Air Transport Issues, table compiled by the authors of the report, p. 98.

to be a problem yet to be solved. There are two other issues which also threaten the health and welfare, not only of the European, but the global airline industry.

The first of these is terrorism. The potential of further terrorist outrages against civilian passenger airliners is a constant worry and one that continues to deter some people from air travel. Another 9/11 disaster would wreak further havoc on the airline industry with consequences for the established airlines, particularly those with transoceanic routes, that are very difficult to calculate precisely. However, a revisiting of the statistics for the aftermaths of the first Gulf War and 9/11 provided in Chapters 7 and 8 would give one some idea of what would be likely. And even without such catastrophes, the security costs which were added to the industry in the aftermath of 9/11 are here to stay.

Finally, and rather sadly for those who have a sentimental affection for the airline industry, there has been a further catastrophe in waiting for many years: emission pollution. European Commission President, Jose Manuel Barroso, has recently taken up the issue of pollution and global warming and wants to make the EU the world pioneer of green issues.[5] This is not new for the Commission. In its 2001 White paper, it argued in favour of 'environmentally favourable' modes of transport and that 'air traffic must therefore be brought under control'.[6] Estimates by the Intergovernmental Panel on Climate Change in its report 'Aviation and the Global Atmosphere' indicated that aviation contributed 3.5 per cent to global climate change in 1992.[7] Since then, the airline industry has expanded massively. Britain generates more international passengers than any other country in the world, and estimates suggest that if left unchecked total flights in and from the UK will rise from 200 million a year in 2003 to 500 million in 2030.[8] In 2003–04 alone there was a rise of 8.9 million passengers in Britain on scheduled flights. Many believe that the planet, never mind Europe, cannot sustain this level of unrestrained activity in the airline market. Currently aviation emissions are not controlled by the Kyoto Protocol, nor is aviation fuel taxed, nor are airline tickets subject to VAT. One does not need to look very far to see what politicians might do to curb the general public's love affair with air travel. And when one says general public, in fact, it refers to a very specific class of the general public. Cheap airfares, which have been delivered in Europe through the changes wrought by the SEAM and the entrepreneurialism of no-frills, low-cost airlines, have been received by the wealthy middle classes. Low-income travellers are relatively few and far between. And even the number of business travellers is dwarfed by leisure travellers who account for over 70 per cent of the airline travelling public. How are any politicians disposed to defending the current status quo going to justify it when cheap air travel, predominantly for the well-off, and overwhelmingly for leisure, is making such a significant contribution to climate change?

A radical transformation has occurred in the European airline market since 1979. The regulatory problems that stifled the market have largely gone, and the new lightly regulated liberalized market has flourished. But, it is now a victim of its own success, or it is soon likely to be. If both the planet and the European airline system are to survive there will have to be equally radical change in the

Concluding thoughts 189

future and once again transformations must occur that will make the present system unrecognizable, just as the conservatively regulated system of the post-war years up until the 1980s and 1990s is not recognizable in the current system. In the 1970s Alfred Khan referred to the alternating policies of deregulation and regulation as a 'whirling dervish'. It was never quite like that in Europe, but if one were to apply the same imagery then the system may very well be set to whirl again with the introduction of higher costs and tighter regulations to limit operations in the marketplace. After explaining how the SEAM came about it is rather a sad note to end with predicting that it must all change again. But, it does emphasize just what this work is – history.

Postscript

In December 2006, in the light of rising political hostility, the US Transportation Department felt obliged to withdraw the NPRM. It looked as if the Transportation Department had abandoned attempts to change the rules on ownership and control.

> [T]he [EU] Transport Council expressed its deep disappointment and regret at this decision, reaffirmed its commitment to a goal of securing a first-stage comprehensive air transport agreement and requested the Commission to enter into urgent consultations with the United States as soon as possible to seek elements that could be used to restore a proper balance of interests.[1]

Only ten months earlier, the Transport Council had unambiguously stressed: 'the crucial importance of clear, meaningful and robust policy changes in this area (i.e. ownership and control)'.[2] Without that how could there to be a 'proper balance' of interests? Were face-saving concessions all that remained for the EU to pursue? Had the US successfully called the European bluff? Was getting recognition of the legal status of community airlines so important for the EU that in the end it gave way to the US?

The OAA in part: the first step – the last step?

In early February the Transport Council President, Wolfgang Tiefensee, and Jacques Barrot went to Washington to re-start talks. Two rounds of negotiations followed in February and March, which resulted in agreement, subject to ratification by the EU Transport Council.

> Byerly said the United States viewed the 2005 agreement as fair and balanced because it offered 'huge benefits' to both sides. But to accommodate the EU demand for 'more balance' it agreed to many 'enhancements' to the 2005 text that benefit mostly EU airlines and investors.[3]

Byerly conveniently overlooked the fact that underpinning the 2005 agreement was an understanding on both sides that there would be changes on ownership and control. In fact, the rules on ownership and control (and the law on cabotage) remained substantially unchanged, but Barrot rather surprisingly said he was content with the new measures to adjust the balance of benefit. What was now offered to the Europeans were reciprocal rights to invest up to 49.9 per cent of an airline's total equity, i.e. of voting and non-voting stock, without this being deemed to be control of the airline, and ownership over 50 per cent of total equity would be reviewed on a case by case basis: in both instances however, the limitation on ownership of 25 per cent of *voting stock* still applied. There was agreement to allow EU-owned airlines from non-EU European states and from many African states and airlines from the European Common Aviation Area (ECAA) all to be treated as if they were EU airlines by the US. There was a unilateral grant of 7th freedom passenger rights for EU airlines from a number of non-EU European countries, some access rights to the Fly America Program, provisions for anti-trust immunity to facilitate the development and strengthening of alliances, and new opportunities for EU airlines to wet-lease to US airlines. These concessions and the recognition of the concept of EU community carrier were substantial, but most, along with other provisions for unlimited code-sharing, fifth freedom rights, and removal of pricing and capacity restrictions, were standard components of US open-skies agreements. Furthermore, the one thing that might have persuaded the US to embark upon a more radical path was traded away.

> The US–EU open-skies pact also would remove heavy restrictions on air services between the United States and the United Kingdom established by a 1977 bilateral agreement .... The agreement, which Byerly called an 'abomination', limits operations at London's Heathrow Airport to only two airlines from each side – British Airways, Virgin Atlantic, American and United.
> Under the draft deal, all US and EU carriers would be able to fly to and from Heathrow once they secure landing rights, or slots, including by buying new landing slots or the existing ones from their current owners.[4]

The EU did not get what it had set out to achieve: it had also traded in its key bargaining chip – access to Heathrow. From one perspective it might be argued that movement on the ownership and control issue and cabotage was always highly unlikely, and that it would have to await a later stage in the process of negotiations. However, having apparently traded away access to Heathrow, it is difficult to see what the EU might offer in order to induce US concessions on these issues in the future.

The reaction from BA was outrage. BA Chairman, Martin Broughton, declared the agreement to be a 'con trick' engineered by 'greedy Americans'. Of the extra concessions that the Americans had made, Broughton dubbed them 'crumbs' that did not 'come anywhere near balancing up the inherent imbalance in the open skies model'. He accused the Commission of putting its legal obligation to get the US to recognise the EU single market ahead of the EU's economic interest. Once the US have achieved their prime negotiating objective of an open skies deal, their motivation to liberalize further will evaporate.[5]

In slightly more measured terms Steve Ridgeway, Chief Executive Officer of Virgin Atlantic, commented that: 'We would love to see full and proper open skies but this draft agreement doesn't come anywhere near that. This appears at first glance to be a missed opportunity to create a truly competitive transatlantic aviation market.'[6] As the crucial decision approached to reject or ratify the agreement by the EU's Transport Council on 22 March, anxiety deepened at BA. Its Chief Executive Officer, Willie Walsh, wrote to both Barrot and the UK Transport Secretary, Douglas Alexander, that benefits to consumers offered by the deal were outweighed by the imbalance in the agreement in favour of US interests. Alexander seemed at least partly persuaded by such arguments as he in turn spoke of a phased approach that would create some benefits now, but would also lock parties into a process that would eventually yield full liberalization, i.e. access to the US domestic market. There was even talk of Prime Minister Blair contacting President Bush to explain that Britain could not sign up to the deal unless the US committed itself to liberalizing access to its own market. However, such defensive manoeuvring would be out-flanked if the EU allowed the decision in the Transport Council to be taken by qualified majority voting.[7]

In the event, the decision was unanimous in favour of acceptance, but the British managed to insert some important last-minute changes. A five month delay was agreed, which will put implementation back to 30 March 2008. More importantly, again on British insistence, Jacques Barrot made clear that if there were no movement on US ownership and control in the follow-on stages of negotiations by 2010, then the EU would have the option of withdrawing from the agreement. If that scenario were to materialize it could stir up a veritable hornet's nest. British Transport Secretary Alexander said it would be up to each individual Member State to decide what rights to withdraw if the US did not move on ownership and control, but that would clearly not be acceptable to the Commission as it would again lead to a lack of uniform commercial rights in external aviation relations and would run contrary to Community law.[8] It is the EU and the Commission that may have difficult decisions to take in 2010, rather than individual Member States.

Where the EU and the US go from here is not easy to predict. The OAA as negotiated will bring very significant changes, though the inherent congestion at Heathrow, even taking its imminent expansion into account, might limit US airlines more than they expect because of scarcity of take-off and landing slots. BM on the other hand will be a big winner with its large number of existing slots and potential to shift them from domestic to international use. Recognition of community airlines by the US will extinguish the threat to existing open-skies agreements and alliances, but transatlantic investment, merger and take-over opportunities remain either tightly restricted or prohibited. The Commission's role in the SEAM and its authority have both been buttressed, but there is still a lot to play for and it will be a hard game to win for the Europeans because it is difficult to see what might persuade a US administration, never mind the US Congress, to change ownership and control regulations and/or open US cabotage. And the Europeans cannot offer access to EU cabotage in return as an incentive because with unlimited fifths granted and existing fifths grandfathered, the US already has de facto access to EU cabotage.

Notes

1 Airlines and the European Community

1 Text of remarks of Jeffrey N. Shane, Under Secretary for Policy, US Department of Transportation, International Aviation Club, Washington DC, 12 September 2006 (courtesy of EC Directorate for Transport and Energy, DG TREN (also known as DG VII for much of the life of the Commission), p. 1.
2 The EU came into being in November 1993. Its origins stretch back to 1952 and to the creation of the European Coal and Steel Community, the 1957 Treaties of Rome that created the EEC and the European Atomic Energy Community (EURATOM). The 1965 Merger Treaty brought the three communities under one governing umbrella and the term European Community came into common use. The OAA was previously referred to as the Transatlantic Common Aviation Area (TCAA).
3 AEA represents the interests of the European national airlines. Its origins date back to 1952 when a small group of European members of IATA got together and created the Air Research Bureau (ARB). After the Strasbourg conference on coordination of the aviation industry in Europe in 1954 and the creation of ECAC, the ARB became the mouthpiece of the airline industry in ECAC and then later the name AEA was adopted. Until 1981, all members had to belong to IATA. IATA was established in Havana in April 1945 and its membership is made up by most of the world's scheduled airlines. Until the 1980s, its main role was to facilitate price-fixing through rate conferences. ICAO was established by the 1944 Chicago Conference on international aviation and it deals largely with the technical and safety matters. ECAC was established in 1955 by the European members of ICAO to pursue a similar brief to the parent organization, but with the primary focus on European matters.
4 Good introductions to integration theory are B. Rosamond, *Theories of European Integration*, Basingstoke, Palgrave, 2000; A. Wiener and T. Diez (eds), *European Integration Theory*, Oxford, Oxford University Press, 2004, and D. Beach, *The Dynamics of European Integration: Why and When EU Institutions Matter*, Basingstoke, Palgrave, 2005. The classics include D. Mitrany, *A Working Peace System: An Argument for the Functional Development of International Organization*, London, Royal Institute for International Affairs, 1943; E.B. Haas, *Beyond the Nation State: Functionalism and International Organization*, Stanford, Stanford University Press, 1964; A.S. Milward, *The European Rescue of the Nation State*, London, Routledge, 1992; A. Moravcsik, 'Preferences and Power in the European Community: A Liberal Inter-governmentalist Approach', *Journal of Common Market Studies*, 31:4, 1993, 473–524. A benchmark study of the work of non-governmental dynamics is J. Greenwood, *Interest Representation in the European Union*, Basingstoke, Palgrave, 2003.
5 Treaty of Rome, 25 March 1957, preamble and Article 2.
6 Ibid., Articles 2(f) and 74–84.
7 'The Community and Transport Policy', European File 10/85, May 1985 and

'Expanding Horizons: A Report by the *Comité des Sages* for Air Transport to the European Commission', Brussels, January 1994, p. 9.
8 Few works deal specifically with the European airline industry, but the following speak about this issue to one degree or another: J. Erdmenger, *The European Transport Policy*, Aldershot, Gower, 1983; G. Majone (ed.), *Deregulation or Re-Regulation? Regulatory Reform in Europe and the United States*, London and New York, Pinter and St Martins, 1990; F. McGowan and C. Trengove, *European Aviation: A Common Market?*, London, Institute for Fiscal Studies, 1986; P.P.C. Haanappel et al. (eds), *EEC Air Transport Policy and Regulation and Their Implications for North America*, Deventer, Kluwer, 1989; P. Forsyth, 'Airline Deregulation in the United States: The Lessons for Europe', *Fiscal Studies*, 4 November 1983, 7–21; S. Wheatcroft and G. Lipman, *Air Transport in a Competitive European Market: Problems, Prospects and Strategies*, London, Economist Intelligence Unit, Economist Publications Ltd., 1986; R. Pryke, *Competition Among International Airlines*, Aldershot, Gower, 1987; D. O'Reilly and A.S. Sweet, 'The Liberalization and European Re-regulation of Air Transport' in W. Sandholtz and A.S. Sweet (eds), *European Integration and Supranational Governance*, Oxford, Oxford University Press, 1998; H. Stevens, *Transport Policy in the European Union*, Basingstoke, Palgrave, 2004; K. Button et al., *Flying Into the Future: Air Transport Policy in the European Union*, Cheltenham, Edward Elgar, 1998.
9 Treaty of Rome, Article 84(2).
10 COM(73)1725, 'Development of the Common Transport Policy', 1975.
11 'Expanding Horizons', op. cit., p. 5.
12 Interview with Cyril Murphy, Vice President for International Affairs, UA, 1 July 1991.
13 Cmd. 266, 'Convention Relating to International Air Transport', 1919. See also A.P. Dobson, *Peaceful Air Warfare: The United States, Britain, and the Politics of International Aviation*, Oxford, Clarendon Press, 1991, Chapters 1 and 2.
14 Ibid., Chapters 5 and 6; D. Mackenzie, 'The Bermuda Conference and Anglo-American Aviation Relations at the End of the Second World War', *Journal of Transport History*, 12:1, 1991, 61–73; M.L. Dierikx, 'Shaping World Aviation: Anglo-American Civil Aviation Relations 1944–46', *Journal of Air Law and Commerce*, 57, 1992, 795–840.
15 Cmd. 6747, 'US, UK, Civil Air Services Agreement Bermuda', 1946. H.A. Raben, 'Deregulation: a Critical Interrogation', in H.A. Wassenbergh and H.P. van Fenema (eds) *International Air Transport: A Legal Analysis*, Deventer, Kluwer, 1981.
16 Interview with Robert Ebdon, Head of Government Affairs, British Airways, 5 August 1991.
17 The Treaty of Rome, 1957, Article 3, Title 4 Transport Articles 74–84, and Rules on Competition Articles 85–102.
18 'Report on Competition in Intra-European Air Services', 1982, Paris, ECAC, CEAC Doc. No. 25, p. 20, hereafter COMPAS Report.
19 Pryke, op. cit., p. 10.
20 L. Gialloreto, *Strategic Airline Management: the Global War Begins*, London, Pitman Press, 1988; R. Pryke, op. cit.; S. Shaw, *Airlines and Management*, London, Pitman, 1985; Raben, op. cit., pp. 1–24. R. Doganis, *Flying Off Course: The Economics of International Airlines*, London, Allen and Unwin, 1985.
21 Available Tonne Kilometres measures the airline's total capacity (both passenger and cargo).
22 *Expanding Horizons*, p. 51.
23 In the mid-1950s, for example, Derby Aviation, which later developed into BM and launched a service Derby–Birmingham–Ostend, B. Gunston, *Diamond Flight*, London, Henry Melland Ltd., 1988, p. 27.

24 US National Archives, Nixon Project (hereafter Nixon Project), Transitional Taskforce Reports 1968–69, box 1, folder: Report of the President Elect's Taskforce on Transportation.
25 Rigidity was not as severe as in Europe, however, as the CAB did not control frequency, scheduling and capacity (though it approved inter-carrier capacity reductions in the early 1970s), and there were no pooling agreements.
26 Nixon Project, WHCF, CA, folder: CA 5/20/69–12/31/69, Flanigan to van der Beugel and his reply 4 August and 19 September 1969. The most dramatic defensive measure was Britain's unilateral denouncement of the Bermuda Agreement in June 1976, A.P. Dobson, 'Regulation or Competition? Negotiating the Anglo-American Air Service Agreement of 1977', *The Journal of Transport History*, 15:2, 1994, pp. 144–65.
27 Nixon Project, WHSF, WHCF, CF, box 3, folder: Civil Aviation 1969–70, Flanigan to Nixon, 14 August 1970.
28 'Statement of International Air Transportation Policy of the United States', 22 June 1970, text from official copy, Nixon Project, Papers of Hendrix Houthakker, box 51.
29 A. Greenspan, 'The Assault on Integrity', in A. Rand, *Capitalism the Unknown Ideal*, New York, New American Library, 1967, pp. 118–22, at p. 121.
30 For more detail of the positions of the major European airlines which fall into the regulatory conservative category, see H.-L. Dienel and P. Lyth (eds), *Flying the Flag: European Commercial Air Transport Since 1945*, Basingstoke, Macmillan, 1998, Chapters 2, 4 and 6.
31 Interview with Frederik Sorensen, 21 February 2000.
32 Ibid.
33 *House of Commons Debates*, 1979–80, vol. 989, cols 547–8, John Nott introducing third reading of the Civil Aviation Bill, 23 July 1980.
34 In fact two flag carriers – British European Airways and British Overseas Airways Corporation – until 1974 when they merged to form British Airways.
35 Cmd. 4018, '[Edwards] Report of the Committee of Inquiry into Civil Air Transport', 1969.
36 *Flight International*, 29 June 1972, 'National's Capacity Cut', p. 96.
37 For more detail, see A.P. Dobson, *Flying in the Face of Competition: the Policies and Diplomacy of Airline Regulatory Reform in Britain, the USA and the European Community 1968–94*, Aldershot, Avebury, 1995, pp. 27–8.
38 Interview with Raymond Colegate, UK CAA (retired) 25 March 1991.
39 Greenwood, op. cit., pp. 2–3 and 4–5.
40 Ibid., pp. 28 and 74.
41 Ibid., pp. 98–101.
42 Interview with R. Fennes, 21 February 2000. See Stevens, op. cit., 2004, pp. 147–50 and Wheatcroft and Lipman, op. cit., pp. 45–7 for views that ECAC was more liberal.
43 J.W.F. Sundberg, 'Inter-Governmental Relations Between EEC and Non-EEC Countries', in Haanappel, op. cit., pp. 159–210, at p. 164. See also Chapter 2.
44 Colegate Interview, 25 March 1991.
45 S. Stadlmeier, 'Convergence of Scheduled and Non-Scheduled Air Services', *Austrian Journal of Public and International Law*, 45, 1993, 159–93.
46 O'Reilly and Sweet, op. cit., p. 171.
47 Sorensen Interview, 21 February 2000.
48 AETR 1970 European Court of Justice Case 22/70. For its implications, see Chapters 7–9.
49 *House of Lords Session 1990–91, Ninth Report Select Committee on the European Communities Conduct of the Community's External Aviation Relations*, 23 April 1992, p. 10. Views expressed here are drawn largely from C.O. Lenz, Advocate General, European Court of Justice, 'The Decision of the European Court of Justice

on the Applicability of the Rules of the Treaty of Rome to Air Transport', in Haanappel *et al.*, op. cit., pp. 33–48, at pp. 33–4.
50 Interview with official from DG IV, 22 May 1991. Regulation No. 17, 6 February 1962 and Regulation No. 141, 26 November 1962, *Official Journal of the European Community* (hereafter *OJ*), pp. L13/204 and L124/2751 respectively. On 19 July 1968 Regulation 1017 re-applied Regulation 17 to inland transport.
51 Sorensen Interview, 21 February 2000. See also Nicholas Argyris, 'EEC Competition Law Rules and Their Impact on Air Transport Services Ancillary Thereto', in Haanappel *et al.*, op. cit., pp. 73–80 at p. 75.
52 'European Community's Transport Policy', 2nd edition, November 1983, *Periodical 3/1984*, p. 16; 'Development of the CTP', *EC Bulletin Supplement* 16/73.
53 K. Button *et al.*, op. cit., p. 36.
54 Sorensen Interview, 21 February 2000.
55 Case 167/73, *Commission v. France*, 1974 ECR, 359.

2 After the French Seamen's case 1974–84: the market, member states, and the voices of aviation interests

1 Murphy Interview, 1 July 1991.
2 Sorensen Interview, 21 February 2000.
3 Colegate Interview, 25 March 1991.
4 Many of the factors bearing on the leadership capabilities of the Commission are drawn from Beach, op. cit. p. 3.
5 M. Feldstein, 'The Retreat from Keynesian Economics', *The Public Interest*, Summer 1981, 92–105.
6 Button, op. cit., p. 25. For more detail on US developments, see Dobson, op. cit. (1995), pp. 147–78.
7 Jimmy Carter Presidential Library (hereafter Carter Library), Staff Offices, Domestic Policy Staff, Eizenstat box 148, folder: Aviation Airline Regulatory Reform, Message to Congress 4 March 1977, attached to Eizenstat to Carter, 22 February 1977.
8 Kahn testimony to Aviation Subcommittee of the House Committee on Public Works and Transportation, 6 March 1978, *Congressional Digest*, June–July 1978, p. 180.
9 Alfred E. Kahn, 'Deregulation and Vested Interests: The Case of the Airlines', in R.G. Noll and B.M. Owen (eds), *The Political Economy of Deregulation: Interest Groups in the Regulatory Process*, Washington DC, American Enterprise for Public Policy Research, 1983, pp. 132–51, p. 149.
10 Kahn testimony to Aviation Sub-Committee of the House Committee on Public Works and Transportation, 6 March 1978, *Congressional Digest*, June–July 1978, p. 186.
11 CAB order 78–6–78, 12 June 1978.
12 Lipmann and Wheatcroft, op. cit., p. 105.
13 For a detailed account of IATA's response to the SCO, see C. Jonsson, *International Aviation and the Politics of Regime Change*, London, Francis Pinter, 1987, pp. 119–51.
14 Ibid., p. 139.
15 P.P.C. Haanappel, *Policy and Capacity Determination in International Air Transport: A Legal Analysis*, Maryland, Kluwer, 1984, Chapter 2.
16 Quoted from Haanappel, op. cit., 1984, p. 160.
17 Murphy Interview, 1 July 1991.
18 Pryke, op. cit., pp. 52–3.
19 N.K. Taneja, *US International Aviation Policy*, Lexington: Heath, 1988, p. 14.
20 Murphy Interview, 1 July 1991.

21 John R. Steele speech ECAC-EU Dialogue, 29 April 2005, www.prismaconsulting.com/EC accessed 7 December 2005.
22 B.S. Peterson, *Bluestreak: Inside Jetblue, the Upstart that Rocked the Industry*, New York, Portfolio, 2004, p. 101.
23 J. Erdmenger (DG VII), 'A New Dimension to Civil Aviation Through European Economic Integration', in Wassenbergh and Fenema, op. cit., pp. 36–52, at p. 36.
24 Forsyth, op. cit., p. 20.
25 Ibid.
26 In this section I have drawn liberally on R. Baldwin, *Regulating the Airlines: Administrative Justice and Agency Discretion*, Oxford, Clarendon, 1985.
27 Cmd. 6400, 'Future Civil Aviation Policy', 1976.
28 Letter from Boyd-Carpenter to Shore printed in Written Answers, *House of Commons Debates*, vol. 905/6, col. 107, 23 February 1976.
29 Cmd. 4899, 'Civil Aviation Policy Guidance', 1972.
30 Interview with Edmund Dell, 8 December 1989.
31 *House of Commons Debates*, vol. 989, col. 547, John Nott introducing third reading of the Civil Aviation Bill, 23 July 1980; Baldwin, op. cit., pp. 238–50; see Civil Aviation Bill 1979/1980, House of Commons Bill 68, 31/10/79 and Civil Aviation Amendment Bill 1981/1982, House of Commons Bill 1, 5/11/81.
32 Interviews with Michael Colvin MP, Chairman, Conservative Backbench Aviation Committee, 7 December 1989 and Sir Michael Bishop, Chairman BM, 15 March 1991.
33 Colegate Interview; Gunston, op. cit., p. 83; Bishop Interview.
34 Cited from Lippman and Wheatcroft, op. cit., p. 57.
35 Colegate Interview; Stevens, op. cit., p. 151.
36 Ibid., exchange between Colvin and Ridley, House of Commons Debates, vol. 65, 30 July 1984, cols 3–6; and D. Campbell-Smith, *Struggle for Take-Off: the British Airways Story*, London, Hodder and Stoughton, 1986, pp. 156–7, 161 and 168.
37 Cmd. 9366, 'Airline Competition Policy', 1984.
38 Ibid.
39 The position of the CAA is interesting. Generally, it tended to be more liberal than the government, especially with regard to the need to reduce BA's dominant position in the marketplace. However, it was the general concerns about nurturing the right regulatory environment for competition that occasionally made it look more regulatory minded and maybe for short periods of time under the Thatcher regime, it actually was. Interview with Andrew Gray, Managing Director, Air UK, 26 March 1991 and Interview with senior official, UK CAA, Economic Regulation Group, 23 May 2001: official 1.
40 Cmd. 9366, 'Airline Competition Policy', 1984.
41 Greenwood, op. cit., pp. 39 and 48–9.
42 O'Reilly and Sweet, op. cit., pp. 171–2.
43 Loder Collection, HE9797A2, Karl-Heinz Neumeister speech at Moscon Conference, 20–1 April 1994.
44 Ibid., Loder to Bethell, 5 July 1988.
45 Ibid.
46 *House of Lords Reports*, 14 June 1995, cols 1839–40.
47 *Lord Bethell v. The Commission*, 10 June 1982, Case 246/81, ECR 2277, p. 2289; Lenz, op. cit., pp. 36–7; see Chapter 3.
48 *Bethell v. The Commission*, 10 June 1982, Case 246/81.
49 Jego Quere, 3 May 2002, Case T-177/01 considered by Greenwood in op. cit., p. 64.
50 Fennes Interview 21 February 2000: he worked for the Dutch interests before joining DG7.
51 CAB order 80-4-113, 15 April 1980.

52 ICAO Document 8681, 10 July 1967.
53 US-ECAC Memorandum of Understanding on North Atlantic Air Tariffs, signed May 1982, entered into force 1 August 1982, Articles 2 and 3.
54 H. Stevens, *Liberalization of Air Transport in Europe: a Case Study in European Integration*, London, European Institute, LSE, 1997, pp. 5, 10–11.
55 Loder Collection, HE9777.7, 'ECAC First in Liberal Skies: the COMPAS Group – a Reminiscence by John Loder', undated.
56 *COMPAS Report*, p. 3.
57 Ibid., pp. 9, 12.
58 Sorensen Interview, 21 February 2001.
59 *COMPAS Report*, p. 3.
60 Ibid., p. 26.
61 Ibid., p. 33.
62 Ibid., p. 47.
63 Ibid., p. 1.
64 Sorensen Interview, 21 February 2001.
65 Wheatcroft and Lipman, op. cit., p. 46.
66 Stevens, op. cit., 1997, p. 11.
67 Interview CAA official 1, 23 May 2001.
68 Interview with Barry Humphreys, former UK CAA official and then a senior executive with Virgin Atlantic, 6 September 2001.
69 Fennes Interview, 21 February 2000; Sorensen Interview, 21 February 2000.
70 Sorensen Interviews, 21 February 2000 and 12 September 2001.
71 Interview with senior official, UK Transport Department, 7 September 2001: official 1.

3 Tentative moves towards a common transport policy in aviation 1974–84: the European institutions

1 COM(81)398 Final, 'Scheduled Passenger Air Fares in the EEC', 23 July 1981, p. 11.
2 See Chapter 4.
3 Lipman and Wheatcroft, op. cit., p. 49.
4 Sorensen Interview, 12 September 2001.
5 See below and in Chapter 4.
6 Council Decision, 20 December 1979, 'Setting up a Consultation Procedure on Relations Between Member States and Third Countries in the Field of Air Transport and On Action Relating to Such Matters Within International Organizations', (80/50/EEC), No. L 18/24, 24 January 1980.
7 Inter-Regional Services, OJ No. L 237, 26 August 1983.
8 Directives 80/1266/EEC and 80/51/EEC OJ No. L18, 24.01. 1980, p. 26.
9 EEC Commission 1975, 'Report and Proposed Decision on a Programme of Action for the European Aeronautical Sector', OJ C265; McGowan and Trengove, op. cit., p. 83.
10 See Chapter 8.
11 Stevens, op. cit. (1997), p. 4.
12 Luxembourg Council, 462nd Session, 28/29 June 1977.
13 'European Airline Traffic after 1993', presentation by F. Sorensen, VII.C.1 – 839/90, 8 April 1991: copy courtesy of Sorensen.
14 'The European Union's Transport Policy', *Periodical*, 3, 1984, 36–7. The list of priorities included: noise reduction; simplification of formalities; uniform technical standards; regulation of competition and state aids; mutual recognition of crew licenses; better working conditions; freedom of establishment; improvement of interregional services; and mutual assistance in the event of accidents.

200   Notes

15   'Review of Competition Policy', Air Transport Policy Unit, CEC, 7th, 1978, p. 38.
16   'The European Community's Transport Policy', *Periodical*, 3, 1984, p. 36.
17   Sorensen Interview, 21 February 2000.
18   Memorandum 1, 'Contributions of the EC to the Development of Air Transport Services', COM(79) 311, 6 July 1979, Supplement 5/79 EC Bulletin, 8139/79.
19   *Flight International*, 22 December 1979, p. 20.
20   The European Community's Transport Policy, *Periodical 3/1984*, p. 38.
21   Stevens, op. cit. (1997), p. 6 and Lipman and Wheatcroft, op. cit., p. 50.
22   Sundberg in Haanappel, op. cit., p. 168.
23   McGowan and Trengove, op. cit., p. 84.
24   Interview with official from DG IV, 22 February 2000.
25   Sorensen Interview, 21 February 2000.
26   'The European Community's Transport Policy', *Periodical*, 3, 1984, p. 17.
27   Council Decision, 'Consultation Procedure', 20 December 1979, No. L 18/24–25, 80/50/EEC, OJ 24/1/80.
28   Ibid.
29   See Chapter 4.
30   'A Better Transport Network for Europe', European File, 5/81, March 1981, p. 7. Directive on Licensing of Inter-regional Air Services, 83/416, July 1983, OJ 237, 26 August 1983.
31   Ibid.; Lipman and Wheatcroft, op. cit., p. 126, citing views of Sorensen and statistics from *AEA Yearbook 1985*; McGowan and Trengove, op. cit., p. 85.
32   Sorensen Interview, 21 February 2000.
33   Loder Collection, HE 9797A2, 'European Community: Commission Proposal for a Community Air Transport Policy', John Loder, UK Department of Transport, Analysis of Memorandum 2, September 1983.
34   'A Better Transport Network for Europe', *European File, 5/81*, March 1981, p. 7.
35   Memorandum 1, 'Contributions of the EC to the Development of Air Transport Services', COM(79) 311, 6 July 1979, Supplement 5/79 *EC Bulletin*, 8139/79, Annex 2.
36   *House of Commons Debates*, 1979–80, vol. 989, col. 548, John Nott introducing third reading of the Civil Aviation Bill, 23 July 1980.
37   COM(81)398, Final, 'Scheduled Passenger Air Fares in the EEC', 23 July 1981, pp. 51, and 54–5.
38   'Proposal for a Council Regulation Applying Articles 85 and 86 of the Treaty to Air Transport', COM(81)396, 31 July 1981; Commission Report, COM(81)398, 23 July 1981; Haanappel, op. cit., Chapter 2; Lipman and Wheatcroft, op. cit., p. 50.
39   Stevens, op. cit. (1997), p. 7.
40   *Parliament* v. *Council*, ECJ Case 13/83; Stevens, op. cit. (2004), p. 55.
41   Loder Collection, HC240.9. Note for the Attention of DG VII, Application of the competition rules to the fixing of fares in the air sector, from B. van der Esch and G.L. Close, 22 May 1981.
42   Ibid.
43   Ibid.
44   *Bethell* v. *The Commission*, 246/81.
45   Ibid.
46   Loder Collection, HC240.9, Draft letter, undated, Peter Sutherland for Commission to BA.
47   Ibid., 3 February 1982, Council, Opinion of the Legal Service.
48   Ibid., HE 9797A2, 'European Community: Commission Proposal for a Community Air Transport Policy', John Loder Analysis of Memorandum 2, September 1983.
49   Wheatcroft and Lipman, op. cit., p. 123.
50   'Progress Towards the Development of a Community Air Transport Policy', COM(84)72, 15 March 1984, otherwise known as Memorandum 2.

51 Ibid., Annexes 4 and 5.
52 Sorensen Interview, 12 September 2001.

4 The single market and the reaction to Memorandum 2

1. COM(84)72, Final, 'Civil Aviation Memorandum 2: Progress Towards the Development of a Community Air Transport Policy', 15 March 1984, p. i.
2. Loder Collection, HC240.9, Steele to Davis, 'Tactical Considerations Relevant to the Current Discussions on Aviation Policy', 29 April 1985.
3. Sorensen Interview, 21 February 2000.
4. D. Dinan, *Europe Recast: A History of European Union*, Basingstoke: Palgrave Macmillan 2004, p. 205.
5. M. Thatcher, *The Downing Street Years*, London: Harper Collins, 1993, p. 547.
6. European Parliament, *Draft Treaty establishing the European Union*, Luxembourg, February 1984, Article 53 (b), p. 32. The draft Treaty was adopted 14 February 1984 by a vote of 237 to thirty-one with forty-three abstentions.
7. Greenwood, op. cit., p. 101.
8. Dinan, op. cit., pp. 216–17.
9. Ibid., p. 547.
10. Thatcher, op. cit., p. 553.
11. White Paper 'Completing the Internal Market', COM(85)310, May 1985, paragraphs 109–10.
12. Williams, in Haanappel (ed.), op. cit., p. 19.
13. Fennes Interview, 21 February 2000.
14. Ibid., Loder Collection HE 9797A2, 'European Community: Commission Proposal for a Community Air Transport Policy', John Loder, UK Department of Transport, Analysis of Memorandum 2, September 1983.
15. COM(84)72 Final, 'Progress Towards the Development of a Community Air Transport Policy', Civil Aviation Memorandum No. 2, 15 March 1984, p. 50.
16. Ibid.
17. Ibid.
18. Cmd. 9366, 'Airline Competition Policy', 1984.
19. Sorensen Interview, 21 February 2000.
20. *EC Bulletin* 9–1985, p. 79, Parliament, Strasbourg 9–13 September, Jan Klinkenborg.
21. Loder Collection, HC 240.9, Committee on Transport [of the European Parliament] Draft Report on Memorandum 2, Rapporteur J. Klinkenborg, 14 March 1985, Klinkenborg Report, EP Doc. A-86/85.
22. Ibid., p. 31.
23. Loder Collection, HE 9777.7, *An Analysis of US Deregulation of Air Transport with Its Inferences for a More Liberal Air Transport Policy in Europe*, Professor P.P.C. Haanappel, 21 May 1984, for the European Parliament Committee on Economic Affairs and Development, p. 62.
24. Ibid., p. 60.
25. Ibid., pp. 62–5.
26. *Flight International*, 17 May 1986, pp. 4–5.
27. Memorandum 2, COM(84)72, p. 26.
28. Klinkenborg, Draft Report on Memorandum 2, 14 March 1985, p. 26.
29. Ibid., p. 25.
30. Ibid., p. 27.
31. Ibid.
32. Ibid., p. 49.
33. Ibid., p. 27.
34. Ibid., p. 34.

35 Ibid.
36 Ibid., pp. 35–6.
37 Ibid., p. 36.
38 Ibid., p. 43.
39 Ibid., p. 47.
40 Ibid.
41 Ibid., pp. 51–2.
42 Stevens, op. cit. 1997, p. 20.
43 *EC Bulletin* 9–1985, p. 80.
44 R. Branson address to IEA Conference, 6 October 1993.
45 Kahn, in Noll and Owen (eds), op. cit., p. 140.
46 Pryke, op. cit., pp. 38–61 and 95–106.
47 Forsyth, op. cit., p. 20; S.D. Barratt, 'Deregulating European Aviation – A Case Study', *Transportation*, 16, 1990, 311–27.
48 Interview with DG IV official, 22 February 2000.
49 Loder Collection, HE 9777.7INS, 13 October 1988, Institute of Air Transport Marrakesh, Scoozza until recently had been Assistant Secretary for International Affairs, US Department of Transportation.
50 Loder Collection, HE 9797A2, Information AEA, 'AEA Completes Comparative Study of European and US Market', 8 May 1987 and comments by Karl-Heinz Neumeister, Secretary General of AEA.
51 Ibid., p. 6.
52 John Steele speech ECAC-EU Dialogue, 29 April 2005, www.prismaconsulting.com/EC accessed 7 December 2005.
53 Gowan and Trengove, op. cit., p. 89.
54 Sorensen Interview, 21 February 2000.
55 Quoted from Gowan and Trengove, op. cit., p. 89.
56 R. Branson address to IEA Conference, 6 October 1993.
57 Cmd. 9366, 'Airline Competition Policy', 1984.

5 Achieving the first package of reform

1 *European File*, 'Air Transport and Aeronautics: Towards a Europe of the Skies', CEC 1989 2/89, p. 7.
2 Sorensen Interview, 21 February 2000.
3 Loder Collection, HE 9797A2, Loder to Bethell, 5 July 1988.
4 Ibid., Information AEA 'AEA Completes Comparative Study of European and US Market, 3 June 1987, comments by Secretary General Neumeister, p. 6.
5 D. Swann, *The Retreat of the State: Deregulation and Privatisation in the UK and the US*, Hemel Hempstead, Harvester Wheatsheaf 1988, p. 243.
6 Loder Collection, HE 9797A2, Loder to Bethell, 25 November 1984.
7 Sorensen Interview, 21 February 2000.
8 *EC Bulletin*, 1984–5, 2.1.170.
9 Stevens, op. cit. 1997, pp. 16–17.
10 Wheatcroft and Lipman, op. cit., pp. 110–12.
11 Stevens, op. cit. 1997, p. 17.
12 Wheatcroft and Lipman, op. cit., pp. 54–5.
13 *EC Bulletin*, 1984–12, 2.1.208.
14 Stevens, op. cit. 1997, p. 20.
15 *European Parliament* v. *Council*, case 13/83, ECR 1513 and Gowan and Trengove, op. cit., p. 90.
16 Loder Collection, HC 240.9, Statement by the Commission Representative at the 1006th session of the Council (Transport), 23 May 1985, 7087/85.

17 Loder Collection, HC 240.9, John R. Steele, Note for the Attention of Mr S. Clinton Davis, 29 April 1985, p. 1.
18 Ibid., p. 2.
19 Ibid., pp. 2–3.
20 Ibid., attached Draft Speaking Note/Press notice: Aviation Policy 29 April 1985, for Clinton Davis.
21 Ibid.
22 Ibid.
23 Ibid.
24 Stevens, op. cit. 1997, p. 17.
25 *EC Bulletin* 1985–9, 2.1.123.
26 Stevens, op. cit. 1997, p. 17, citing Press Release IP(85)385, 11 September 1985.
27 *EC Bulletin* 1985–11, 2.1.160.
28 Stevens, op. cit. 2004, p. 152; ECAC Policy Statement on Intra-European Air Transport, Paris, 1985.
29 Ibid.
30 *EC Bulletin* 1986–1, 2.1.128.
31 Ibid., 1986–3 2.1.49.
32 Cases 209–213/84, *Ministère public* v. *Lucas Asjes et al., Nouvelles Frontières*.
33 Loder Collection, HC 240.9, 12 May 1986, Legal Service memorandum to Members of the Commission: Judgement Court of Justice, 30 April 1986, Joined Cases 209 to 213/84, *Nouvelles Frontières*, p. 8.
34 *Flight International*, 14 June 1986, 'Practically Nothing Expected from Brussels', p. 5.
35 Ibid.
36 Ibid.
37 *EC Bulletin*, 1986–6, 2.1.233.
38 COM(86)338, final.
39 Quoted from Wheatcroft and Lipman, op. cit., p. 59.
40 *EC Bulletin* 1986–6, 2.1.233.
41 Wheatcroft and Lipman, op. cit., p. 61; Stevens, op. cit. 1997, p. 23.
42 *Flight International*, 17 May 1986, Nouvelles Frontières: Where Europe is Headed', pp. 4–5.
43 Loder Collection, HC 240.9, Draft letter, Peter D. Sutherland for Commission to BA, undated.
44 Wheatcroft and Lipman, op. cit., p. 128; EC Bulletin – 7/8, 1986, 2.1.211.
45 *Flight International*, 22 November 1986, 'European Law Threatens European Cartels', pp. 6–7; Stevens, 1997, op. cit., p. 24.
46 Quoted from *Flight International*, 22 November 1986, 'European Law Threatens European Cartels', pp. 6–7.
47 Ibid.
48 Ibid.
49 Ibid.
50 *EC Bulletin* 1986–12, 2.1.303.
51 Ibid.
52 Stevens, op. cit. 1997, p. 26.
53 *EC Bulletin* 1987–3, 2.1.200 and 2.1.201.
54 Directives 87/601/EEC and 87/602/EEC; Regulations 3975/87 and 3976/87.
55 *Flight International*, 13 February 1988, 'Europe's New Rules: Substance or Illusion?', p. 9.
56 *EC Bulletin* 1987–12, 2.1.280.
57 *Flight International*, 13 February 1988, 'Europe's New Rules: Substance or Illusion?', p. 9.
58 *EC Bulletin* 1987–12, 2.1.280.

6 Receiving Package 1: delivering Package 2

1. Sir Leon Brittan paper presented Aviation Conference, Marrakesh, 1–3 June 1989.
2. Interview with three Commission officials from DG TREN, 25 September 2006, official 1.
3. Regulation (EEC) No. 2671/88, OJ L239/9, 6 July 1988; enforcement provisions were promulgated in Regulation 4261/88.
4. Regulations (EEC) Nos. 2673/88 and 2672/88, OJ Nos L239/17 and L239/13, 26 July 1988.
5. Loder Collection, HE 9797A2, Loder to Bethell, 5 July 1988.
6. Ibid.
7. Ibid.
8. Loder Collection, HE 9797A2, Bethell to Tugendhat and his reply on 24 February and 24 March 1988.
9. Ibid., Loder to Bethell, 10 April 1988.
10. Ibid.
11. Ibid.
12. *Flight International*, 'UK CAA Defines Competition Policy', 6 February 1988, p. 14.
13. Rules reproduced in the *House of Commons Session 1987–88 Transport Committee Third Report Airline Competition: Computer Reservation Systems vol. 1*, appendix 18, pp. 49–51, London, HMG Stationery Office, 1988.
14. *Flight International*, 10 October 1987, 'Sabre Crusades for Neutral CRS in Europe', pp. 6–7; for major inquiry into operation of US CRSs, see *Airline Competition: Impact of Computerized Reservation Systems, United States General Accounting Office Report to Congressional Requesters*, May 1986, GAO/RCED-86-74, Washington DC, 1986. As we shall see later in this chapter, the dispute was settled out of court with Sabre adopting the ECAC code for displays to run alongside its standard display, Interview with Arnold Grossman, Vice President for International Affairs, AA, 12 April 1991.
15. David Moss, Under Secretary, Department of Transport, evidence before *House of Commons Transport Committee Session 1987–88, Third Report Airline Competition: Computer Reservation Systems, vol. 2, Minutes of Evidence*, London, HMSO, 28 July 1988, p. 211.
16. Interview with senior official, UK Department of Transportation, 25 September 1991.
17. The Regional Services Directive was updated and brought into line with Package 1 by Directive 89/463/EEC, 18 July 1989, following proposals submitted by the Commission to the Council in March 1988.
18. COM(88)447 final, Proposal for a Council Regulation (EEC) on a code of conduct for computerised reservation systems, 14 October 1988.
19. Loder Collection, HE 9797A2, Loder to Bethell, 5 July 1988.
20. 'Air Services Agreement Between the Government of the United States of America and the Government of the United Kingdom and Northern Ireland including Amendments through 1980', US Department of Transportation, Washington DC, 1981. For detailed analysis of the replacement of TWA and Pan Am. with AA and UA, see A.P. Dobson, 'The USA, Hegemony and Airline Market Access to Britain and Western Europe, 1945–96, *Diplomacy and Statecraft*, 9(2), 1998, 129–59.
21. As we noted in Chapter 2, an exception to this was BM, which was deemed to have a grandfathered right to international operations out of Heathrow on rather dubious but politically expedient grounds.
22. BM, in particular, was keen to get more and better scheduled slots at Heathrow and argued that among other ways this could be done by increased efficiency which would allow the number of slots to grow. BM had the second largest number of aircraft movements at Heathrow after BA.
23. Dobson, 1998, op. cit.

24 Interview with Lord King, 17 May 1991.
25 Loder Collection, HC 240.9, Loder to Goodman, 28 May 1989.
26 COM(89)476 final, Report on the first year (1988) of implementation of the aviation policy approved in December 1987. Directives 87/601/EEC (1) (fares) and 87/602/EEC (2) (capacity/market access) require Commission to submit a report by 1 November 1989.
27 Ibid.
28 Ibid.
29 Ibid.
30 Loder Collection, HE 9797A2, Loder to Bethell, 5 July 1988.
31 EFTA was formed in 1960, largely by British leadership and with Austria, Switzerland, Portugal, Norway, Sweden and Denmark as members. It was supposed to be a free trade alternative to the EEC, without commitments to integration.
32 Loder Collection, HC 240.9, Communication to the Commission from Van Miert, draft letter 27 July 1989.
33 COM(90)17, final Proposal for a Council Decision on Consultation and Authorization Procedure for Agreements Concerning Commercial Aviation Relations Between Member States and Third parties, 23 February 1990.
34 COM(89)417, 8 September 1989 and OJ C258, 29 September 1989, p. 7.
35 Stevens, op. cit. 1997, p. 31.
36 Argyris in Haanappel (ed.), op. cit. 1989, p. 75.
37 Ibid., Sundberg, p. 170.
38 Ibid., Weber, p. 62.
39 European Court of Justice Information Office, Press Summary, 11 April 1989. Judgement of the Court in case 66/86, the Ahmed Saeed case.
40 Argyris in Haanappel, op. cit., p. 77; *EC Bulletin* 1989, No. 7/8 2.1202.
41 COM(90)17, Final Proposal for a Council Decision on Consultation and Authorization Procedure for Agreements Concerning Commercial Aviation Relations Between Member States and Third Parties, 23 February 1990.
42 *EC Bulletin* 1990, No. 1/2, 1.1256.
43 Ibid.
44 Ibid.
45 Ibid.
46 AETR Case ECJ Case 22/70, March 1971; *House of Lords Session 1990–91. Report Select Committee on the European Communities,* 23 April 1991. Conduct of the Community's External Aviation Relations, 23 April 1992. Report on 5080/90 (COM(90)17), p. 5.
47 Loder Collection, HE 9762.5, Explanatory Memorandum on European Community Legislation 5080/90 COM(90)17, Patrick M'Loughlin, Parliamentary Under Secretary of State, Department of Transport, 28 March 1990.
48 *House of Lords Session 1990–91. Report Select Committee on the European Communities, 23 April 1991. Conduct of the Community's External Aviation Relations*, 23 April 1992. Report on 5080/90 (COM(90)17), p. 27.
49 Interview with senior official DG IV, 22 May 1991.
50 Loder Collection, HE 976L-5 Air Transport Relations with Third Countries (Communication to the Council – preliminary version, subject to linguistic verification) 1992.
51 European Court of Justice Opinion 1/94.
52 COM(90)18, final, 14 February 1990, Recommendation for a Council Decision: The Opening of Negotiations Between the European Economic Community and EFTA Countries on Scheduled Air Passenger Services; Frederik Sorensen, 'European Airline Traffic After 1993', 8 April 1991, p. 10.
53 *House of Lords Session 1990–91, 9th Report Select Committee on the European*

Communities: Conduct of the Community's External Aviation relations, 23 April 1992, p. 27.
54 Ibid.
55 Frederik Sorensen, evidence before *House of Commons Transport Committee Session 1987–88, Third Report Airline Competition: Computer Reservation Systems, vol. 2, Minutes of Evidence*, HMSO, London, 28 July 1988, p. 176.
56 COM(88)447 final, Proposal for a Council Regulation (EEC) on a Code of Conduct for Computerised Reservation Systems, 14 October 1988.
57 Nicholas Argyris, evidence before *House of Commons Transport Committee Session 1987–88, Third Report Airline Competition: Computer Reservation Systems, vol. 2, Minutes of Evidence*, HMSO, London, 28 July 1988, p. 172.
58 Stevens, op. cit. 2004, p. 156.
59 COM(88)447 final, Proposal for a Council Regulation (EEC) on a Code of Conduct for Computerised Reservation Systems, 14 October 1988, p. 3.
60 Council Regulation 2299/89.
61 Council Regulation 3089/93, 11 December 1993 was the first major update. There was a further flurry of activity in 1997, but by then the problems of CRSs had been brought largely under control.
62 Argyris in Haanappel, op. cit., p. 80; *EC Bulletin* 1990, No. 12, 1.3.276, COM(90)576.
63 *Flight International*, 12 December 1990, 'EC Climbdown on Slots Forced By Airlines', p. 6.
64 Stevens, op. cit. 2004, p. 159.
65 COM(90)63 final, 8 March 1990, Proposal for a Council Regulation on the Operation of Air Cargo Services; Council Regulation 294/91, 4 February 1991.
66 Argyris in Haanappel, op. cit., p. 78.
67 *Independent*, 31 July 1989, 'Sharing the Pie in the Sky'.
68 *Independent*, 5 August 1992, 'EC airlines still clinging to state subsidies', p. 21.
69 Loder Collection, HC 240.9, Communication to the Commission from Van Miert, 27 July 1989, draft letter.
70 Stevens, op. cit. 1997, p. 30.
71 Loder Collection, HE 9762.5, Nicholas Argyris address to European Air Law Association, London, 27 July 1990.
72 Ibid. HC 240.9, Loder to Powell, 1 December 1989.
73 Thatcher, op. cit., p. 756; on 5 June 1989, there was a Resolution calling on all Member States to join Eurocontrol, but that was only the beginning of trying to sort out the troubles that would afflict European airline traffic control for many years.
74 Portillo quoted in Stevens, op. cit. 1997, p. 34, no source provided; Circular from Moorhouse, 'Cheaper Air Fares thanks to British Initiative', 8 December 1989. For more detailed views of the UK Department of Transport on Package 2, see Loder Collection, HE 9762–5, Transport Select Committee Inquiry: Developments in European Community Air Transport Policy, Memorandum by Department of Transport, December 1990.
75 Loder Collection, HC 240.9, Loder to Powell, 1 December 1989.
76 Ibid. and Stevens, op. cit. 1997, pp. 32–3. Loder places the meetings on 13 and 14 not 15 and 16 November as in Stevens.
77 Loder Collection, HC 240.9, Loder to Powell 1 December 1989.
78 Regulation EEC, No. 2342/90, 24 July 1990.
79 Regulation EEC, No. 2343/90, 24 July 1990.
80 Frederik Sorensen, 'European Airline Traffic After 1993', 8 April 1991, p. 4.
81 Regulation EEC, No. 2343/90, 24 July 1990.
82 Loder Collection, HE 9762.5, Nicholas Argyris address to European Air Law Association, London, 27 July 1990.

83 Ibid.
84 Interview with senior official from the UK CAA, 23 May 2001.
85 Fennes Interview, 21 February 2000.
86 Stevens, op. cit. 1997, pp. 33–4.
87 Interview with senior official DG IV, 22 February 2000.
88 Argyris in Haanappel, op. cit., p. 78.
89 *Flight International*, 7 November 1990, p. 12.
90 Ibid.
91 Remarks by Lord King, Royal Aeronautical Society 125th Anniversary Banquet, 16 May 1991.
92 Loder Collection, HE 9762–5, C. Paice, CAA Group Director, Economic Regulation Group, to A.H. Doherty, clerk to the Transport Committee, House of Commons, 31 October 1990.
93 Interview with Andrew Gray, 26 March 1991.
94 COM(90)100 final, 22 May 1990.
95 Frederik Sorensen, 'European Airline Traffic After 1993', 8 April 1991, p. 5.

7 Package 3: delivery in 1992

1 Interview with senior official DG IV, 22 May 1991.
2 *Flight International*, 21 July 1993, 'Twelve Wise Men', p. 22.
3 Loder Collection, HE 9762.5, Argyris address to European Air Law association, 27 July 1990; for the US experience, see 'Secretary's Taskforce on Competition in the US Domestic Airline Industry', February 1990, US Department of Transportation, Washington DC, Office of the Secretary of Transportation.
4 Ibid., UK Department of Transportation, memorandum, December 1990.
5 Ibid.
6 Loder Collection, HE 9762.5, 'Turbulence in European Aviation', LCB Consultants Ltd. Aviation Industry Study Group, April 1988.
7 *Flight International*, 13 January 1993, 'Kahn Warns Europe on Deregulation Dangers', p. 8.
8 E. Sochor, *The Politics of International Aviation*, London, Macmillan, 1991, p 197, citing source Wolfgang Weinert, corporate strategist for Lufthansa, address to Airline Business Conference, London, 28 March 1988.
9 Interview with senior official DG IV, 22 February 2000.
10 *Flight International*, 25 March 1991, editorial, 'Competing Views', p. 3.
11 Stevens, op. cit. 1997, p. 44, citing 'Aviation State Aid' briefing by UK Department of Transport, 5 October 1995.
12 Loder Collection, HE 9762.5, UK Department of Transportation, memorandum, December 1990.
13 A.P. Dobson, 'Aspects of Anglo-American Aviation Diplomacy 1976–93', *Diplomacy and Statecraft*, 4:2, 1993, 235–57 at pp. 246–54.
14 *Flight International*, 25 March 1991, editorial, 'Competing Views', p. 3.
15 Ibid., 13 February 1991, 'European Airlines Declare 1990 Losses', p. 12.
16 Ibid., 20 January 1993, Airline Apocalypse', p. 25 and 28 April 1993, 'Aerospace Apocalypse', p. 26.
17 H.-L. Dienel and P. Lyth (eds), op. cit., pp. 40–1.
18 *Flight International*, 20 February 1991, 'Where Have all the Airline Jobs Gone?', p. 22.
19 Ibid., 13 February 1991, 'Community Considers State Aid for Airlines', p. 13.
20 Ibid., 15 May 1991, 'No European Competition Yet', predicts Tugendhat', p. 10.
21 Loder Collection, HC 240.9, Sorensen, 'EEC Internal and External Aviation Policy',

10 June 1991; COM(91)275 final, 'Completion of the Civil Aviation Policy in the European Communities Towards Single Market Conditions', 18 September 1991.
22. Loder Collection, HC 240.9, Sorensen, 'EEC Internal and External Aviation Policy', p. 3, 10 June 1991.
23. COM(91)275, 'On licensing of Air Carriers' pp. 19–38; 'On Access', p. 48. There could only be like-for-like competition, that is, only another 80-seat aircraft would be allowed entry to compete.
24. Sorensen, 'European Airline Traffic After 1993', 8 April 1991, p. 8.
25. Sorensen's position on fares between April and June does not seem to have changed. In a presentation in April, he had simply spoken of a double disapproval system being implemented. Sorensen, 'European Airline Traffic After 1993', 8 April 1991, p. 7.
26. Ibid., p. 15.
27. Ibid., p. 5.
28. Loder Collection, HC 240.9, Sorensen, 'EEC Internal and External Aviation Policy', 10 June 1991, p. 9.
29. Ibid., p. 10.
30. Ibid., p. 11 and COM(91)275, p. 7.
31. Interview with three Commission officials from DG TREN (previously DG VII), 25 September 2006, official 1.
32. *Flight International*, 24 July 1991, 'EC in New Liberalisation Move', p. 8.
33. Ibid.
34. Ibid., 7 August 1991, 'Liberalising Europe's Skies', p. 22.
35. Ibid.
36. Ibid.
37. Interview with senior official DG IV, 22 February 2000; *Flight International*, 1 April 1992, European Ministers Back Lower Air Fares, p. 11; *Independent,* 27 March 1992, 'EC accepts free pricing for air fares', p. 9.
38. *EC Bulletin* 1992, No. 4 1.3.75.
39. *Flight International*, 1 April 1992, 'European Ministers Back Lower Air Fares', p. 11.
40. Ibid., 1 July 1992, 'EC Compromises on Air Competition', p. 6.
41. Ibid., 21 July 1992, 'Not Liberal Enough?', p. 23.
42. Interview with three Commission officials from DG TREN (previously DG VII), 25 September 2006, official 2.
43. *Financial Times,* 23 June 1992, 'EC Pact May Trigger Air Fare Cuts'.
44. EC Regulations 2407/92, 2408/92, 2409/92, 23 July 1992.
45. Flight International, 21 July 1992, 'Not Liberal Enough?', p. 23.
46. *Financial Times*, 24 June 1992, 'Clouds over Open Skies', p. 18.

8 Impact and developments after Package 3

1. L. Jones, *EasyJet: The Story of Britain's Biggest Low-Cost Airline*, London, Aurum, 2005, p. 16.
2. *Flight International*, 15 July 1992, p. 23; *Financial Times* 24 June and 2 September 1992, pp. 18 and vii respectively.
3. Bishop quoted in *Financial Times*, 24 June 1992, 'Clouds over open skies', p. 18.
4. *Financial Times*, 5 April and 10 May 1995, 'Showdown over French skies', p. 9 and 'France opens up Orly air routes', p. 2.
5. European Commission White Paper 'European Transport Policy for 2010: Time to Decide', COM(2001)370, 2001. Significantly, however, the White Paper talked about environmental matters and sustainability, which held some serious challenges for the future of civil aviation. These challenges were being fully articulated in 2006.
6. EasyJet took its first booking in October 1995, see Jones, op. cit., p. 12.
7. This list by no means exhausts the catalogue of problems and challenges that

remained or arose over the following years. They will be briefly mentioned in the final chapter, but these were the most significant issues as perceived by the reformers and Commission officials at the time.
8 Interview with three Commission officials from DG TREN (previously DG7), 25 September 2006, official 1.
9 *Flight International*, 20 February 1991, 'Community views European airline aid agreements', p. 13.
10 DG VII/C/2–448/92, Communication of the Commission of the EC on Guidelines for the Evaluation of State Aids in the Aviation Sector, Executive Summary, 20 April 1993; and Annex 4 of 2nd Memorandum on Aviation Policy, COM(84)72.
11 *Independent*, 5 August 1992, 'EC airlines still clinging to state subsidies', p. 21.
12 *Daily Telegraph*, 25 September 1993.
13 *Flight International*, 5 October 1993, 'Disclosures to the Wise', p. 24.
14 Ibid., 21 July 1993, 'Twelve Wise Men', pp. 22–3.
15 *Expanding Horizons: A Report by the Comité des Sages for Air Transport to the European Commission*, January 1994, p. 17.
16 *Financial Times*, 2 December 1993, p. 3.
17 *Expanding Horizons*, p. 21.
18 *Financial Times*, 5 April 1995, 'Showdown over French skies', p. 9.
19 *Flight International*, 10 September 1997, 'Blanc quits over privatisation', p. 12.
20 Summary Report DG TREN, Analysis of the European Air Transport Industry 2003. Final Report January 2005, p. 22.
21 *Financial Times*, 10 November 1994, 'Struggle at the airport gates', p. 22.
22 *Aerospace International*, August 1998, p. 7.
23 *Financial Times*, 11 March 1997, 'Freedom to go a little crazy', p. 19.
24 *Observer*, 22 September 2002, 'Airlines Fear Gathering Storm', *Business* p. 4; *Aerospace International*, October 2001, 'Airlines suffer', p. 8.
25 Interviews with three Commission officials from DG TREN (previously DG7), official 1 and two officials from the DG for Competition (formally DG4) official 2, both 25 September 2006.
26 *Observer*, 23 September 2001, 'EU wants shake-outs, rather than handouts', *Business*, p. 4.
27 *Aerospace International*, July 2002, p. 4; not surprisingly Air France was compensated beyond the 4-day period and later investigated by the Commission.
28 *Guardian*, 'Belgian Airline goes bust with loss of 12,000 jobs', 8 November 2001.
29 COMPAS Report 1982, p. 47; Klinkenborg, Draft Report 14 March 1985, p. 27.
30 Richard Branson, Address to the IEA Conference, 6 October 1993. He delivered something similar to the European Aviation Club in Brussels a few days later reported in *Flight International*, 20 October 1993, with headline, 'Branson rages at Europe', p. 12.
31 Ibid., 27 January 1993, 'A better slot', editorial.
32 Loder Collection, HE 9797 A2, Paper on Slots by R.J.C. Ebdon, Head of Commercial and Government Affairs, BA, 21 May 1992.
33 Council Regulations (EEC) No. 95/93, 18 January 1993 and No. 1617/93, 1 July 1993.
34 *Expanding Horizons*, p. 20.
35 *Financial Times*, 11 March 1997, 'Freedom to go a little crazy', p. 19.
36 Button *et al.*, op. cit., p. 85.
37 The other factor was the failure to reach agreement on an open-skies agreement between the US and the UK. Proposed alliance was announced on 11 June 1996 but raised serious questions about the dominance of BA and AA on transatlantic routes and at Heathrow. By November, there was talk of the two airlines having to give up slots at Heathrow, and in December, the number bruited about was 168, but BA and

AA were far from happy with such proposals. In the end, the European Commission said yes to the alliance in the autumn of 1998, but set the price at 267 weekly slots from Gatwick and Heathrow with 220–30 from the latter, which effectively made the alliance too expensive to consummate. *Financial Times* 12 June 1996, 'A day for eating words', p. 23 and editorial; *Independent Business* 'Those Desperate Men in their flying machines', p. 1 and 16 November 1997, 'Ayling airline seeks flight from failure', p. 6 and *Independent News*, 29 September 1996, 'Open skies cloud the issue for BA deal', p. 2 and 8 December 1996, 'BA and American to pursue link-up', p. 2; *Aerospace International*, December 1998, 'AA-BA on hold', p. 4, the two airlines decided on a looser relationship through the Oneworld Alliance. Matters had become extremely fraught in Anglo-American talks for replacing Bermuda 2 with an open-skies agreement. *Observer*, Business, 17 June 2001, 'BA and AA kiss and make up', p. 4.

38 AEA Information, 19 January 1998, 'Airline chiefs in talks with competition Commissioner'.
39 Karel Van Miert, Speech, 'Competition policy in the air transport sector', April 1998, copy courtesy of the Royal Aeronautical Society, London. The same message was repeated to Loyola De Palacio two years later when she met with airline executives. They warned her about weakening Europe's major airlines in their bid to compete globally by favouring new entrants and withdrawing slots from them: AEA Information, 31 October 2000, on meeting at Madrid 27 October 2000.
40 *Observer*, 21 April 2002, 'BA buys up Heathrow slots'.
41 COM(2001)0335, final Proposal for the European Parliament and the Council amending Council Regulation (EEC) No. 95/93 of 18 January 1993 on common rules for the allocation of slots at Community airports.
42 Coopers and Lybrand, 'Application and Possible Modification of Council Regulation 95/93 on Common Rules for the Allocation of Slots at Community Airports', 17 October 1995.
43 AEA Information, undated, reporting on Neumeister speech 'Better Use of Airport Slots in the EU', Düsseldorf, Hochtief AirPort Symposium, 17 September 2001.
44 COM(2001)0335, final Proposal for the European Parliament and the Council amending Council Regulation (EEC) No. 95/93 of 18 January 1993 on common rules for the allocation of slots at Community airports.
45 A report for DG TREN claimed that the reform only had 'limited institutional impact', *ASSESS: Assessment of the contribution of the TEN and other transport policy measures to the mid-term implementation of the White Paper on the European Transport Policy for 2010*. Transport and Mobility Leuven, 28 October 2005. Annex XIV, Qualitative Analysis of Air Transport Issues. Commission of the European Communities White Paper 12 September 2001, Europe Transport Policy for 2010, COM(2001)370 final.
46 Loder Collection, HE 9780, DG7 Discussion Document, Subject: Revision of Council Regulation 95/93, 11 April 1996.
47 Council Regulation 793/2004 of the European Parliament and the Council, 21 April 2004 amending Council Regulation (EEC) No. 95/93 on common rules for the allocation of slots at Community airports.
48 Interview with senior Commission officials DG TREN, 25 September 2006, official 1 and with senior officials DG for Competition, official 2.
49 *Assess: Assessment of the contribution to TEN and other transport measures to the mid-term implementation of the White paper on European Transport Policy for 2010*, Transport and Mobility Leuven, 28 October 2005 for DG TREN, Annex XIV, p. 45.
50 *Flight International*, 15 July 1992, 'Airlines Dissatisfied with European ATC', p. 9.
51 Ibid.
52 Ibid., 31 July 1991, 'EC wants EUROCONTROL changes', p. 6.

53 Ibid., 25 March 1992, 'Second-course EATCHIP cleared by ECAC', p. 10.
54 *Expanding Horizons*, p. 23.
55 Ibid.
56 AEA Information, 'Still too much national influence in Eurocontrol, say airspace users', 14 February 1997.
57 *Air Transport Action Group News*, September 1997.
58 COM(1999)614 final, 'The Creation of the Single European Sky', 1 December 1999.
59 Speech by Michael Ayral, Director Air Transport, EC, 'European Air Transport Policy: Examining the external constraints imposed on ATM by liberalisation, environmental protection, defence, security requirements and economics'. ATC 2000 Conference, 22–3 February 2000, Maastricht.
60 European Parliament Session Document, Final A5–0141/2000, 26 May 2000, report on COM(1999)614, Committee for Regional Policy, Transport and Tourism, Explanatory Statement by Rapporteur, Sir Robert Atkinson.
61 *Flight International*, 19 September 2000, 'Privatisation the answer to ATC difficulties says IATA', p. 12.
62 European Commission Directorate-General Energy and Transport, 'Single European Sky: Report of the high-level group', Brussels, November 2000.
63 Ibid., pp. 3–4.
64 *Aerospace International*, July 2003, 'Clear the skies', p. 14.
65 EC Regulations Nos. 549/2004, 550/2004, 551/2004 and 552/2004, effective 20 April 2004.
66 www.cfmu.eurocontrol.int/cfmu/g.
67 *Aerospace International*, January 2003, p. 4, and EC Regulations Nos. 549/2004, 550/2004, 551/2004 and 552/2004.
68 EUROCONTROL 'The Single European Sky', www.eurocontrol.int/ses/public/standard_page/sk_ses.html.
69 Ibid.
70 *Assess: Assessment of the contribution to TEN and other transport measures to the mid-term implementation of the White paper on European Transport Policy for 2010*, Transport and Mobility Leuven, 28 October 2005 for DG TREN, Annex XIV, p. 28.
71 *Flight International*, 9 September 1992, 'Carriers at loggerheads over BA deal', p. 14.
72 *International Aviation Developments, Second Report*, 'Transatlantic Deregulation: the Alliance Network Effect', US Department of Transportation, Office of the Secretary, October 2000.
73 'Air transport relations with third countries', COM(92)434, 21 October 1992, and *Flight International*, 28 October 1992, 'BA/US Air purchase 'concerns' Europe', p. 8.
74 Loder Collection, HE 9797 A2, Memo of Consultations, 4 September 1992, Protocol amending 3 April 1957 Bilateral Air Service Agreement between the Netherlands and the USA.
75 *Aerospace International*, December 2001, p. 5.
76 *International Aviation Developments, Second Report*, op. cit., pp. 2–5.
77 Ibid., p. 5.
78 Loder Collection, HE 9762.5, Argyris address to European Air Law Association: Seminar on Airline Mergers and Competition in the EC, 27 July 1990.
79 Sorensen Interview, 12 September 2001.
80 Interview with senior BA official, February 2002 and H.W. Bashor, 'A New Legal Order in Air Transport', *Journal of Diplomatic Language*, 2: 2005, www.jdonline.org/IIBashor.html, p. 16.
81 Sorensen Interview, 21 February 2002.

212 *Notes*

82 SkyTeam subsumed the old Wings Alliance and in 2006 consisted of Air France/ KLM, Alitalia, Continental, CSA, Delta, Northwest Airlines, Korean Air, Aeroflot, and Aeromexico. It flew 14,615 flights a day to 728 destinations in 149 countries.
83 Interview with two senior officials DG for Competition, 25 September 2006, official 1. The officials explained that the Commission's scepticism in early 1990s concerning the theory of contestability, which had largely been developed in the USA, had changed by 2006 because of changes in the marketplace. A more open and flexible market made contestability more potent.
84 *EC Bulletin*, Supplement 3/93, 1993, 'The future development of the common transport policy: A global approach to the construction of a Community framework for sustainable mobility'.
85 COM(94)218 final, 1 June 1994, 'The way forward for civil aviation in Europe', p. 3.
86 CAP 654 'The Single European Aviation Market: Progress So Far', September 1995, UK CAA, London, p. vii.
87 *Financial Times*, 20 September 1995, 'Europe's Airlines', p. 21.
88 Ibid.
89 COM(96)415 final, 'Impact of the Third Package of Air Transport Liberalisation measures and European Commission Spokesman's Service, 24 October 1996, 'Commission's report on impact of third and final stage of liberalisation from 1993–1996'.
90 AEA Information, 27 January 1998, 'Meeting the Global Challenge – the Outlook for Civil Aviation in the EU – the view from Brussels', Karl-Heinz Neumeister, Forum Europe Conference, Brussels, 27 January 1998.
91 COM(1999)614 final, 'The creation of the single European sky', p. 20. Figures given here are taken from COM(1999)614 final and from CAP 685, 'The Single European Aviation Market: the First Five Years', London, UK CAA, 1998.
92 *Observer*, 21 May 2001, Escape, pp. 10–11.
93 Speech by Michael Ayral, Director Air Transport, EC, 'European Air Transport Policy: Examining the external constraints imposed on ATM by liberalisation, environmental protection, defence, security requirements and economics'. ATC 2000 Conference, 22–3 February 2000, Maastricht, p. 2.
94 European Commission Spokesman's Service, 24 October 1996, 'Commission's report on impact of third and final stage of liberalisation from 1993–1996'.

9 External relations and the SEAM

1 *House of Lords Session 1990–91, 9th Report Select Committee on the European Communities: Conduct of the Community's External Aviation Relations*, 23 April 1992, p. 5.
2 D. Calleja, Director Air Transport Directorate, European Commission, speech to International Aviation Club Washington, 16 November 2004, text courtesy of the European Commission.
3 EEC 69/494, 16 December 1969 and EEC 80/50, 20 December 1979.
4 Loder Collection, HE 9780, Minister for Aviation and Shipping, Lord Caithness to Derek Prentice, IOCU Air Transport Committee, 25 June 1992.
5 Loder Collection, HE 9762.5, Robert Ebdon, Head of Commercial and Government Affairs, BA, 'European Community External Air Transport Policy: the ICC View', International Chamber of Commerce Paper, 17 December 1991, Doc. No. 310/390.
6 Many of the points made here are drawn from Loder Collection, HE 9762.5, Richard Gardiner, UK Department of Transport, 'Conduct of Community's External Relations', 15 January 1991.
7 Ibid., 'Air Transport Relations with Third Countries: Communication to the Council', preliminary version undated and COM(92)434, 21 October 1992.
8 Loder Collection, HE 9762.5, letter 1 March and 2 July 1990, and DG VII Working

papers, 6 December 1990 and 27 March 1991, letter to Member States 26 September 1989, see also supra Chapter 6.
9 COM(92)434, 21 October 1992.
10 *Flight International*, 16 September 1992, 'Dutch gain from open skies', p. 34.
11 *Flight International*, 2 December 1992, 'EC set to issue bilateral proposals', p. 4.
12 COM(92)434, 'Air Transport Relations with Third Countries', 21 October 1992 and 'Air Transport: Relations with Third Countries', *EC Newsletter*, December 1992.
13 COM(92)434. On 12 January 1993, the Commission submitted a communication to the Council on air transport with third countries accompanied by the amended version of COM(90)17, but still based on Article 113 of the Treaty of Rome.
14 Ibid.
15 Loder Collection, HC 2409, European Communities, The Council, 10 March 1993, from COREPER to Council Transport, 15 March 1993, regarding COM(92)434 final.
16 Ibid., p. 6.
17 *EC Bulletin*, March 1993, 1.2.70.
18 European Court of Justice Opinion 1/94.
19 *Expanding Horizons*, p. 34.
20 *Flight International*, 7 June 1995, p. 16.
21 M. Staniland, 'The United States and the external aviation policy of the EU', *Journal of European Public Policy*, 2:1, 1995, 19–40, p. 23.
22 *Aerospace International*, December 2001, p. 5.
23 Interview with Jeffery Shane, Assistant Secretary for Policy and International Affairs, US Department of Transportation, 5 April 1991.
24 There were numerous other advantages which the British garnered from the talks. All US airlines including AA and UA were outraged at the results, but things were politically awkward because Britain was busy standing shoulder to shoulder with the US in the Gulf War. See Dobson, op. cit. 1993, and Memorandum of Consultations 7–11 March 1991 and agreed amendments to US–UK Air Services Agreement [Bermuda 2], text supplied courtesy of UK Department of Transport.
25 The request was to extend the scope of EEC 3975/87 and 3976/87 to transport between the Community and third countries.
26 Speech by Karel Van Miert, April 1998, text courtesy of the Royal Aeronautical Society.
27 Ibid., p. 2.
28 Ibid., p. 3.
29 Ibid., p. 4.
30 COM(1999)182, 'The European Airlines Industry: From Single Market to Worldwide Challenges'.
31 AEA Policy Statement, 'Towards a Transatlantic Common Aviation Area', September 1999 and AEA Information, 'AEA Assembly Spells Out Priorities in Madrid', 31 October 2000.
32 COM(2001)370, Final, 'European Transport Policy for 2010: Time to Decide', 12 September 2001.
33 Commission versus Austria etc. cases C-466/98 to C-476/98., and *Aerospace International*, December 2002, p. 4.
34 *ASSESS: Assessment of the contribution of the TEN and other transport policy measures to the mid-term implementation of the White Paper on the European Transport Policy for 2010*. Transport and Mobility Leuven, 28 October 2005. Annex XIV, Qualitative Analysis of Air Transport Issues, p. 100.
35 COM(2002)649, Final, 'Communication from the Commission on the consequences of the Court judgements of 5 November for the European air transport policy', 19 November 2002, p. 6.
36 Ibid., p. 8.

214 *Notes*

37 Of the 25 Member States, fifteen had open-skies agreements with the US; five did not, namely the UK, Spain, Ireland, Greece and Hungary; and five had no ASAs with the US at all, namely, Cyprus, Slovenia, Lithuania, Latvia and Estonia.
38 *Aerospace International*, November 2001, 4.
39 Ibid., April 2003, 'The rise and rise of the low-cost airlines', pp. 14–16.
40 COM(2002)649, p. 7.
41 COM(2003)94, Final, 'Communication from the Commission on relations between the Community and third countries in the field of air transport', 26 February 2003, p. 5.
42 Ibid., p. 2.
43 EC Regulation No. 847/2004 of the European Parliament and of the Council, 'On the negotiation and implementation of air service agreements between Member States and third countries', 29 April 2004; and Speech by Daniel Calleja to International Aviation Club, Washington DC, 16 November 2004, text courtesy European Commission.
44 EC Regulation 847/204 and interview with senior Commission official from DG TREN, 25 September 2006, official 4.
45 P. Stephen Dempsey, *European Aviation Law*, the Hague, Kluwer, 2004, p. 89.
46 *Flight International*, 4 January 2005, 'EC warns four nations to terminate bilaterals', p. 9.
47 Calleja speech, 16 November 2004, p. 7.
48 Brattle Group, 'The Economic impact of an EU–US open aviation area', report for DG TREN, 2002.
49 Interview with senior Commission official from DG TREN, 25 September 2006, official 4.
50 Remarks of Jeffrey N. Shane, Under Secretary for Policy, US Department of Transportation, International Aviation Club, Washington DC, 12 September 2006, text courtesy of DG TREN, p. 3.
51 Ibid.
52 Ibid.
53 Quoted from speech by Daniel Calleja, 16 November 2004, p. 18.
54 Ibid., pp. 13–14.
55 Ibid., pp. 17 and 15.
56 Ibid., p. 19.
57 Jacques Barrot, speech at the European Institute Washington DC, 22 March 2005. ec.europa.eu/commission_barosso/barrot/discours_en.htm.
58 US Department of Transportation, Secretary's Office, Docket No. OST-30–15759–15, Title: Actual control of US carriers, NPRM.
59 Remarks of Jeffrey N. Shane, Under Secretary for Policy, US Department of Transportation, International Aviation Club, Washington DC, 12 September 2006, text courtesy of DG TREN, p. 2.
60 Extract from Minutes of the Transport Council, 9 June 2006. See also extracts from 5 December 2005 and 27 March 2006. Texts courtesy of the European Commission.
61 Remarks of Jeffrey N. Shane, Under Secretary for Policy, US Department of Transportation, International Aviation Club, Washington DC, 12 September 2006, text courtesy of DG TREN, p. 3.
62 Interview with senior Commission official from DG TREN, 25 September 2006, official 4.
63 Lisbeth Kirk, 'Transatlantic aviation deal faces delay', 15 May 2006, www.euobserver.com.
64 Remarks of Jeffrey N. Shane, Under Secretary for Policy, US Department of Transportation, International Aviation Club, Washington DC, 12 September 2006, p. 3, text courtesy of DG TREN.

65 Ibid.
66 Ibid.
67 Ibid.
68 E-mail from Commission DG TREN official to author 24 November 2006.
69 Remarks of Jeffrey N. Shane, Under Secretary for Policy, US Department of Transportation, International Aviation Club, Washington DC, 12 September 2006, p. 5, text courtesy of DG TREN.
70 Ibid., p. 4.

10 Concluding thoughts: The dervish shall whirl again

1 *ASSESS: Assessment of the contribution of the TEN and other transport policy measures to the mid-term implementation of the White Paper on the European Transport Policy for 2010.* Transport and Mobility Leuven, 28 October 2005. Annex XIV, Qualitative Analysis of Air Transport Issues, p. 12.
2 Ibid., p. 16.
3 Interview with two senior officials DG for Competition, 25 September 2006.
4 EC Regulation 261/2004 superseding 295/91 denied boarding compensation; 889/2002 air carrier liability for accidents; 868/2004 protecting against unfair competition from third parties; and Directive 2002/30 noise directive.
5 *Observer*, Business, 26 November 2006, 'Europe accepts its role as the green pioneer of the world', p. 5.
6 European Commission White Paper 'European Transport Policy for 2010: Time to Decide', COM(2001)370, 2001, p. 21.
7 www.grida.no/climate/ipcc/aviation/index.htm.
8 Jones, op. cit., p. 176.

Postscript

1 EC DG TREN Information Note 6 March 2007, 'Air Transportation Agreement between the EU and US'.
2 Extract from Minutes of the Transport Council, 9 June 2006. See also extracts from 5 December 2005 and 27 March 2006. Texts courtesy of the European Commission.
3 'Draft Air Services Liberalization Deal Would Benefit U.S., EU', current issues 5 March 2007, usinfo.state.gov
4 Ibid.
5 www.dailymail.co.uk/pages/live/articles/news.html?in_article_id=440153 Accessed 14/03/07.
6 news.bbc.co.uk/2/hi/business/6417277.stm. Accessed 14/03/07
7 www.telegraph.co.uk/money.jhtml?xml=/money/2007/03/19/cnba19.xml. Accessed 19/03/07.
8 'EU backs "open skies" pact', uk.reuters.com/article/businessNews/idUKL 222729952007032?src=032207_1. Accessed 22/03/07

Bibliography

Books

Ashworth, W. and P. Forsyth, *Civil Aviation and the Privatisation of British Airways*, London, Institute for Fiscal Studies, 1985.
Baldwin, R. *Regulating the Airlines: Administrative Justice and Agency Discretion*, Oxford, Clarendon, 1985.
Beach, D. *The Dynamics of European Integration: Why and When EU Institutions Matter*, Basingstoke, Palgrave, 2005.
Button, K. et al., *Flying Into the Future: Air Transport Policy in the European Union*, Cheltenham, Edward Elgar, 1998.
Campbell-Smith, D. *Struggle for Take-Off: The British Airways Story*, London, Hodder and Stoughton, 1986.
Dempsey, P.S. *Law and Foreign Policy in International Aviation*, New York, Transnational Publishers, 1987.
Dempsey, P.S. *European Aviation Law*, The Hague, Kluwer, 2004.
Dienel, H.-L. and P. Lyth (eds), *Flying the Flag: European Commercial Air Transport Since 1945*, Basingstoke, Macmillan, 1998.
Dinan, D. *Europe Recast: A History of European Union*, Basingstoke: Palgrave Macmillan 2004.
Dobson, A.P. *Peaceful Air Warfare: The United States, Britain, and the Politics of International Aviation*, Oxford, Clarendon Press, 1991.
Dobson, A.P. *Flying in the Face of Competition: The Policies and Diplomacy of Airline Regulatory Reform in Britain, the USA and the European Community 1968–94*, Aldershot, Avebury, 1995.
Doganis, R. *Flying Off Course: The Economics of International Airlines*, London, Allen and Unwin, 1985.
Erdmenger, J. *The European Transport Policy*, Aldershot, Gower, 1983.
Gialloreto, L. *Strategic Airline Management: the Global War Begins*, London, Pitman Press, 1988.
Gidwitz, B. *The Politics of Air Transport*, Boston, Heath, 1980.
Greenwood, J. *Interest Representation in the European Union*, Basingstoke, Palgrave, 2003.
Gunston, B. *Diamond Flight*, London, Henry Melland Ltd, 1988.
Haanappel, P.P.C. *Pricing and Capacity Determination in International Air Transport: A Legal Analysis*, Maryland, Kluwer, 1984.
Haanappel, P.P.C. et al. (eds), *EEC Air Transport Policy and Regulation and Their Implications for North America*, Deventer, Kluwer, 1989.

Haas, E.B. *Beyond the Nation State: Functionalism and International Organization*, Stanford, Stanford University Press, 1964.
Jones, L. *EasyJet: the Story of Britain's Biggest Low-cost Airline*, London, Aurum, 2005.
Jonsson, C. *International Aviation and the Politics of Regime Change*, London, Francis Pinter, 1987.
Majone, G. (ed.), *Deregulation or Re-Regulation? Regulatory Reform in Europe and the United States*, London and New York, Pinter and St Martins, 1990.
McGowan, F. and C. Trengove, *European Aviation: A Common Market?* London, Institute for Fiscal Studies, 1986.
Milward, A.S. *The European Rescue of the Nation State*, London, Routledge, 1992.
Mitrany, D. *A Working Peace System: An Argument for the Functional Development of International Organization*, London, Royal Institute for International Affairs, 1943.
Noll, R.G. and Bruce M. Owen (eds), *The Political Economy of Deregulation: Interest Groups in the Regulatory Process*, Washington, DC, American Enterprise for Public Policy Research, 1983.
Peterson, B.S. *Bluestreak: Inside Jetblue, the Upstart that Rocked the Industry*, New York, Portfolio, 2004.
Pryke, R. *Competition among International Airlines*, Aldershot, Gower, 1987.
Rand, A. *Capitalism the Unknown Ideal*, New York, New American Library, 1967.
Rosamond, B. *Theories of European Integration*, Basingstoke, Palgrave, 2000.
Sampson, A. *Empires of the Sky: the Politics, Contests and Cartels of World Airlines*, London, Hodder and Staughton, 1984.
Sandholtz, W. and A.S. Sweet (eds) *European Integration and Supranational Governance*, Oxford, Oxford University Press, 1998.
Shaw, S. *Airlines and Management*, London, Pitman, 1985.
Sochor, E. *The Politics of International Aviation*, London, Macmillan, 1991.
Stevens, H. *Liberalisation of Air Transport in Europe: a Case Study in European Integration*, London, European Institute, LSE, 1997.
Stevens, H. *Transport Policy in the European Union*, Basingstoke, Palgrave, 2004.
Swann, D. *The Retreat of the State: Deregulation and Privatisation in the UK and the US*, Hemel Hempstead, Harvester Wheatsheaf, 1988.
Taneja, N.K. *US International Aviation Policy*, Lexington: Heath, 1988.
Thatcher, M. *The Downing Street Years*, London: Harper Collins, 1993.
Wassenbergh, H.A. *Public Air Transport in a New Era*, Deventer, Kluwer, 1976.
Wassenbergh, H.A. and H.P. van Fenema (eds) *International Air Transport: A Legal Analysis*, Deventer, Kluwer, 1981.
Wheatcroft, S. and G. Lipman, *Air Transport in a Competitive European Market: Problems, Prospects and Strategies*, London, Economist Intelligence Unit, Economist Publications Ltd, 1986.
Wiener, A. and T. Diez (eds), *European Integration Theory*, Oxford, Oxford University Press, 2004.

Articles and papers

Barratt, S.D. 'Deregulating European Aviation – A Case Study', *Transportation*, 16, 1990, 311–27.
Bashor, H.W. 'A New Legal Order in Air Transport', *Journal of Diplomatic Language*, 2:1, 2005, www.jdonline.org/IIBashor.html.

218 Bibliography

Dierikx, M.L. 'Shaping World Aviation: Anglo-American Civil Aviation Relations 1944–46', *Journal of Air Law and Commerce*, 57, 1992, 795–840.
Dobson, A.P. 'Regulation or Competition? Negotiating the Anglo-American Air Service Agreement of 1977', *The Journal of Transport History*, 15:2, 1994, 144–65.
Dobson, A.P. 'Aspects of Anglo-American Aviation Diplomacy 1976–93', *Diplomacy and Statecraft*, 4:2, 1993, 235–57.
Dobson, A.P. 'The USA, Hegemony and Airline Market Access to Britain and Western Europe, 1945–96, *Diplomacy and Statecraft*, 9:2, 1998, 129–59.
Forsyth, P. 'Airline Deregulation in the United States: The Lessons for Europe', *Fiscal Studies*, 4 November 1983, 7–21.
Feldstein, M. 'The Retreat from Keynesian Economics', *The Public Interest*, Summer 1981, 92–105.
Kirk, E. 'Transatlantic Aviation Deal Faces Delay', 15 May 2006, www.euobserver.com
Mackenzie, D. 'The Bermuda Conference and Anglo-American Aviation Relations at the End of the Second World War', *Journal of Transport History*, 12:1, 1991, 61–73.
Moravcsik, A. 'Preferences and Power in the European Community: A Liberal Inter-Governmentalist Approach', *Journal of Common Market Studies*, 31:4, 1993, 473–524.
Stadlmeier, S. 'Convergence of Scheduled and Non-Scheduled Air Services', *Austrian Journal of Public and International Law*, 45, 1993, 159–93.
Staniland, M. 'The United States and the External Aviation Policy of the EU', *Journal of European Public Policy*, 2:1, 1995, 19–40.

Newspapers and weekly/monthly publications

Aerospace International
Air Transport Action Group News
Airlines International (*IATA*)
Daily Telegraph
ECAC News
The Economist
Financial Times
Flight International
ICAO Journal
Independent
Observer

Primary sources

'A Better Transport Network for Europe', European File, 5/81, March 1981.
AEA Information Memoranda.
AEA Policy Statement, 'Towards a Transatlantic Common Aviation Area', September 1999.
'Air Services Agreement Between the Government of the United States of America and the Government of the United Kingdom and Northern Ireland Including Amendments thru 1980', US Department of Transportation, Washington DC, 1981.
Airline Competition: Impact of Computerized Reservation Systems, United States General Accounting Office Report to Congressional Requesters, May 1986, GAO/RCED-86-74, Washington DC, 1986.

Argyris, N. Address to European Air Law Association, London, 27 July 1990.
Assess: Assessment of the Contribution of the TEN and Other Transport Measures to the Mid-Term Implementation of the White Paper on European Transport Policy for 2010. Final Report, Annex XIV Qualitative Analysis of Air Transport Issues. DG TREN 28 October 2005. Project contractor: Transport and Mobility Leuven. Authors Hansjochen Ehmer, Wolfgang Grimme and Björn Zeppenfeld.
Ayral, M. Director Air Transport, EC, 'European Air Transport Policy: Examining the External Constraints Imposed on ATM by Liberalisation, Environmental Protection, Defence, Security Requirements and Economics.' ATC 2000 Conference, 22–3 February 2000, Maastricht.
Branson, R. Address to IEA Conference, 6 October 1993.
Brattle Group, 'The Economic Impact of an EU–US Open Aviation Area', report for DG TREN, 2002.
Brittan, Sir L. Paper presented Aviation Conference, Marrakesh, 1–3 June 1989.
Calleja, D. Director Air Transport Directorate, European Commission, speech to International Aviation Club Washington, 16 November 2004, text courtesy of the European Commission.
CAP 685, 'The Single European Aviation Market: The First Five Years', London, UK CAA, 1998.
Carter, J. Presidential Library Staff Offices, Domestic Policy Staff.
Cmd. 266, 'Convention Relating to International Air Transport', 1919.
Cmd. 6747, 'US, UK, Civil Air Services Agreement Bermuda', 1946.
Cmd. 4018, '[Edwards] Report of the Committee of Inquiry into Civil Air Transport', 1969.
Cmd. 4899, 'Civil Aviation Policy Guidance', 1972.
Cmd. 6400, 'Future Civil Aviation Policy', 1976.
Cmd. 9366, 'Airline Competition Policy', 1984.
Coopers and Lybrand, 'Application and Possible Modification of Council Regulation 95/93 on Common Rules for the Allocation of Slots at Community Airports', 17 October 1995.
EC/EU documentation includes Commission Communications, and Council Decisions, Regulations and Directives as cited in the footnotes.
'European Airline Traffic after 1993', presentation by F. Sorensen, VII.C.1 – 839/90, 8 April 1991: copy courtesy of Sorensen.
EUROCONTROL 'The Single European Sky', www.eurocontrol.int/ses/public/standard_page/sk_ses.html.
European Commission White Paper 'Completing the Internal Market', COM(85)310, 1985.
European Commission White Paper 'European Transport Policy for 2010: Time to Decide', COM(2001)370, 2001.
European Commission Directorate-General Energy and Transport, 'Single European Sky: Report of the High-Level Group', Brussels, November 2000.
European Community Bulletin.
European Community's *Official Journal*.
European Economic Community Commission 1975, 'Report and Proposed Decision on a Programme of Action for the European Aeronautical Sector', OJ C265.
European File 10/85, The Community and Transport Policy, May 1985.
Expanding Horizons: A Report by the Comité des Sages for Air Transport to the European Commission, Brussels, January 1994.

European Court of Justice Cases.
European Parliament, *Draft Treaty Establishing the European Union*, Luxembourg, February 1984.
Extract from Minutes of the Transport Council, 9 June 2006. See also extracts from 5 December 2005 and 27 March 2006. Texts courtesy of the European Commission.
House of Commons Debates.
House of Commons Session 1987–88 Transport Committee Third Report Airline Competition: Computer Reservation Systems vol. 1, London, HMG Stationery Office, 1988.
House of Commons Transport Committee Session 1987–88, Third Report Airline Competition: Computer Reservation Systems, vol. 2, Minutes of Evidence, London, HMSO, 28 July 1988.
House of Lords Reports.
House of Lords Session 1990–91, Ninth Report Select Committee on the European Communities Conduct of the Community's External Aviation Relations, 23 April 1992.
ICAO Document 8681, 10 July 1967.
International Aviation Developments, Second Report, 'Transatlantic Deregulation: the Alliance Network Effect', US Department of Transportation, Office of the Secretary, October 2000.
King, Lord, Remarks at Royal Aeronautical Society 125th Anniversary Banquet, 16 May 1991.
Loder, John, Papers, University of Wales Swansea Library.
Memorandum of Consultations 7–11 March 1991 and agreed amendments to US–UK Air Services Agreement [Bermuda 2], text supplied courtesy of UK Department of Transport.
Moorhouse, J. 'Cheaper Air Fares Thanks to British Initiative', 8 December 1989.
'Report on Competition in Intra-European Air Services', 1982, Paris, ECAC, CEAC Doc. No. 25, the COMPAS Report.
'Review of Competition Policy', Air Transport Policy Unit CEC 7th, 1978.
Shane, J.N. Under Secretary for Policy, US Department of Transportation, remarks at International Aviation Club, Washington DC, 12 September 2006, text courtesy of EC, DG TREN.
Summary Report DG TREN, Analysis of the European Air Transport Industry 2003. Final Report January 2005.
Steele, J.R. Speech ECAC-EU Dialogue, 29 April 2005, www.prismaconsulting.com/EC, accessed 7 December 2005.
'The European Union's Transport Policy', Periodical 3/1984.
US CAB Orders.
US *Congressional Digest*.
US Department of Transportation, Secretary's Office, Docket No. OST-30-15759-15, Title: Actual control of US carriers, NPRM.
US–ECAC Memorandum of Understanding on North Atlantic Air Tariffs, May 1982.
US National Archives, Nixon Project Papers of Hendrix Houthakker Transitional Taskforce Reports 1968–69.
WHCF.
WHSF.
Van Miert, K. Speech, 'Competition Policy in the Air Transport Sector', April 1998, copy courtesy of the Royal Aeronautical Society, London.

Interviews

Raymond Colegate, UK CAA (retired) 25 March 1991.

Michael Colvin MP, Chairman Conservative Backbench Aviation Committee, 7 December 1989.

Sir Michael Bishop, Chairman BM, 15 March 1991.

Edmund Dell, 8 December 1989.

Robert Ebdon, Head of Government Affairs, British Airways, 5 August 1991.

Fennes, R. DG 7, 21 February 2000.

Andrew Gray, Managing Director, Air UK, 26 March 1991.

Barry Humphreys, former UK CAA official and then a senior executive with Virgin Atlantic, 6 September 2001.

King, Lord, Chairman BA, 17 May 1991.

Cyril Murphy, Vice President for International Affairs, United Airlines, 1 July 1991.

Official from DG 4, 22 May 1991; and 22 February 2000.

Frederik Sorensen, DG 7, 21 February 2000; and 12 September 2001.

Senior official BA, February 2002.

Senior official UK CAA Economic Regulation Group, 23 May 2001.

Senior official UK Department of Transportation, 25 September 1991.

Senior official UK Transport Department, 7 September 2001: official 1.

Shane, J.N. Assistant Secretary for Policy and International Affairs, US Department of Transportation, 5 April 1991.

Three Commission officials from DG TREN, 25 September 2006.

Two officials from the DG for Competition (formally DG4), 25 September 2006.

Index

9/11 153, 176, 188

Aer Lingus 116–17, 138
Afghanistan 159
Air Europe 114
Air France 97, 108, 114–15, 130–1, 136, 138–9, 142, 150–4, 160, 162, 168, 182, 187
Air Inter 131
Air Portugal (TAP) 112, 117
air service agreements (ASAs) 5, 32–4, 55, 69–70, 84, 116, 118, 120, 123, 166–71, 175; *see also* US open skies
air traffic control (ATC) 134–5, 144, 150, 157–60, 163; air traffic flow management 159–60; Council High Level Group 159
Air UK 32, 70, 132
airline anti-competitive practices 6–7, 114–15, 160–3; *see also* alliances; code sharing; computer reservation systems; frequent flyer programmes; International Air Transport Association; pooling; Treaty of Rome, competition rules
Alitalia 99, 142
alliances (airline) 102, 135, 160–1, 163, 184, 188; anti-trust immunity 160, 174, 184; Commission's view 162–3; Oneworld Alliance 162; Sky Team 162–3, 186; Star Alliance 160, 162, 186; US Department of Transportation Report 161–2
Amadeus *see* computer reservation systems
America West 139
American Airlines (AA) 26, 124, 140, 155, 160–3, 172, 176, 182
Amsterdam Treaty 46
anti-trust immunity 24–5, 39, 119, 160–1, 188
Arab–Israeli Six Day War 8

Argyris, N. 118–19, 126–7, 131, 134–5
Association of European Airlines (AEA) 2, 14, 36–7, 51, 53, 72, 74, 78–81, 86, 92, 103, 109, 114–15, 128, 141, 156, 164, 174; *see also* Neumeister, K.H.; Veenstra, K.
Association of Independent Air Carriers in the European Community (ACE) 14, 51, 81, 95
Attali, B. 142, 151–2
Austria 118, 122, 175
Austrian Airlines 153, 162
Ayral, M. 158, 165, 178

Barrett, S.D. 79
Barroso, J.M. 183, 188
Barrot, J. 180
Belgium 24, 45, 99, 116, 166, 175
Bennett, R. 161
Bermuda 1 US–UK ASA 5–6, 8, 12, 30
Bermuda 2 US–UK ASA 21, 30, 172
Bethell, Lord 36–8, 44, 52, 54–6, 63, 77, 82, 103, 106, 108–9, 115–16
Bishop, M. 34, 149, 153
Blanc, C. 152
block exemptions *see* Treaty of Rome
BMI Baby 164
Boeing jumbo-jets 8, 12
Bouw, P. 151, 157
Boyd-Carpenter, Lord 21, 29
Braathens 164
Branson, R. 42, 78, 137, 154
Brattle Group 178
Britain 5, 7, 9–13, 17, 19, 22, 44–6, 50, 59–60, 67–70, 74–5, 77–8, 81–2, 84, 87–8, 90, 96–100, 102, 105, 116, 119, 126, 129, 135, 138–40, 147, 151, 166–7, 171, 173, 175, 185–6, 188; ASA with Ireland 79; ASA with Netherlands 69–70; aviation policy 11–13, 21,

28–35, 61–2, 70, 81, 84, 109–11, 118, 121, 127, 136, 140, 162, 171–3; Edwards Report 11; House of Lords 121–2; *see also* UK Civil Aviation Authority
British Air Transport Association (BATA) 14
British Airways (BA) 7, 11, 29, 32–3, 69, 80, 97, 101, 108, 110, 112–15, 124–5, 135, 138–9, 142, 150, 152, 155–6, 160–1, 163, 172, 176; privatization 31, 70, 78, 135–6, 153
British Airways Business System *see* computer reservation systems
British Caledonian Airways (B.Cal.) 12, 29, 70, 80, 110, 136, 155
British European Airways (BEA) 6, 12
British Midland (BM) 7, 32–4, 70, 113, 152, 185
British Overseas Airways Corporation (BOAC) 12
Brittan, L. 106, 108, 125–7, 131, 137, 150
Brymon Airways 115
Browne, S. 8
Bureau Européen des Unions des Consommateurs (BEUC) 14, 81
Burke, R. 48–9
Bush, G.W. 180, 182
Buzz 164
Byerly, R. 178, 182

cabotage 5–6, 28, 128, 143, 146–7, 161, 173; *see also* packages of reform; United States, access to US cabotage
Calleja, D. 178, 180
capacity 6–7, 40–1, 57–9, 76, 83, 127–30, 143–8, 164–5; *see also* packages of reform
cargo services 54, 118, 125, 127, 130, 132, 136, 181
Carter J. 23–5, 27, 161
Cathay Pacific Airlines 32
Channon, P. 126–7
Charles de Gaulle (airport) 132
charter airlines 14
Chataway, C. 138
Chicago School 22
China 177
Cino, M. 182
Civil Reserve Air Fleet (CRAF) 173, 180–1
Close, G.L. 55–6
Cockfield, Lord 32, 66, 88
code sharing 111, 150, 160, 163
Cohen, M. 25
Colegate, R. 110

Colombo, E. 64
Colvin, M. 33
Committee of Permanent Representatives (COREPER) 15, 51, 128, 170; Working Party 48–9, 55, 57
common transport policy (CTP) 3–4, 6, 16–17, 19, 52, 60, 72, 74, 88
Community carriers *see* Single European Aviation Market, licensing
COMPAS Report *see* European Civil Aviation Conference
computer reservation systems (CRSs) 27, 35, 101–2, 105, 107–8, 111–13, 118, 123–5, 127, 130, 132, 134, 144, 175–6, 183
contestability 138–9, 163
Continental 162, 182
Contogeorgis, G. 54, 88
Convention Relating to the Regulation of Air Navigation 5
Coopers and Lybrand 156–7
Crandall, R. 123
Cundiff, C. 161

Dan Air 112, 136
Dauvignon, E. 65
Davis, S.C. 29, 61, 80, 88–9, 91–2
De Croo, H. 99–100, 151; *see also* European Commission, *Comité des Sages*
De Palacio, L. 153, 158–9, 176
Debonair 164
Delebarre, M. 131
Dell, E. 12–13, 30–1, 34, 113
Delors, J. 13, 65, 83; Commission President 65–6, 127
Delta Airlines 26, 162, 172, 182
Denmark 62–3, 67, 101, 115, 118, 129, 175
Deutsche BA 160, 172, 174
DG IV *see* European Commission
DG VII *see* European Commission
DG for Competition *see* European Commission
DG TREN *see* European Commission
Dooge, J. 65; Committee 65–7
Douffiagues, J. 99
Draft Treat Establishing the European Union 64
Dubai 182

Easyjet 164–5, 176, 185–6
Economic and Social Committee 13, 17, 51, 53, 147

Erdmenger, J. 55
Esch, V.D. 55–6
EUROCONTROL 47, 68, 157–60; CFM 158; EATCHIP 158; Single European Sky 158
European Civil Aviation Conference (ECAC) 2, 13–14, 25, 52, 74, 76, 78–81, 86, 88, 90–100, 103, 186; COMPAS Report 37–44, 47, 51, 53, 57, 68, 92, 98, 154; computer reservation systems 124; tariff agreements 14, 38–44, 54, 58, 69, 75
European Commission 1, 4, 11, 13–19, 21–2, 36, 45–7, 52, 61–3, 73–4, 87–93, 107–9, 115–16, 121–2, 129, 131, 134, 139, 156, 167–8, 174–6, 186; *Comité des Sages* 151–2, 155, 158, 170–1; Directorate General for Competition (DG IV)/(DG for Competition) 17, 38, 47–8, 51, 59, 77–9, 83, 88–9, 91, 97, 104, 115, 118–19, 126–7, 138–9, 146, 185, 187; Directorate General for Transportation (DG VII)/(DG TREN) 11, 17–18, 22, 27, 38, 46–8, 52–6, 77–8, 84, 89, 91–2, 97, 104, 115, 132, 139, 141–2, 146, 153, 157, 160, 168, 185; Legal Service 38, 47, 49, 55, 57, 59, 77, 93–4, 126; Memorandum (1) 46–52, 57, 83, 184–5; Memorandum (2) 34, 39, 43, 47, 57–81, 83, 87–8, 91, 95–6, 150; Memorandum (2) and High Level Group(HLG) 85–7, 92–3, 103; Single European Sky 158–9; White Paper (2001) 150, 175, 188; *see also* packages of reform; Single European Aviation Market
European Community 2–3, 7, 10, 12–14, 27, 35, 45, 69, 88, 104, 185; competition rules *see* Treaty of Rome
European Constitution 178
European Council 15, 146–7; *see also* European summits
European Council of Ministers 13–18, 21, 32, 45–7, 49–50, 52, 54–5, 64, 72, 87, 90, 95–103, 107–8, 112, 118–19, 126–9, 131, 144–7, 154, 156, 168–71, 175, 177–9, 181–2, 185; Directive on consultation procedures 52, 59; Directive on regional services 52–3, 57, 59–60, 68, 72, 76, 87, 97, 112; Luxembourg Compromise 15, 63; qualified majority voting 67; *see also* packages of reform
European Court of Justice 15–16, 19, 48, 93, 104, 133, 150, 152, 170, 174–5, 182, 185–6; AETR case 16, 121, 175; Ahmed Saeed case 118–19; Bethell case 37–8, 56; French Seamen's case 18–19, 21, 35, 49, 184–5; *Nouvelles Frontières* case 46, 68, 73, 83, 85, 91, 93–9, 103; Parliament case 55, 88–9, 91
European Economic Community 6
European Free Trade Area 118, 122, 127, 129–30, 168
European Parliament 13, 15–19, 46, 51, 53, 54–5, 61, 67, 127, 147, 186; Crocodile Club 63; Kangaroo Group 64; Klinkenborg Report 71–8, 84, 91–2, 154
European Round Table of Industrialists (ERTI) 13–14
European Single Market 3, 13, 36, 62–8, 91, 95, 102–3, 107; Cockfield White Paper 66–7, 88
European Summits: Fontainbleau 65–6; Hague 16, 95, 97; Luxembourg 67; Stuttgart 64
European Union (EU) 1, 14, 174, 177–84; Member States 1, 3, 9–10, 17, 21, 43, 45, 54, 60, 83, 104, 107, 126, 132, 141

fares *see* rates
Federal Express 125, 136
Federation of Air Transport User Representatives of the European Community (FATUREC) 14, 36, 77, 81
Fennes, R. 42
Finland 122, 175, 177
First Framework Programme for Research and Development 65
Flanigan, P. 8
Fly America Program 173, 180
Forsyth, P. 79
France 9, 63, 85–6, 96, 98, 100, 107–8, 127–32, 136, 142, 147, 150–3, 160, 177–8; open-skies with US 162, 171
Freedom of the Skies Campaign 14, 36–7, 77, 103
freedoms of the air 5–6
frequent flyer programmes (FFPs) 35, 135, 160–1, 163

Galileo *see* computer reservation systems
Gatwick airport 7, 33, 112, 114, 155–6
Genscher, H.D. 64
Germany 9, 24, 45, 60, 74, 96, 100, 107, 116, 147, 160, 166, 172; open-skies with US 171, 174–5, 177

Index 225

Gibraltar 102
globalization 2, 4, 7, 9, 19, 63–8, 107, 132, 176, 186–7; airline losses 141–2, 153, 176
Go 164, 186
Goodman, H. 114
Gray, A. 132
Greece 63, 65, 67, 87, 101
Gulf War 139, 141–2, 146, 150, 172

Haanappel, P.P.C. 72–3
Haji-Ioannou, S. 164
Heath, E. 11–12, 21, 29
Heathrow airport 7, 11, 32, 34, 70, 112–14, 132, 136, 140, 155–6, 172–3, 182
High Level Group 170; see also European Commission, Memorandum (2)
hub and spoke 26–7, 73
Humphreys, B. 42
Hussein, S. 136

Iceland 122
integration 2
interest groups 13–14, 36–43, 45, 103, 106–7
Intergovernmental Panel on Climate Change 188
interlining 114–15
International Air Transport Association (IATA) 2–3, 142, 176; CRSs 113; fares 2–3, 5, 7–8, 13–14, 30, 40–1, 43, 51, 55, 69, 72, 74–5, 78, 80–1, 86, 92, 99, 106, 112, 114–15; liberalization 24–5; Show Cause Order (SCO) 24–5, 44, 54; slots 125, 154
International Civil Aviation Conference Chicago 5, 14
International Civil Aviation Organization (ICAO) 2, 68, 124
Iraq 159, 182
Ireland 45, 63, 98, 100, 116, 128–9, 179
Italy 87, 101, 147, 177

Jeans, T. 149
Jenkins, R. 48

Kahn, A. 23–5, 40, 79, 137, 189
King, Lord 33, 70, 114, 131, 136, 140
Keynesian economics 19, 22
Kinnock, N. 153, 171
KLM *see* Royal Dutch Airlines
Kohl, H. 65
Kroes, N.S. 91

Kuwait 136
Kyoto Protocol 188

Laker, F. 12, 32–3, 36–7, 44, 54, 70, 103, 112, 186; Skytrain 12, 29–31, 40
Lawson, N. 33
Le Goy, R. 10, 17, 19, 21, 32, 49, 54
Lipman, G. 151
Loder. J. 36, 40, 108–9, 114–15, 127–8
London European 108–9
Lufthansa 115, 142, 153, 155, 160–2, 168, 176, 187
Lumsden, G. 40
Luton airport 7, 114, 186
Luxair 153
Luxembourg 45, 60, 87, 90, 96, 116, 166, 175

Maastricht Treaty 46, 64
McDonnell Douglas 33, 112
Mack, K. 157–8
Maersk Air 112, 116, 164, 185
Member States *see* European Union
Mineta, N. 181–2
Mitterand, F. 65, 128, 130
Moore, J. 85, 96–101, 126
Moorehouse, J. 127
Moscow 172
Mugnozzo, C. 48

Netherlands 7, 9–10, 17, 19, 24, 34, 40, 43, 45–6, 60, 74, 77, 84, 87–90, 95, 98, 116, 129, 138–40, 147, 178, 185; open-skies with US 161, 168
Neumeister, K.H. 82, 156, 164
Nixon, R. 7
no-frills airlines *see* Easyjet; Ryanair
noise emissions 52
non-governmental organizations (NGOs) 2, 13–14, 35, 45–6, 104, 106–7, 141
Nordio, U. 99
Northwest Airlines 162, 182
Norway 118, 122, 127, 130, 146
notice of proposed rule making 181–2
Nott, J. 11, 31–2

Olympic Airways 152
O'Mahoney, D. 86
Open Aviation Area (OAA) 1, 163, 168, 177–84
open-skies *see* United States, open-skies
Orly aiport 150
Ornstein, J. 155

Pacific Southwestern Airlines 23
packages of reform: first 1, 62, 82–118,
    139; reaction to first package 115–17,
    169; second 1, 101, 107–8, 118–33, 136,
    139; second and High Level Group
    128–30; third 1, 133–65, 168, 170
Pan American World Airways (Pan Am)
    26–7, 33, 112–13, 131, 140, 172
Parkinson, C. 127
Peña, E. 88
People's Express 139
pollution 188–9
pooling 6, 68, 83, 127–30, 143–8; *see also*
    packages of reform
Portillo, M. 127
Portugal 63, 101, 116, 177, 185
Price-Waterhouse-Cooper 156
Pryke. R. 79

Qantas 172

Raben, H. 40, 87
rates 5–7, 24–5, 40–1, 50, 54–9, 69–70,
    76, 127–30, 143–8, 164–5, 175–6, 183;
    fixing 54–6, 69, 75, 80–1, 83; *see also*
    IATA; packages of reform
Reaganomics 19
Ridley, N. 32–3, 35, 69, 91, 96
Rifkind, M. 91, 97, 140
routes 6–7, 12, 21, 23, 30–2, 40–1, 57–9,
    70, 76, 83, 127–30, 143–8, 164–5; *see
    also* packages of reform
Royal Aeronautical Society 131
Royal Dutch Airlines (KLM) 8, 10, 19, 69,
    97, 112, 142, 152–5, 160, 162, 172, 182,
    187
Ryanair 149, 164–5, 185–6

Sabena 97, 108–9, 114–15, 142, 150–1,
    153, 155, 160, 162, 168, 172
sabre *see* computer reservation systems
SARS 159
Scandinavian Air Services (SAS) 7, 97,
    112, 115, 118, 122, 129, 142, 152–3
Schiphol airport 10, 19, 101
Scocozza, M. 74, 79
Scrivener, C. 127
Shane, J.N. 171–2, 182–4
Shore, P. 12, 21, 29, 31, 88
Single European Act 15, 45–6
Single European Aviation Market (SEAM)
    1–5, 10, 16, 21, 30, 35–6, 42, 48–9, 57,
    60ff; comparisons with US civil aviation
    7, 72–4, 79–80, 137–8, 143, 146, 163–4,
176–7; external relations 16, 57, 69,
    102, 105, 117–23, 127, 129–30, 140–1,
    143–5, 147, 165–85; impact of 163–6,
    186; licensing (Community carriers)
    107, 118, 126–7, 130–1, 135–6, 143–9,
    168, 178–83; mergers 186–7; Regional
    Air Services Directive (1983) 34;
    relations with US 176, 178–85; *see also*
    air traffic control; cabotage; capacity;
    packages of reform; pooling; rates;
    routes; slots; subsidies
slots (take-off and landing) 105, 107,
    113–14, 118, 125, 130, 132, 135, 140,
    144, 147, 150, 154–7, 163, 175, 183
Solemn Declaration on European Unity 64
Sorensen, F. 43, 48–51, 53, 57, 70, 80, 82,
    95, 104, 129, 137, 141–5, 162–3, 185
Southwest Airlines 7
Spain 63, 101–2, 179, 185
Spinelli, A. 64
Stansted airport 7, 114
Steele, J. 27, 32, 54, 57, 61, 89–91, 97, 150
Stevens, H. 86–7, 128
subsidies 75, 135, 139, 142, 147, 150–4,
    163
Sutherland, P. 83, 87, 91, 92, 97–8, 100,
    104
Sweden 118, 122–3, 127, 130, 146, 175
Swiss International Airlines 187
Swissair 162
Switzerland 118, 122

TAT 155, 160
Tebbit, N. 33, 50
terrorism 188
Thatcher, M. 10, 31–3, 65–6, 70, 126–7;
    Thatcherism 11, 19, 62–4, 66
traffic distribution rules (TDRs – London
    airports) 30, 34, 113
Trans World Airlines (TWA) 26–7, 33,
    112–13, 131, 140, 172
transatlantic common aviation area
    (TCAA) 171, 174–5
Transavia 155
Treaty of Rome 2–3, 63, 74, 76, 78,
    99–100, 104, 121, 142, 150; article 113,
    121–2, 140, 169–70, 183; block
    exemptions from competition rules 89,
    93–4, 100–1, 107–9, 114–15, 119, 131;
    competition rules 3–4, 6, 13, 16–18, 21,
    37–8, 45–6, 54–6, 69, 76–9, 84–5,
    89–90, 93–4, 97, 118, 126, 140;
    transport title 3–4, 51, 55
Tugendhat, C. 109–10, 142

89–90, 93–4, 97, 118, 126, 140; transport title 3–4, 51, 55
Tugendhat, C. 109–10, 142

Union de Transport Aérien 131, 155
United Airlines (UA) 5, 7, 136, 140, 160–2, 172, 182
United Kingdom (UK) *see* Britain
United Kingdom Civil Aviation Authority (CAA) 12, 21, 29–36, 42, 70, 110, 113, 132–3, 138–40, 142; reports on SEAM 164–5; *see also* Chataway; Colegate; Tugendhat
United Parcel Service 125, 136
United States (US) 5, 7, 105, 117, 153, 161, 167, 171, 182–3; access to US cabotage 172–3; Airline Regulatory Reform Bill/Act (1978) 23; anti-trust immunity 24–5, 39, 119, 160; Britain 5–6, 8, 12, 21, 30, 171–3; Civil Aeronautics Board (CAB) 8, 12, 23–5, 29; deregulation 7–10, 22–8, 44, 48, 73, 79–81, 100, 102, 137, 161; Fly America Program 28; International Air Transportation Competition Act (1979) 24; liberal ASAs 24, 28, 44; open-skies 161–2, 166–8, 171, 174; ownership and control 179–84; relations with SEAM 176, 178–85; Show Cause Order *see* IATA; *see also* Bermuda 1 US–UK ASA; Bermuda 2 US–UK ASA; European Civil Aviation Conference
US Air 161, 172

value added tax (VAT) 16, 149, 153, 188
Van der Beugel, E. 8
Van der Maaten 40
Van Hasselt, L. 169
Van Miert, K. 126–7, 137, 142, 145–6, 148, 151, 153, 155, 157, 161, 173–4
Veenstra, K. 94–5
Venables, R. 32
Veres, R. 146
Virgin Atlantic 42
Virgin Express 155, 164
Volpe, J. 8

Weber, J. 155–6
Weck, J. 161
West Germany *see* Germany
wet leasing 28, 173, 180
Wilson, H. 11–12

Yom Kippur War 8, 12, 29

eBooks – at www.eBookstore.tandf.co.uk

A library at your fingertips!

eBooks are electronic versions of printed books. You can store them on your PC/laptop or browse them online.

They have advantages for anyone needing rapid access to a wide variety of published, copyright information.

eBooks can help your research by enabling you to bookmark chapters, annotate text and use instant searches to find specific words or phrases. Several eBook files would fit on even a small laptop or PDA.

NEW: Save money by eSubscribing: cheap, online access to any eBook for as long as you need it.

Annual subscription packages

We now offer special low-cost bulk subscriptions to packages of eBooks in certain subject areas. These are available to libraries or to individuals.

For more information please contact webmaster.ebooks@tandf.co.uk

We're continually developing the eBook concept, so keep up to date by visiting the website.

www.eBookstore.tandf.co.uk

For Product Safety Concerns and Information please contact our EU representative GPSR@taylorandfrancis.com
Taylor & Francis Verlag GmbH, Kaufingerstraße 24, 80331 München, Germany

www.ingramcontent.com/pod-product-compliance
Lightning Source LLC
Chambersburg PA
CBHW071824300426
44116CB00009B/1428